The Story of
ALABAMA
in
FOURTEEN
FOODS

The Story of

ALABAMA

in

FOURTEEN

FOODS

EMILY BLEJWAS

The University of Alabama Press | Tuscaloosa

The University of Alabama Press
Tuscaloosa, Alabama 35487-0380
uapress.ua.edu

A curriculum guide with English and social studies lessons for
grades 10 and 11 is available at www.fosterdickson.com.

The recipes in this book are intended to be followed as written
by the author. Results will vary.

Inquiries about reproducing material from this work should be
addressed to the University of Alabama Press.

Typeface: Bembo

Cover design: Michele Myatt Quinn

Library of Congress Cataloging-in-Publication Data

Names: Blejwas, Emily, author.

Title: The story of Alabama in fourteen foods / Emily Blejwas.

Description: Tuscaloosa : The University of Alabama Press, [2019]
| Includes bibliographical references and index.

Identifiers: LCCN 2018048158| ISBN 9780817320195 (cloth)
| ISBN 9780817392314 (ebook)

Subjects: LCSH: Cooking—Alabama—History. | Food—
Alabama—History. | Cooking, American—Southern style.
| Alabama—History. | LCGFT: Cookbooks.

Classification: LCC TX715.2.S68 B548 2019
| DDC 641.59761—dc23

LC record available at https://lccn.loc.gov/2018048158

To Alabamians, especially my favorite five:
Andrew, Stan, Andrew, Leo, and Katie

And in memory of
Bill Allen
Bea Carlton
Annie Cooper
Billie Crumly
Dora Finley
Vince Henderson
Ruthie Smith
Robert Thrower
Bud Williams

A place at the table is like a ringside seat at the historical
and ongoing drama of life in the region.

—John Egerton

Contents

Recipes

Acknowledgments

RESEARCH FOR THIS BOOK was supported by the Alabama Association of Resource Conservation and Development Councils.

A book like this depends entirely on the generosity of others. Time and again, I was humbled by the willingness of so many people to freely open their lives, hearts, and schedules to me, with no expectation of return. A grateful thanks to the following for providing information and support and for snowballing me in the right direction: Amber Alvarez, John Aplin, Ray Barnett, Shirley Baxter, James Bedsole, Peter Berg, Cora Berry, Mike Bethune, Lakin Boyd, Joey Brackner, Sharon Brakefield, Lecia Brooks, Valerie Pope Burnes, Lorraine Capers, Deborah Casey, Al Cason, Joyce Cauthen, Cappi Chambers, Tom Chesnutt, Jennifer Chism, Midge Coates, Lauren Cole, Peggy Collins, Richard Collins, John Cooper, Billie Crumly, Jerry Curran, Debra Davis, Rebekah Davis, Deidra Dees, Avis Dunbar, Connie Floyd, Glenda Freeman, Frye Gaillard, Darlene Gatlin, James Giesen, Gloria Good, Steve Grauberger, Sandy Greene, Brian Grubbs, Tim Hamer, Wayne Hammond, Glen Harrison, David Helms, Mark Hersey, Jonathan Hinton, Roger Howard, Clinton Hyde, Tory Johnston, Norwood Kerr, Bettye Kimbrell, Anne Knight, Jacob Laurence, Mary Linneman, Jan Longone, Sara Love, Ellen Gray Massey, Bill Mathews, Robby McClure, Meredith McLemore, Mark Moberg, Mike Moody, Robert Moss, Gina Myers, Linda Nelson, Becky Nichols, Aubrey Pearce, Beth Poole, Chris Raley, Dewayne Raper, Christina Rausch, Neil Ravenna, Lori Rockhold, Mike Roden, Jessica Roth, Amy Ryan, Vivian Santangelo, Cornelia Schnall, Justin Sessions, Harriet Sharer, John Soluri, Mary Sternberg, Stephanie Sutton, Louisa Terrell, Susan Thomas, Michael Thomason, Carrie Threadgill, and Ann Toplovich.

And then there are those who breathed this book into being. A profound thanks to Bill Allen, Alex Alvarez, Steve Barnett, Rebecca Beasley, Joey Boyd, Bea Carlton, Wayne and Doris Dean, Barbara Drummond, the

East Limestone Volunteer Fire Department, Dora Finley, Lula Hatcher, Martha Hawkins, Vince Henderson, Al Hooks, Tom Kelly, Nelson Malden, Eddy, Susan, and Forrest Morris, Steve Mussell, Jimmy Pollard, Dave Raley, Fred Richardson, Becky Robertson, Robert Thrower, Steven Toomey, Vinh Tran, Tricia Wallwork, Virginia Whitfield, and Bud Williams.

A heartfelt thanks to my editors, Dan Waterman and Wendi Schnaufer, for seeing this project through all of its stages. To my reviewers for providing critical advice. To Foster Dickson for creating an incredible curriculum guide to make this book more meaningful to our most important readers. And to Valerie Downes for her friendship and artistic grace.

A deep, sweet thanks to all of my friends and family for their support, especially my Hannon Avenue neighbors, my dad for reading the early, sketchy drafts, the ladies for all the title help, my kids for keeping me simultaneously grounded and light, and, most of all, my husband, who taught me how to think outside the box and gives me the boost, every day, to get there.

The Story of
ALABAMA
in
FOURTEEN
FOODS

Map of Alabama, including key counties, regions, places, cultural areas, and waterways featured in the book

Introduction

EVER SINCE HERNANDO DE SOTO brought thirteen pigs to the Florida shore in 1539, Native, European, and African Americans have blended and shaped each other's food traditions to create a food identity that is uniquely southern. "Southern food" emerged from this cultural collision in the Southeast, which mingled African spices, native plants, and European recipes. Yet, southern food not only encompasses the dishes served but crops raised, trade routes, cultural movements, and pastimes. Each food tradition is a mix of converging factors, including cultural, social, economic, legislative, and environmental. Today, forces as variable as soil content, Catholic tradition, and southern literature continue to shape southern food.

To fully understand southern food, then, requires us to examine the culture surrounding the food in its totality, with all of the nuances and complexities that birthed the southern food identity. We must consider environment, economy, politics, social movements, geography, and heritage. Only then can we understand why sweet potatoes and collards grace the Thanksgiving table, or how banana pudding became the ubiquitous southern dessert, or what enabled the plain old peanut to once reverse economic fortunes.

Southerners will tell you this is work worth doing. Food has always occupied a primary place in southern culture, in every walk of life. Art, music, film, and literature in the South teem with food references and symbolism. Southerners use food as a badge of honor and identity, one deeply connected to a sense of family, community, and self. Hurricane Katrina proved the point, when after the "floodwaters receded, the first volumes residents bought to replace their waterlogged, moldy collections were often beloved cookbooks."[1]

Food is embedded in southern identity at every historical step. For hundreds of years, food operated at the center of southern life. Though the Deep South conjures up cotton plantations in the minds of many, few lived this reality. From its inception until World War II, the South was largely populated by subsistence farm families who spent most of their hours planting, harvesting, and processing the foods needed to stay alive. Food was central to southerners because it demanded nearly all of everyone's time. It was important because life depended on it.

In this rural existence, where travel was local, communication slow, and townships outspread, food-centered gatherings also provided a vital social outlet. Cane grindings and peanut boils became major fellowship opportunities for rural communities. Some traditional southern foods, like chicken stew and barbecue, are cooked long and slow, providing ample time for visiting. Over time, these rural food-centered gatherings grew into traditions emblematic of southern identity, so that even when southerners moved to urban and suburban places, they still gathered for fish fries.

Food also grew into the southern identity via hospitality: a fundamental belief among southerners that everyone who comes to the door should leave well fed. Scholars have various theories on the origins of southern hospitality. Culinary historian Jessica Harris believes it grew from West African notions brought to the South by American slaves. Journalist John Egerton attributes it to historic struggles with hunger and poverty. Either way, southerners are likely to agree with Egerton's assessment that nothing better characterizes the South than "the spreading of a feast of native food and drink before a gathering of kin and friends."[2]

The Civil War further solidified food's place in southern identity. When widespread poverty introduced wealthy southerners to foods previously consumed only by the poor, the concept of southern food fused across economic and racial lines. Southerners also greatly expanded their vegetable repertoire during the war, eating anything they could grow or find wild, which continues to inform southern cooking today. Finally, the South's defeat gave food traditions a new gravity among southerners. As Eugene Walter, a chef, poet, musician, actor, and general jack-of-all-cultural-trades from Mobile, Alabama, writes of the South, "during the years after the Civil War the region took its tone, set its style, cocked its snoot, *decided* to become set in its ways and pleasurably conscious of being so. Traditions became doubly important; the

Plowing a field at Palmerdale, Alabama, 1937 (photo by Arthur Rothstein, Library of Congress, LC-USF34-005891-E)

South set about glamorizing its past and transforming anecdote into legend. And among the rites and observances, none was more important than those of the table."[3]

As Walter notes, the Civil War forever altered the South, and southerners responded by using traditions as touchstones in the face of bleak uncertainty and economic chaos. But this instinct was not confined to postbellum years. World War II also dramatically changed the South, as southerners abandoned rural life in droves. Though they embraced new convenience foods like canned vegetables and prepackaged bread, southerners still held tight to traditional fare, especially at Sunday dinners and downtown cafés that served up "home cooking."

In fact, once most southerners had left farming, home cooking became more than taste preference and comfort food. It became historic preservation. The cooking that everyone's mama and granny used to do as daily habit was suddenly under threat of extinction, and as it flickered, southerners fought hard to save it. The 1970s saw a renaissance of barbecue joints, which had languished in the face of fast food, as well as a surge in farmers' markets, food-centered festivals, and food writing.

Southerners' efforts to preserve their food heritage captured national attention. Among southerners and northerners alike, interest in southern food has exploded in the past few decades, inspiring a spate of cookbooks and culinary tours. Barbecue cook-offs have reached biblical proportions. *Cornbread Nation*, a compilation of the best in southern food writing, saw its seventh edition in 2014. The increasingly louder calls to eat local have also spotlighted southern food, which has been anchored in seasonal, homegrown ingredients for centuries. In recent years, many talented chefs, food writers, and locavores have provided rich accounts of and instructions for capturing the southern food experience.

With the existing, excellent scholarship on southern food as its foundation, this book aims in a new direction. Neither a cookbook nor a food travelogue, this book uses fourteen foods as a lens for exploring the histories and cultures of one southern state: Alabama. In this book, food traditions act as gateways to Alabama customs, cultures, regions, movements, and events. Each featured food is deeply rooted in Alabama identity and tells a story with both local and national resonance. Chapters are arranged chronologically to allow the story of Alabama to unfold.

This book is grounded in the premise that every food has a story to tell, but I was especially interested in lesser-known stories. Thus, the book illumines the lives of Poarch Creeks, Creoles of color, wild turkey hunters, Alabama club women, frontier squatters, Mardi Gras revelers, sharecroppers, and Vietnamese shrimpers. It explores Mobile's banana docks, chicken stew

Poarch Creek Pow Wow Club dancers (photo by Emily Blejwas)

sales in the Tennessee Valley, the Great Depression in Birmingham, Sumter County barbecue clubs, Appalachian Decoration Days, cane syrup making, peanut boils, and eggnog parties. And it profiles the lives of Alabama notables such as George Washington Carver and Georgia Gilmore.

To collect these stories, I traversed Alabama from the Gulf Coast to Sand Mountain, from grassy peanut country to urban blocks, and along Alabama's Black Belt, cinched across its middle. I learned, as Alabama native and chef Scott Peacock contends, that "the state of Alabama is a small town, but many countries."[4] Alabama holds a stunning diversity of history, culture, environment, and experience, which is expressed in its food. Fried cornbread and layer cakes are Wiregrass specialties. Seafood gumbo reigns along the coast. Stack cakes belong to the Appalachian foothills. Tennessee Valley chicken stew is made in just a handful of north Alabama counties. Cornmeal is yellow in the north and white in the south. Syrup is sorghum in the north and cane in the south. The state is home to at least six distinct regional variations of barbecue sauce.

I wrote this book both to articulate and pay homage to this complexity in a state too often categorized as simply "Deep South." Alabama food traditions are united under a southern identity but customized according to local experience. As chef Bill Neal reminds us, since the South's creation, "the cooking, like the society, was never homogenous."[5] Food traditions in Alabama reflect these intricacies, revealing the intrigue of Alabama itself: its startling variety, cultural fusion, weighty history, and spectrum of stories to tell.

ONE

Roasted Corn

The Creek Nation in Alabama

ON THANKSGIVING DAY, the Poarch Creek Thanksgiving Pow Wow opens under blue skies and a mild sun, with tribal members and non-Natives alike ambling onto the reservation. Held on the only remaining Creek land in Alabama, the ceremonial mound is flanked by an eclectic mix of living history exhibits, food booths, and vendors selling Native American wares. One stand offers Indian face painting, and a woman from Florida has lugged along her corn mill, which hums loudly as it separates corn into three troughs: cornmeal, grits, and chicken feed. Just inside the entrance gate, local historian Larry Tupperville is smoking out a canoe. No one taught him how, he says; he just decided one day to try it.

Roasted corn is the Pow Wow's signature dish, prepared by members of the McGhee family who use only the freshest corn, which in late November requires importing thousands of ears from California. On arrival, the corn is soaked in cold water for a few hours so it retains moisture and stays tender when roasted in the husk over an oak wood fire. The husk is then removed,

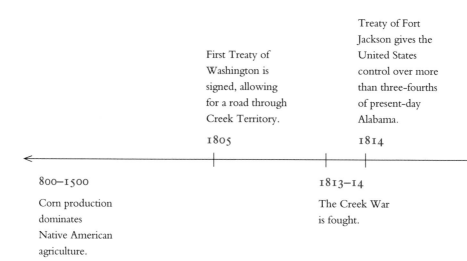

First Treaty of
Washington is
signed, allowing
for a road through
Creek Territory.

1805

Treaty of Fort
Jackson gives the
United States
control over more
than three-fourths
of present-day
Alabama.

1814

800–1500

Corn production
dominates
Native American
agriculture.

1813–14

The Creek War
is fought.

the bright yellow ear dipped in butter, and the corn served hot, with salt shakers provided.[1] The McGhee family has perfected their methods over the years through trial and error, eventually building a pit on the reservation expressly for the purpose of roasting corn.

Shortly after the inaugural Pow Wow in 1971, Poarch Creek leaders recruited tribal member John Arthur McGhee to roast corn annually at the event. McGhee knew nothing about roasting corn when he began, but agreed to do it because he recognized corn as the most emblematic food of Creek culture, one that was part of every traditional Creek dish, and it was hard to imagine an authentic Pow Wow without it. In fact, roasted corn at the Poarch Creek Pow Wow reflects the titanic connection between Native Americans and corn, one that made corn the most significant food in the South for over a thousand years.

When corn cultivation began in earnest in the Southeast, it revolutionized Native American life. In the Mississippian Era (800–1500 CE), the sharp increase in corn production (coupled with an increase in bow and arrow warfare) created a food surplus that yielded a population surge, prompting Native Americans to abandon nomadic lifestyles and establish permanent agrarian

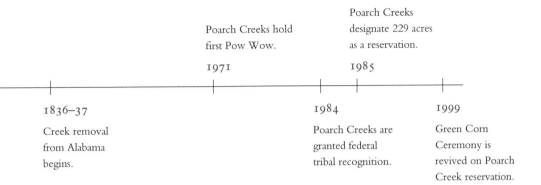

Poarch Creeks hold
first Pow Wow.

1971

Poarch Creeks
designate 229 acres
as a reservation.

1985

1836–37
Creek removal
from Alabama
begins.

1984
Poarch Creeks are
granted federal
tribal recognition.

1999
Green Corn
Ceremony is
revived on Poarch
Creek reservation.

Roasting and eating corn at the Poarch Creek
Thanksgiving Pow Wow (photos by Emily
Blejwas)

societies. A complex social and political structure emerged that relied on centralized authority and economic redistribution. Settlements became large and fortified, and adjoining settlements grouped into political territories with permanent offices of leadership. These societies maintained trade networks, engaged in war, established shared symbols and rituals, and practiced elaborate ceremonies.

The second largest of these prehistoric Mississippian communities was located in present-day Moundville, Alabama, along the Black Warrior River. At its height, the Moundville settlement was a bustling city of three thousand inhabitants encompassing three hundred acres. As described by John Blitz in *Moundville*, it was massively productive and traded at great distances. At its

Moundville Archeological Park (drawing by Steve Patricia)

heart lay a central plaza with more than twenty earthen ceremonial mounds, surrounded by small wood and thatch homes in clusters of five to twenty. Then came the encircling fortifications and beyond those: fields of corn.

Though Native Americans hunted, fished, gathered, and planted a variety of fruits and vegetables, corn remained the linchpin of diet, society, and economy during the Mississippian Era.[2] As the core food staple, corn was raised in an abundance of varieties and colors and consumed in various ways, including raw, boiled, fried, and roasted. Corn was ground into meal, flour, and grits and mixed with vegetables to make stew. *Sofkee*, a thick corn porridge, was a common dish, and a pot of it was kept on hand in most households. Dried corn was stored in elevated cribs to last throughout the winter.

Mural of corn in Native American life, by John Augustus Walker, 1939 (Auburn University Libraries)

All of this work, the planting, harvesting, and cooking of corn, was done primarily by women. They owned the fields and controlled the harvest, while men acted as hunters, warriors, and diplomats. The women raised corn alongside streams, where the soil was naturally renewed each year by annual spring floods. They interspersed beans and squash among the corn plants, and together, these "three sisters" of the Native American diet provided Mississippians with essential nutrients.

Corn cultivation not only radically reconfigured Native American lives, however. It would dramatically shape the lives of all Southerners. When Europeans began settling in the Southeast in the early 1600s, corn spared them from starvation when their crops of wheat and barley failed, and Native Americans taught them how to plant, harvest, process, prepare, and store it. Through several winters of famine, white settlers relied almost entirely on corn for their survival.

A symbol of life and death in colonial America, corn remained the mainstay of the Southern diet throughout frontier years. Every pioneer's first step was to clear enough land to plant a crop of corn. Sometimes, frontier men would venture ahead to plant the first crop, then return for their wives and children. Pioneers even marked the seasons by corn. In 1808, a woman in present-day Limestone County, Alabama, described the time of year as "when the first crop of corn was in good roasting ear state and every stalk was cut and burned."[3]

Corn was the primary crop in every colony and every state, prompting historian Nicholas Hardeman to dub it "the great common denominator of agriculture."[4] Every southern farm devoted more than half its acreage to corn, most of which provided basic sustenance for families and livestock and never reached the marketplace. Though settlers did hunt, fish, and grow vegetables, they traded meat and produce for corn in times of need. In fact, the American economy revolved around corn, which passed as currency anywhere in the hemisphere and was frequently used to pay taxes, rents, and marriage licenses. As Hardeman notes, "corn was coin" in America, whether it appeared as ears, meal, or whiskey.[5]

Appearing "on the southern table in some form at practically every meal," corn was eaten raw, pickled, and boiled.[6] It was ground into flour for bread (known as pone, ashcake, johnnycake, hoecake, and dodgers), fritters, dumplings, and tortillas.[7] Corn was consumed as hominy, grits, roasting ears, popcorn, soup, mush, succotash, pudding, and porridge. It provided a foundation for beer and whiskey, a batter to fry fish, a starch, and a sweetener.

Corn's utility also extended beyond the table. Corn silks served a medicinal purpose. Husks were turned into chair seats, horse collars, baskets, dolls, and paper. Corncobs met a range of household needs as scrubbing brushes, handles for small tools, bowls for tobacco pipes, jug stoppers, firewood, fertilizer, and livestock feed. Fermented corn became lamp fluid and antifreeze. Houses were built from cornstalks.[8]

Cornfield in Cullman County, Alabama, 1926 (Auburn University Libraries, 71.14.4.4)

By 1849, the South had eighteen million acres planted in corn compared with five million in cotton. During the 1850s, the combined value of cotton, tobacco, wheat, and rice claimed only two-thirds the value of corn. During the lean years of the Civil War and Reconstruction, corn again shielded southerners against starvation. In fact, corn remained the most significant component of the southern diet until World War II.[9] Corn, truly, was king, inspiring anthropologist David Hurst Thomas to call the emergence of corn cultivation in the Southeast "a watershed event in American history."[10] Yet, what had become of the Native Americans who gave starving Europeans the gift of corn that spared their lives and shaped their diet, economy, and culture for the next three hundred years?

In the early seventeenth century, prompted in part by the influx of Europeans, confederations began to emerge out of hundreds of Native American societies in the Southeast. In what is now Alabama, Creeks were by far the largest and most significant tribe, with no sizable groups of Cherokee, Chickasaw, or Choctaw in the region until the early nineteenth century. In fact, Creeks were one of the most powerful tribes in all of North America. The Creek Nation occupied nearly all of what is present-day Alabama and Georgia and parts of the Florida Panhandle, controlling millions of acres of land.

Creeks referred to themselves as Muskogee but were dubbed Creeks by early British settlers who noted their habit of establishing settlements along fertile creek banks. The Creek Nation operated as a loose confederation of independent tribes united by Muskogee language, culture, and common interest. Always in flux, the confederation sometimes also included non-Muskogee tribes. In what is now Alabama, Creeks controlled a vast frontier defended by sixty or so scattered towns. In 1775, after devastating losses caused by European disease followed by a steady regrowth, the Creek population there numbered around twelve thousand.[11]

Though the Creek Nation flourished at the end of the 1700s, change came with the dawn of the new century. The First Treaty of Washington, signed in 1805, allowed the US government to construct a horse path through

Map of the southern United States, 1813 (Hargrett Rare Book and Manuscript Library, University of Georgia, Map 1813, M4)

Creek lands to connect Washington, DC, to Mobile and New Orleans. Running through the heart of Creek territory, the new postal road gave thousands of white settlers an easy route into what is now Alabama. In 1810, when the road became a military road (the Federal Road), the number of white settlers traversing the Creek Nation, living along its borders, and encroaching on Creek land soared.[12]

Reactions to the road were mixed among Creeks. A minority of Creeks benefited from the increased white presence, which provided access to the European economy. These Creeks were predominantly *métis* (mixed white and Creek) who had settled in the Tensaw region in the late 1700s and begun a vigorous trade with the Spanish. Tensaw was the Creek name for the fertile valleys along the lower reaches of the Alabama River, in present-day Baldwin County.

In the Tensaw, Creeks continued to grow corn in communal fields and adhere to Creek constructs of kinship, gender roles, and religion but also adopted aspects of white culture and became immersed in the European economy. They grew and shipped indigo and cotton, raised cattle and hogs in pens, traded deerskins for tools, cloth, and guns, owned slaves, bred horses, intermarried with white settlers, traveled by flatboat, and wore European clothing. Some worked as guides, interpreters, river pilots, and postal riders, and some owned stores, inns, and taverns. One operated a horse track. As historian Karl Davis writes, Tensaw Creeks existed in a "curious mix of tradition and innovation" in which they resembled white people culturally in some ways but "remained distinctly Creek."[13]

Tensaw Creeks recognized that their prosperity depended on the white economy, and though most rejected assimilation into white culture, they saw nothing to gain from conflict with white people.[14] Most Creeks (including many within the Tensaw region), however, viewed white settlers flooding into Creek territory as a direct threat to their homeland and way of life.[15] Divisions between the two Creek factions intensified as the settlers continued to pour into Creek lands, Tensaw Creeks became more prosperous, and the US government stepped up its "plan of civilization."

The plan of civilization called for Native Americans to assimilate into white society, abandon hunting, raise cattle, and grow cotton. It purported to benefit Native Americans by training them to become successful small farmers but was truly purposed to enable the US government to acquire vast Native lands no longer needed for hunting and redistribute them to white settlers.[16] As archaeologist Gregory Waselkov notes, the plan "called for a radical reorientation of native society" that encouraged Creeks to forfeit traditional constructs and subscribe to "American notions of education, justice, religion, and private property."[17]

In the plan, most Creeks saw a thinly veiled effort "to steal their ancestral land and destroy their culture."[18] Dubbing themselves Red Sticks after the traditional color of the Creek war club, this faction demanded a return to tradition, calling on fellow Creeks to reject American values, fight white expansion, and revitalize Creek culture. They began attacking white travelers throughout Creek Territory and destroying goods and cattle owned by Tensaw Creeks, who had gained wealth in the white economy and were suspected of colluding with the US government.[19] By the summer of 1813, civil war appeared inevitable.

The Creek War of 1813–14 played out on what is now Alabama soil and impacted the fate of all southeastern tribes as well as the development, economy, and culture of Alabama. In August 1813, in the Battle at Fort Mims (in present-day Baldwin County), 700 Red Sticks killed 250 Tensaw defenders and civilians in a grisly surprise attack. Though the battle was truly between Creek factions (and even between Creek family members), the media portrayed it as an unprovoked massacre of white people. A wave of anti-Indian sentiment ensued, despite the fact that several hundred white settlers and Creeks had peacefully coexisted for years in the Tensaw. As Waselkov notes, "that dream ended in blood and fire at Fort Mims."[20]

Panic now raged in the Mississippi Territory (present-day Alabama and Mississippi). Many white people, especially those who lacked prior contact with Creeks, sought revenge for the Fort Mims atrocity. Within weeks, thousands had volunteered to fight the Red Sticks, now cast in their minds as savages. In fact, observes Waselkov, the "imagery generated by the myth of Fort Mims—of hundreds of helpless white settlers slaughtered by inhuman savages—fueled passions for American conquest of all native peoples for the rest of the century."[21] Fort Mims provided a tool to incite white citizens to fight, divide, and destroy the Creek confederacy and ultimately to drive all Creeks from their lands.[22] And no one understood this better than Andrew Jackson.

As commander of the Tennessee militia, Jackson used the brutality at Fort Mims to justify equally brutal tactics. Under his command, the Creek civil war quickly became a war of Indian extermination.[23] By March 1814, following several battles, Jackson had gathered a force of American militia and allied Creeks and Cherokees strong enough to challenge the Red Sticks at the village of Tohopeka (located in a turn of the Tallapoosa River known as Horseshoe Bend, in present-day Tallapoosa County). The battle swiftly became a slaughter, as Jackson and his allies killed nearly all of the nine hundred Red Stick warriors, "the highest number of Native American fatalities of any battle in North American history."[24] Jackson then headed to the heart of Creek territory, the junction of the Coosa and Tallapoosa Rivers, where he established Fort Jackson and dispatched troops to attack every Creek they encountered and burn every town in the Upper Creek nation.[25]

The Red Sticks' defeat at Horseshoe Bend permanently destroyed Creek power in Alabama. On August 9, 1814, despite objections from Creek chiefs in attendance, the Treaty of Fort Jackson gave over twenty-two million acres of land (more than half of the entire Creek nation) to the US government. Over nine million acres (including all of the Tensaw) came from allied Creeks. It was the largest seizure of Native lands in American history to date. Further, over the next decade, Jackson would spearhead eight more treaties to remove Native Americans from their homelands in order to clear the Southeast for white settlement, giving the United States control over three-quarters of what is now Alabama.

Thousands of white settlers from Tennessee, Georgia, and the Carolinas poured into former Creek lands. In 1810, the non-Native population in what is now Alabama numbered 9,000. By 1820, it had increased more than 1,000 percent to reach 150,000 (with two-thirds of the growth coming after 1815). By 1830, the state population had doubled, reaching 310,000.[26] Yet, as Alabama historians note, this was "more than just a population explosion." By opening vast, fertile lands for white settlement, the Creek War paved the way for an economy based on the cotton trade and slave labor that would shape Alabama politics, economics, and culture for years to come.[27]

The Creek War also made Jackson a national hero to many, propelling him to win the presidency in 1828.[28] In 1830, one year after taking office, Jackson pushed the Indian Removal Act through both houses of Congress despite considerable opposition. As Waselkov keenly notes, "we tend to think of American history as a series of inevitabilities, but many white Americans in the 1820s and 1830s opposed Indian Removal, and Congress only narrowly passed the legislation which enabled that national shame to occur. Indian Removal derived largely from Andrew Jackson's political popularity and his unshakeable will."[29]

The Indian Removal Act gave the president power to negotiate removal treaties with tribes living east of the Mississippi River. Most Creeks, however, refused to emigrate. In 1832, a number of prominent Creek chiefs negotiated the Treaty of Washington, in which Creeks ceded all five million acres of their land to the United States but retained legal title to two million acres reserved for Creek plantations and farms. In the treaty, the US government pledged to protect Creek lives and property.

The United States violated the treaty within days, failing to protect Creeks from white settlers who invaded Creek lands, killing, raping, and stealing, and from speculators who cheated Creeks out of their land. Further, the state of Alabama did not enforce the treaty, continuing "its strategy of making conditions so miserable for the Creeks that they would choose to remove." In Alabama, Creeks had "no legal protection. Their oaths were not accepted in court, so they had no legal redress when wrongs were committed against them."[30]

When destitute Creeks began stealing livestock and crops from white settlers, violent clashes erupted, which President Jackson used to justify removing all Creeks from Alabama. In 1836, the secretary of war ordered Creek removal as a military necessity.[31] Nearly all Creeks, regardless of their participation in violence, previous aid to the US military, or legal claim to land, were rounded up and sent to "gathering places" to await removal. Soon, "weakened by starvation, defrauded of their lands and swindled out of most of their possessions, thousands of Creeks were on their way from Alabama to what is now Oklahoma."[32] In 1836–37, over fourteen thousand Creeks were removed from their Alabama homelands and relocated west.

When Tensaw Creeks returned home following the Creek War, "they found their houses and farm buildings burned, their livestock killed or missing, and their fields overgrown."[33] Land disputes with white settlers erupted immediately. But in 1817, a small group of Tensaw Creeks secured twenty-four US land grants in recognition of their long service to the American government. Thanks to this tiny group from the Tensaw, Creeks maintained a presence in the Southeast: Tensaw Creeks were the only Creeks to retain land in Alabama during removal and would become the sole Creek community east of the Mississippi.[34]

By the time Tensaw Creeks received their land in 1836, no acreage remained in the Tensaw, which was well populated and home to a growing timber industry. They were forced to obtain land in the pine forests twenty miles inland from the Alabama River, in present-day Escambia County, fifty-three miles northeast of Mobile. It was here they became known as the Poarch Creeks, named for a nearby railroad stop called Poarch Switch. (Poarch was likely the surname of a British railroad man.)

During the late nineteenth century, the Poarch Creek community became increasingly defined as local settlements evolved "into a geographically concentrated, highly intermarried, kinship-based group" that numbered roughly 150 members in the 1900 census.[35] Yet, Poarch Creeks lived in a world of intense racial discrimination and segregation that afforded few economic opportunities and consigned them to a meager existence. Natives were hired only as migrant laborers, mostly farming cotton. Lou Vickery, a Poarch Creek tribal member, explains: "There were few, if any, cultural and economic arguments . . . to self-identify as Indian. In fact, most of the Poarch Creeks, during this era, were treated by the white community as second-class citizens. Those identifying as 'Indian' attended inferior schools. They had restricted opportunities for employment. They had minimal chances for participation in the power structure of the community. They experienced prejudices of the first order."[36]

As a result, many Poarch Creeks hid their heritage well into the twentieth century. As Poarch Creek cultural director Robert Thrower relates, from the Civil War through the Great Depression, Poarch Creeks referred to themselves as "the Lost Creeks" because few white people realized Indians still existed in Alabama. Even Thrower's grandmother, the last native Muskogee speaker in the region and daughter of a medicine woman, did not openly reveal her heritage.[37]

Toward midcentury, however, things began to change. In 1929, the Episcopal Church began a mission program in the area. They constructed four churches, provided much-needed medical services, and consolidated the four local Creek schools in 1939. The school consolidation bound the community closer together and planted seeds of Creek pride. Poarch Creeks also suffered less isolation in the 1930s with the emergence of new job opportunities in forest related industries (particularly timber and pulpwood), on new railroad lines, and at the Alabama Dry Docks in Mobile. Military service during World War II also broadened Poarch Creek horizons.

In the early 1940s, when the Poarch Creek community had grown to four hundred members, Calvin McGhee was elected as the first official *mekko* (leader). A charismatic leader, McGhee worked tirelessly toward social and educational reforms within the community and in Washington, DC. He championed school desegregation, revived lost land claims, and sought federal recognition for the tribe. In 1948, McGhee spearheaded a community-wide boycott of local public schools until Poarch Creeks received a new schoolhouse and a bus so they could attend the nearby junior high and high schools, allowing them to attend school past sixth grade.

In 1952, after McGhee went door-to-door collecting signatures of support, Poarch Creeks won a Supreme Court case that made them eligible for Creek Indian Land Claims. Payments were dispersed in 1972, and most recipients donated the money to a community fund. Though the payments were relatively small, the recognition of land lost, the unity generated by filing the claims, and the ability to invest in the future of Poarch Creeks bolstered community pride.[38] Combined with a cultural landscape changed by the civil rights movement and the American Indian movement, the land claim payments sparked a renaissance in the Poarch Creek community. At long last, tribal members began to seek out and celebrate their heritage.

However, Creek removal and racial discrimination had buried Creek traditions in Alabama for generations. In fact, when Calvin McGhee donned Indian clothing in the 1950s and 1960s to display pride in his Creek heritage, he was actually wearing a Plains-style headdress. Thus, reconnecting with their heritage required Poarch Creeks to consult Creeks in Oklahoma, where Creek traditions and language had remained intact. Oklahoma Creeks were instrumental in bringing cultural knowledge to their Alabama brethren in the 1970s and 1980s.

By the time Calvin McGhee died in 1970, his cultural revitalization efforts spanning three decades had provided the Poarch Creek community with incredible momentum. A group of young leaders, including some of the first Poarch Creek high school graduates, carried the torch.[39] In 1971, Poarch Creeks held their first Thanksgiving Pow Wow. In 1974, they adopted their official name: the Poarch Band of Creek Indians. In 1975, they petitioned for federal tribal recognition, followed by five years of genealogical research to produce the necessary documentation. After five more years of waiting, federal tribal recognition was granted on August 11, 1984. The following year, the tribe designated 229 acres as the Poarch Creek reservation.

Today, Poarch Creeks are the only federally recognized Indian tribe in Alabama and reside on the only official Creek land in the state. Most of the three thousand tribal members live on or near the reservation, which now boasts a cultural center that offers a range of Creek heritage classes, including Muskogee language, patchwork, river cane basketry (river cane is grown on the reservation), shell carving, and ribbon shirt making. Robert Thrower made it his mission to grow the corn original to Creek ancestors in Alabama and obtained kernels of blue corn from a colleague in Oklahoma that are identical to the variety that kept Creeks alive on the Trail of Tears.

"Cultural revival is gaining momentum daily," relates Alex Alvarez, hired as a full-time cultural educator in 2006. Alvarez has focused on developing

Calvin McGhee (second from right) at the White House, 1962 (Calvin McGhee
Cultural Authority)

youth programming, after "falling in love with what teaching culture does for
kids" while working for an Indian Aid program in Kansas. Further, the power
of cultural knowledge is "contagious," says Alvarez. "It's a chain reaction.
The kids influence their parents. We teach kids about their heritage and identity hoping they will pass the knowledge on to their families."

Alvarez hopes to continue growing the cultural programs, especially
when it comes to Creek language, which has not been openly spoken in the

Poarch Creek community since the 1890s. Today, there are only four thousand Muskogee speakers worldwide. In Poarch Creek schools, Creek language is now part of the weekly curriculum from preschool to middle school, but Alvarez has even loftier goals. He envisions a Creek language immersion school on the reservation, enabling students to achieve fluency in Muskogee by high school graduation.[40]

Though the Pow Wow draws competitive drummers and dancers from tribes across the nation, the morning is devoted to celebrating Poarch Creek heritage. Local preschoolers count to ten and sing songs in Muskogee. Poarch Creek Pow Wow Club dancers, ages ten through sixteen, sport brightly colored regalia and perform energetically to cheers from the crowd. The club boasts forty members, who practice twice weekly and dance at a dozen competitions annually, traveling throughout the Southeast.

Poarch Creek Pow Wow Club dancers (photo by Emily Blejwas)

Poarch Creek girls, ages nine through eighteen, can also compete in a princess contest, a traditional Creek event. Today's contestants have attended sessions since July, learning about Creek culture and practicing basket weaving and sewing so they could make part of their own ensembles. Last night, they performed in a talent competition and were interviewed about their interests and Creek heritage. Today, each contestant circles the outer edge of the ceremonial mound, wearing traditional Creek clothing and waving to the crowd, while the emcee announces her name, parents' and grandparents' names, school, church, and favorite subjects, foods, and hobbies. When she has completed the circle, she is asked a randomly selected question about Creek heritage. The girls' answers reveal not only their cultural knowledge but a deep commitment to carry on Poarch Creek traditions, to serve and represent the tribe, and to live by Creek values.

Poarch Creek Princess contestants (photo by Emily Blejwas)

The princess title is viewed with gravity. Princesses are esteemed as representatives of their families and tribes and are expected to conduct themselves as role models. Today, the three winning princesses are called to increase cultural knowledge among tribal members, educate others about the tribe, be goodwill ambassadors, and represent Poarch Creeks throughout Pow Wow country. Alvarez reflects on the power of cultural education for youth, provided by the Pow Wow Club and princess contest: "Without a cultural grounding, you try to fill that hole with everything else. Drugs, alcohol, any kind of trouble. I speak from personal experience. But if you can help kids find their identity and link them to the past, it makes them well rounded and gives them a sense of who they are. You see amazing changes in kids who learn their culture, especially for kids who don't fit anywhere else. They find their place."[41]

It's easy to see how finding their place could be a struggle for modern Poarch Creeks, who seem to exist in a cultural mix of traditional and modern, Indian and white, Creek and Christian, evidenced in small details throughout the Pow Wow. Several princess contestants bear the surname McGhee, but their first names are popular: Madison, Hayley, Kennedy, and Mallory. Their hobbies include texting and shopping. Thanksgiving itself is a blended European and Native American celebration. The Pow Wow also bears touches of nationalism, with veterans recognized and the national anthem sung. Both God and the Great Spirit are invoked. Local churches operate the food booths and preschoolers sing "This Little Light of Mine" in Muskogee.

In fact, the vast majority of Poarch Creeks are Christians, Alvarez says. The community possesses a deep sense of gratitude for the Episcopal missionaries who brought vital health services and schools to the community beginning in 1929, and most Poarch Creeks have attended churches ever since. When Alvarez began teaching Creek culture in the community in 2006, some Poarch Creeks were actually suspicious. "You have to have the proper education alongside cultural programs," says Alvarez. "When people realize that Creeks are monotheistic and that practicing Creek heritage does not interfere with church or with Christian beliefs, they become more open to it."[42]

Alvarez views his role as being "a bridge" between the two worlds.

That's why he teaches preschoolers Christian hymns in the Creek language. "You have to do both," he says. "The message is that it's the same God, just different methods of worship. You walk with both your feet, not just one."[43]

The Pow Wow continues with intertribal competitions that last into the night and all day the following day. Participants have traveled from across the United States and Canada to compete in northern and southern styles of dancing and drumming. Thousands of spectators gather to watch, jamming the bleachers and food stands. The final round is featured on ESPN.

But as magnificent as the Pow Wow has become, Alvarez quickly clarifies that the Pow Wow does not define being Creek. "The Pow Wow is a social event," he explains. "It's intertribal, modern. But being Creek is a way of living. You follow a set of rules for fasting, abstaining, honoring your medicines, cleansing."[44] This also includes participating in the Green Corn Ceremony, revived on the Poarch Creek reservation in 1999 and held on secluded ceremonial ground.

The Green Corn Ceremony has been the most significant event of the Creek year since Mississippian times and is the most important rite for Poarch Creeks in Alabama today. "We have nothing in our own calendar of holidays which comes close to matching it in its load of social and cultural meaning," states anthropologist Charles Hudson, who likens the Green Corn Ceremony to Thanksgiving, New Year's Day, Yom Kippur, Lent, and Mardi Gras combined.[45]

Known as the *poskita*, from the Creek word *posketv*, "to fast," the Green Corn Ceremony was traditionally held to celebrate the ripening of the year's first corn, give thanks to the creator, ensure a bountiful harvest, and purify both individuals and villages. It marks the Creek New Year, and as such is a time for renewal, forgiveness, and purification. In the past, whole towns were renewed during a tribal fast. Men repaired and cleaned town buildings while women cleaned houses, clothing, and cooking vessels, extinguishing the home fire and scrubbing the hearth. Animosities were reconciled and crimes forgiven. In the central square, white-clad priests extinguished the sacred fire that had burned all year, cleansing the village of impurities. At the end of the

Green Corn Ceremony, which lasted several days, the sacred fire was rekindled and used to light home fires, symbolizing community oneness.[46]

Ceremonial dances play a critical role in the Green Corn Ceremony. The ribbon dance, performed by women bedecked in ribbons and new handmade clothing, commences the ceremony. This highly revered dance prepares the ceremonial ground for the main events the following day, when, after a ritual cleansing and purification, the men perform feather dances, wielding long river cane poles adorned with blue and white heron feathers. All participants fast from sunrise to sundown, then break the fast with a feast, followed by a night of singing and stomp dancing. The stomp dances of the Green Corn Ceremony, still performed in Creek communities, are believed to be one of the oldest surviving dances in the United States.

Traditionally, the Green Corn Ceremony feast featured the year's first corn. Today, a handful of Poarch Creeks honors this tradition by abstaining from eating new corn from December 31 until the Green Corn Ceremony the following summer. As Alvarez notes, this fast "recognizes that in the old days, there would be no more corn after the harvest was consumed. You couldn't just run down to the Winn Dixie. You had to survive off of one crop. So in honor of that we will only eat old corn, last year's crop, until the new corn comes in."[47]

To Alvarez, however, being Creek means more than honoring the old ways. It requires living by Creek values: sharing, giving to those less fortunate, selflessness, humility, being thankful, unconditional love and respect for your fellow humans, and a sense of connectedness, both to those around you and to other generations. "With every action, you think about the generation before you and the generation after you," Alvarez explains. "You connect yourself into that cycle."

These values "are reflected in corn," Alvarez notes. "Especially equality." A long time ago, he explains, corn was farmed in tribal gardens. The work was shared among large families and everyone helped with the harvest, the wealthy and commoners working side by side. Corn was the great equalizer, a shared burden, harvested for the need and for the good of all.[48]

TWO

||||||||||||||||||||||||||||||||||||||||||||||||||||||||||||||||||||||||||||||||||||||||||||||||||

Gumbo

Africans and Creoles on the Gulf Coast

Sooner or later, Southerners all come home,
not to die, but to eat gumbo.
—Eugene Walter, *Milking the Moon: A Southerner's Story of Life on This Planet*

IN 1940, FOLLOWING A parade in their honor, the first Mobile Mardi Gras
king and queen of color proceeded to the home of Dr. J. A. Franklin. A
prominent citizen in the black community, Franklin was well-known for his
hospitality and often hosted black celebrities who were barred from white-
owned hotels, including Joe Louis, Marian Anderson, Jackie Robinson, Oscar
De Priest, and Paul Robeson. At the Franklin home, the Mardi Gras court
enjoyed a champagne toast and gumbo, the enduring symbol of Creole and
African heritage on the Gulf Coast. Carrying on her grandfather's tradition,
Dora Finley continued to make a large pot of gumbo for family and friends
on the day of the king and queen's parade.

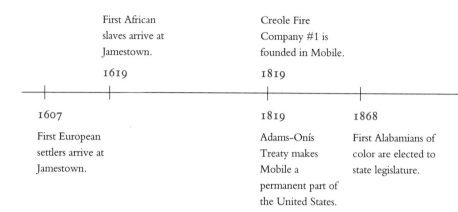

First African slaves arrive at Jamestown.

1619

Creole Fire Company #1 is founded in Mobile.

1819

1607

First European settlers arrive at Jamestown.

1819

Adams-Onís Treaty makes Mobile a permanent part of the United States.

1868

First Alabamians of color are elected to state legislature.

I visit Dora Finley on the seventieth anniversary of that first gumbo, and she stands in her kitchen just as her grandmother Dora Franklin once did. A Mardi Gras tree shimmers in purple, green, and gold in her front window, encircled by shoebox floats Finley made with her grandson. Family members are in town from Atlanta, Jackson, Houston, and as far away as San Francisco. When a cousin calls, Finley begs off the phone, telling him, "I'm knee deep in gumbo. . . . You need to get down here to Mobile."[1] Indeed, though Finley has laid out a large spread, the center of the feast will be the gumbo. She is preparing a large pot, which she assures me will be gone by evening's end.

Finley cooks gumbo in a "pass down pot" inherited from her mother. She has always liked to cook and, as the eldest daughter, was expected to cook for her family. She learned some of her gumbo techniques from her grandmothers, some from friends, and some through plain trial and error. She follows no written recipe but prepares through sight and taste. She cooks the roux, for instance, "'til it's the color of me." She holds out her arm so I can see the desired color. "Every time I cook gumbo, it's a different experience," she says. "It comes out different every time."

"Everything" goes into Finley's gumbo, including shrimp, crab, oysters,

New Alabama
state constitution
disenfranchises
nearly all persons
of color.

1901

Colored Carnival
Association forms
in Mobile.

1939

1908

Creoles of
color are barred
from voting in
Mobile municipal
elections.

1940

First Mardi Gras
king and queen of
color are appointed
in Mobile.

Dora Finley (photo
by Emily Blejwas)

baking hens, Conecuh sausage, and beef. She uses thyme, the Creole holy trinity of vegetables (onion, celery, and green bell pepper), and okra, insisting, "You can't have gumbo without okra." When all of the ingredients are in the pot, Finley dips in a coffee cup to "see what we're missing and what we're not." When she takes a sip, her eyes widen. "It's pretty much dead on," she says. "I can't believe it." As she ladles gumbo into a bowl for me, I ask if this is her favorite part of Mardi Gras: cooking gumbo for scores of family and friends.

She replies, "I love Mardi Gras. How could I not? I see all of my friends and family, the floats line up right outside my front door. But the part that disappoints me is that there are organizations that I can't be a part of because of the color of my skin. Mardi Gras is still segregated in 2010; it's the last stronghold of segregation in Mobile. People skirt around the issue, they say blacks want it that way. But we don't have a choice. Not that I'd run out and join these organizations, you understand, but don't tell me that I can't."[2]

Her words echo those of Mobile native and celebrated chef Vince Henderson, who waged a quiet war against segregation by passing as a white person and joining every private club in downtown Mobile in the 1960s. There were half a dozen of them, and none were open to black residents, who entered only as entertainers. Club owners confronted Henderson when he brought black friends to the clubs, but there was nothing they could do. As a member, he was entitled to bring up to five guests. Henderson often heard racist remarks at the clubs and ignored them. When I ask why he wanted to be part of a racist organization, he replies, "I had to join, just to see if I could do it. It was an act of defiance. Those clubs weren't about being private. They were about keeping blacks out."[3]

The stamp of African tradition on southern cooking is hard to understate. The first Africans arrived in America in 1619, just over a decade after the first European settlers. African slaves, who did the cooking in many southern households, were largely responsible for fusing African, European, and Native American traditions to birth a distinct southern food identity. Further, because most cooks were women, African American women played a pivotal role in creating southern cooking. "The near mythic quality of Southern cookery is to be attributed to the presence of African-American women cooks," writes culinary historian Karen Hess. "They did the cooking; it's as simple as that."[4]

Blending ingredients from three cultures and a new geography, African American women applied African techniques to European recipes, leaving "their thumbprint on every dish they cooked," Hess writes. "They had known other produce, other fragrances, other flavors. Even when they conscientiously followed the recipe as read aloud by the mistress, certain subtle changes were bound to take place."[5]

The dishes created by African American cooks occupied a central place in the new "southern food," consumed by black and white people alike. By the mid-nineteenth century, the most influential and popular American cookbooks all contained recipes featuring African ingredients including okra, field peas, eggplants, greens, cayenne peppers, sesame seeds, and peanuts, as well as African food pairings and techniques. Culinary historian Jessica Harris defines these mainstream American recipes as "culinary refinements of dishes that certainly came from the slave quarters and were transformed in the hands of Big House cooks."[6]

No dish better showcases the African backbone and cultural blend of southern cooking than gumbo, a seafood stew that unites ingredients across continents. Gumbo's soup base is of African or Native American origin. Okra was brought from Africa, hot peppers from the Caribbean, black pepper from Madagascar, and salt from the French and Native Americans. The Spanish introduced tomatoes and red pepper, obtained from the Canary Islands. Native contributions include filé (ground sassafras leaves) made by Choctaw Indians and shrimp, crab, and oysters indigenous to coastal waters.[7]

Gumbo as a cultural mélange is evidenced in its very name. The word *gumbo* stems either from a Choctaw word for filé or an African word for okra. Both are used as thickeners and are essential to gumbo's definition and preparation. First, *gumbo* may trace its roots to *kombo*, the Choctaw word for the sassafras tree, whose leaves possess a flavor resembling thyme or savory. Choctaw women once sold packets of crushed sassafras leaves, dubbed filé by the French, in the streets of Mobile. Sassafras trees still grow wild in the region, lining the bluffs of the Mobile River in northern Mobile County.

Making Gumbo on the Gulf Coast

Gumbo begins with the roux: a combination of equal parts flour and oil browned until it reaches a desired color. Depending on the cook, the color ranges from light brown to almost black. The roux is cooked over low heat, usually in a heavy, cast-iron pot. Cast iron is easily cooled and heated, making it easier to achieve the desired color and consistency. The roux must be cooked slowly and stirred constantly to prevent it from sticking or burning. Gumbo cooks insist that a burned roux must be thrown out. Gumbo cannot begin or succeed without a proper roux.

To the roux is added a seafood stock, a broth most commonly made by boiling shrimp or crab shells. Once the roux and stock have simmered together for hours, the Creole holy trinity of vegetables is added: onion, celery, and green bell pepper. Most cooks also add pepper, salt, and red pepper. After that, a variety of ingredients are added depending on the cook, although cooks agree all ingredients should be as fresh as possible. Common additions include garlic and parsley (sometimes called the devil and the angel), thyme, green onions, bay leaves, rosemary, basil, tomatoes, and hot sauce. Okra and/or filé is then added as a thickener. Okra should be fried or baked beforehand to prevent sliminess. The seafood, which should be fresh and is often

But *gumbo* could also stem from West African words for okra, including *ki ngombo*, *ochingombo*, and *guingombo*, eventually shortened to *gombo*, which was the original French spelling of *gumbo* in the American colonies. Okra, a staple of the West African diet, was used in myriad dishes created by African cooks in America, especially in soups and stews. Okra is an essential ingredient in many gumbo recipes, which appeared in the most popular and influential southern cookbooks of the early 1800s.[8] Today, West Africans continue

obtained locally, includes shrimp, crab, and oysters. Added last, it is
cooked for a short period of time to prevent it from becoming rubbery.

Modern gumbo cooks often add meat to seafood gumbo, in-
cluding gumbo hens, hambones, veal briskets or bones, sausage, or
beef. Gumbo hens (old hens that no longer lay eggs but are still
flavorful) were traditionally bought fresh and still are in commu-
nities where there is a demand. Grocery stores sell them frozen as
"stewing hens" or "baking hens." Sausage is a common gumbo
addition, and many Alabama cooks prefer Conecuh sausage, made
in Conecuh County, located ninety miles northeast of Mobile.

According to culinary historian Jessica Harris, "there are as
many gumbos as there are chefs." In fact, a single chef often makes*
gumbo in infinite variety. Abby Fisher, who worked as a cook in
Mobile during the mid-1800s, included recipes for oyster gumbo,
ochra gumbo, and chicken gumbo in her 1881 cookbook. Mobile
chef Vince Henderson included okra, tomatoes, shrimp, and crab
in his summer gumbo but used filé and oysters in winter. And be-
cause gumbo is a mix of whatever is at hand, many cooks (who
often do not use recipes) find that each batch tastes unique.†

* Harris 1989:151.

† Personal interview with Vince Henderson, 2010, Mobile, AL.

to make a fish soup from dried, ground okra and baobab leaves, which is traditionally paired with rice and resembles American gumbo.[9]

On the Gulf Coast, gumbo emerged as a practical and economical food
for the poor. It relied on common ingredients, stretched expensive ingredients including meat, and allowed for the use of tougher cuts of meat softened
by the long cooking process. "Gumbo was poverty driven," states Henderson.
"It was for people living off the land, the rivers, and the sea. Gumbo is scraps

Gloria's Gumbo

GLORIA GOOD

FOR THE TRINITY

2 celery bunches, chopped in
   very fine pieces
2 whole bell peppers, chopped
   in very fine pieces
1 clove garlic, chopped in very
   fine pieces
1 large onion, diced

FOR THE ROUX

1 cup of Crisco oil
2 cups flour
gumbo filé
Tony Chacheres Creole seasoning

FOR THE SEAFOOD

3 lbs. shrimp, peeled
½ lb. Conecuh sausage, sliced
2 lbs. dark crab meat
6 large blue crabs, cleaned and
   washed
2 pts. chicken broth
large can diced stewed
   tomatoes
½ lb. frozen okra, chopped
4 bay leaves
½ cup olive oil
Salt to taste

TO PREPARE THE TRINITY

1. Mix chopped celery, bell peppers, garlic, and onion together in a ziplock
   plastic bag and place in the refrigerator overnight.

TO PREPARE THE ROUX

1. Place Crisco in a deep cast-iron skillet, heat.
2. Sprinkle flour into hot oil. Stir continuously on low heat.

of food put together. You use what you have. Anything leftover, inexpensive, you use what is seasonal."[10]

From its inception, gumbo was known as a Creole dish. Like gumbo, Creole culture emerged from a unique relationship between European settlers and West African slaves on the Gulf Coast. In Alabama, few slaves accompanied the earliest French settlers to the Gulf Coast in the early eighteenth century. But beginning in 1719, thousands of West African slaves were brought to

3. Stir until color changes to pecan tan. Do not let it get too hot. It will burn easy and turn too dark in color.

4. Sprinkle in gumbo filé for seasoning and Tony Chacheres Creole seasoning in roux. Stir continuously until turning pecan brown.

5. Stir mixture slowly for 45 minutes. Take roux off fire and put it aside.

TO PREPARE THE SEAFOOD

1. Keep peeled shrimp in water until ready for use.

2. Slice Conecuh sausage in ½ inch slices.

3. In a medium pot half full of water, add Conecuh sausage and crabs. Boil for 1 minute. Add shrimp and boil for 1 minute. Turn off fire. Pour entire mixture into large gumbo stock pot.

4. Add roux to the stock pot. Turn stove on medium high and heat for 5 minutes. Stir in chicken broth. Stir for 5 minutes.

5. Add large can of diced stewed tomatoes. Stir.

6. Add more chicken broth if it thickens too much. Stir.

7. Sauté trinity in butter in separate pan. Add okra in with trinity. Stir continuously. Put into stock pot.

8. Add dark crab meat to stock pot.

9. Stir all items in pot and add a dash of salt and Creole seasoning.

10. Add bay leaves and olive oil. Cook slowly until all items are well immersed. (Taste with a separate spoon and wash after each tasting. Gumbo will sour if saliva is on spoon.)

Cover pot and let simmer for 15 minutes.

Mobile and other Gulf Coast settlements to work on newly developing indigo, sugarcane, tobacco, and rice plantations. When these attempts at plantation agriculture failed, however, it dramatically impacted social relations in the region.

With their owners unable to furnish basic necessities, Gulf Coast slaves pushed for maximum autonomy and self-reliance and "within certain parameters, managed to exercise some control over their daily lives," writes southern historian Virginia Gould.[11] Gulf Coast slaves cultivated their own land,

Okra Festival

Since 2000, the small community of Burkville, Alabama, has honored okra with a yearly festival. On the last Saturday of August, when the okra is ripe, festival-goers gather at Annie Mae's Place, an art gallery in rural Lowndes County, for blues and gospel music, storytelling, and, of course, okra. Residents sell everything from gourd art to local history books to homemade preserves. In addition to okra, attendees can feast on gumbo, fried fish, barbecue, pig ears, and homemade ice cream. Amos Paul Kennedy Jr., renowned print artist, attends annually and designs the festival's signature posters.

Okra Festival posters by Amos Paul Kennedy Jr. (photo by Valerie Downes)

provided food, clothing, and housing for themselves and their families, rested on Sundays, and often lived apart from their owners. Relations between slaves and their owners became "a constant struggle over who was in control."[12]

This power struggle generated a looser, more nuanced social order than existed in the broader South. Gulf Coast settlements like Mobile and Pensacola lacked strict boundaries between race and class, which promoted mutual cultural influence. A Creole culture emerged that was a blend of white European, West African, and Native American traditions. The term *Creole* stems from similar French, Spanish, and Portuguese words indicating individuals born in a native location. On the Gulf Coast, *Creole* originally indicated any inhabitant, regardless of ethnic origin, who was not full-blooded Native American. Creoles could be white Creoles or Creoles of color (a mix of West African, European, and/or Native American descent).

Under French or Spanish rule for most of the eighteenth century, Mobile was a city dominated by European culture and Catholic tradition, both of

Boys at the Cathedral Creole School, 1906 (photo courtesy of Rosemary Parker Brazile Butler, Doy Leale McCall Rare Book and Manuscript Library, University of South Alabama)

which supported interracial relationships. The Catholic Church had a liberal conversion policy, seeking to convert all people regardless of race. There was also a shortage of white women on the Gulf Coast throughout the eighteenth century. These conditions conspired to produce a large Creole of color population in Mobile.

A sense of common culture instilled respect between white Creoles and Creoles of color. Nowhere else in the antebellum South did white people treat people of color with as much dignity as in the Gulf Coast settlements. Creoles of color enjoyed the same rights as white citizens in regard to military service, education, property, and inheritance. Creoles of color served in the military as early as 1735. Because the Catholic Church believed in universal education, Creoles of color were educated in racially integrated Catholic schools. Creoles of color could also inherit property from white fathers, and if they were enslaved, white fathers could (and often did) purchase their freedom.

These rights enabled Creoles of color to build a large, prosperous, and powerful society in Mobile. Creoles of color held high social and economic positions and worked in a range of occupations: as doctors, ship owners, merchants, and landowners. Able to obtain land grants from the Spanish, Creoles of color owned extensive tracts of land in Mobile and the surrounding area. Some owned plantations and slaves. They voted in municipal elections and lived in integrated neighborhoods.[13]

One of the most prosperous Creole of color families in Mobile traces its lineage to Pierre Lorendini, who arrived in Mobile in 1719, the same year as the first wave of West African slaves. Of Italian descent, Lorendini was a soldier in the French army under orders to help populate the new colony in America. Upon arrival, when his name was changed to Laurendine, he was twenty-one years old and married with one child. He would eventually father nine more children and become a founding ancestor of Creoles of color in Mobile. In fact, the saying goes that every tenth person you meet on the street in Mobile can trace his or her ancestry to Pierre Laurendine.

Jean Baptiste Jr., Pierre Laurendine's grandson, fathered seven children with Rosita Miraguan, a free Creole of color, to establish the Laurendine

Creole of color lineage in Mobile. Jean Baptiste Jr. owned a massive piece of land called the St. Louis tract, one of the largest land grants ever permitted in the city. He accumulated vast property holdings, including downtown buildings on Royal, St. Charles, and Conti Streets, sailing schooners, and forty head of cattle and horses. The Laurendines even had their own currency, called the "Heraldic Eagle," approved as legal tender for the city of Mobile and the state of Alabama.

In 1819, the Adams-Onís Treaty (or Transcontinental Treaty) between the Spanish and Americans made Mobile a permanent part of the United States. This treaty guaranteed the rights of citizens of the formerly Spanish territory, including Creoles of color, and elevated them above the status of African Americans. In the same year, however, Alabama's new statehood brought an influx of white settlers to Mobile. These new arrivals made no distinction between Creoles of color and African Americans. Largely of rural, English, Protestant, and Puritan heritage, these settlers prized the nuclear family, promoted strict family morals, discouraged marrying beneath one's social status, and denounced racial mixing.

To distinguish themselves and their way of life from the new arrivals, Gulf Coast natives increasingly identified as Creoles. Though racially mixed, Creoles "recognized that they shared a unique culture that had evolved over generations of mutual experience" and included shared language, religion, food traditions, and architecture.[14] But the new settlers saw things differently, and as the prosperity of plantation agriculture, through cotton, finally turned profitable, relations between owners and slaves changed. A stringent slave code emerged in Mobile. Owners could no longer free slaves at will, and slaves could not purchase their own freedom.

Free people of color were increasingly viewed as dangerous to the institution of slavery, which depended in part on preventing slaves from organizing or gaining access to education. When Nat Turner led a slave rebellion in Virginia in 1831, white Americans saw their fears realized. Immediately, the state of Alabama passed laws to restrict access to slaves by free black citizens. The laws prohibited educating persons of color, restricted contact and commerce

Catholic Cathedral of the Immaculate Conception, Mobile, Alabama, between 1900 and 1915 (photo by Detroit Publishing Company, Library of Congress, LC-D4-39536)

between free African Americans and slaves, and enacted speedy trials for the accused.

Though the treaty protecting their rights was only a decade old, Creoles of color in Mobile saw their status slipping. Now, Creoles of color convicted of crimes were whipped or branded instead of charged a fine. Authorities

Creole Fire Department, 1919 (Eric Overbey Collection, Doy Leale McCall Rare Book and
Manuscript Library, University of South Alabama, C7004)

claimed this was because Creoles of color could not pay the fines, but Creoles
of color and white people possessed the same degree of wealth at the time.[15]
In reality, the new laws intended to reduce Creoles of color to the same social
category as African Americans, cleanly splitting the races in Mobile.

During the next twenty years, from 1830 to 1850, Mobile transformed
from a leisurely European port to a bustling American metropolis. The city's
population surged from six thousand to thirty thousand, mostly from a mass
influx of white immigrants from rural areas who dramatically altered Mobile
culture. The population of Creoles of color fell from 9 percent to 3 percent.
By 1850, slaves represented 33 percent of the city's population. The white
population increasingly grouped Creoles of color with African Americans in a

racially polarized society, where neighborhoods were now segregated.

Though 1850 marked the height of economic prosperity for Creoles of color in Mobile, they feared that the losses in social status would eventually shrink economic opportunity. They responded by emphasizing their Creole identity and seeking to distinguish themselves from black residents. As Gould notes, Creoles of color "sought to protect and maintain their distinctiveness" as a way to protect and maintain their rights.[16] They began exclusively marrying each other and joining Creole organizations, including the Creole Social Club and the Creole Fire Company. Already educated alongside white people in Catholic schools and attending mass with them at the cathedral, Creoles of color sought any opportunity to identify and associate with white people and not with African Americans. In 1846, members of the prestigious Creole Fire Company #1 voted to expel any member seen with a black person.

Despite these efforts, however, Creoles of color were severely stripped of their rights beginning in 1850. Anglo-Saxon nationalism, racial prejudice, and anti-Catholic sentiment were at a peak, accompanied by a swell of Protestant revivalism that used the Bible to justify slavery. New pseudoscientific literature defined African Americans as a separate and inferior race to prove that they were suitable for slavery or even benefited from it.[17] This concept was one of the most influential justifications of new restrictive legislation on Creoles of color in Alabama, where white people now controlled the state legislature.

In Mobile, laws reducing the status of Creoles of color were passed partly out of racism and partly because new white arrivals to the city coveted the jobs held by Creoles of color. Under new legislation, Creoles of color needed white Creoles to act as "guardians" to claim their rights. These restrictions began to affect their livelihoods, as they had feared, prohibiting Creoles of color from sampling cotton and selling liquor, among other things. Humiliated, some Creoles of color abandoned the Gulf Coast for Spanish America, Mexico, the Caribbean, Haiti, and France.

Some returned to Mobile after the Civil War, when life appeared briefly hopeful. In 1868, two persons of color (one of them Creole) became the first

African American Queen of Mardi Gras, 1995 (photo courtesy of Marshall Wormley, Doy Leale McCall Rare Book and Manuscript Library, University of South Alabama, C4146)

Alabamians of color elected to the state legislature. But Reconstruction ended swiftly and was replaced by the extreme racism and total segregation of the Jim Crow era. In 1901, the new Alabama state constitution disenfranchised nearly all persons of color. In 1908, Creoles of color were barred from voting in Mobile municipal elections.[18]

In the twentieth century, many Creoles of color in Mobile continued to hold themselves apart from African Americans. Vince Henderson, born in 1939, was a tenth generation Mobilian and a descendant of Pierre Laurendine. When he was growing up in the 1940s and 1950s, Creoles of color still "didn't want to be considered black. They wanted Creole on their driver's licenses and birth certificates. There was an unwritten rule that when you married, your spouse couldn't be darker than a brown paper bag. The parents would hold your arms next to each other to see. You weren't supposed to marry anyone darker than the family."

It was a modern manifestation of the quadroon balls once held in Mobile to introduce white men to young Creole women of color. (A quadroon is a person with one-quarter black ancestry and three-quarters white.) Marked by high society and propriety, the balls were closed to Creole men of color. Mothers who wanted the best matches for their daughters acted as chaperones. Marrying someone with lighter skin was seen as a way to move up the social and economic ladder.

But in twentieth-century Mobile, a society and government dominated by white people made no distinction between Creoles of color and African Americans. When Creoles of color participated in Mardi Gras, Mobile's most significant festival, they attended events sponsored by the Colored Carnival Association, formed in 1939 to create Mardi Gras events for people of color who were shut out of white events.

The resulting celebrations were infused with multiple aspects of Creole and African American heritage, including gumbo, still inextricably linked to Mardi Gras in both communities.[19] "Every Creole family in Mobile owns at least thirty gumbo spoons," Henderson says, describing the silver soup spoons sometimes adorned with decorative motifs. "I could take you to any home during Mardi Gras and they would all be cooking the same four foods: red beans and sausage, baked ham, potato salad, and gumbo." In fact, Laurendine family members gather annually on the Sunday before Mardi Gras to attend mass at the downtown cathedral, located at the nexus of the family's former land, then spend the day at the Mobile Mardi Gras Museum, catching up and eating gumbo.[20]

THREE

||||||||||||||||||||||||||||||||||||||||||||||||||||||||||||||||||||||

Chicken Stew

Frontier Life in the Tennessee Valley

ON THE DAY OF THE East Limestone Volunteer Fire Department's annual chicken stew sale, a Saturday in mid-February, I arrive at the fire department at four fifteen in the morning. It is twenty-eight degrees outside and the sky is black. Firefighter Jonathan Hinton introduces me to Joey Boyd, the fire chief since 1989, and three other firefighters called Al, Jacob, and Cricket. They are unloading two fifty-gallon cast-iron pots from the back of a truck and setting them over portable gas burners. A laminated copy of the department's chicken stew recipe, given by one of the original East Limestone firefighters and modified by founder David Scates's wife, Carolyn, is taped to the wall of the station.

David Scates founded the department in 1974, after a futile attempt to fight a house fire in rural Limestone County with the only tool at hand: a short garden hose. As the house blazed in front of them, Scates and the home-owner could do nothing but sit on the lawn and cry. By the time the Athens Fire Department arrived, the house was completely destroyed. Shaken, Scates

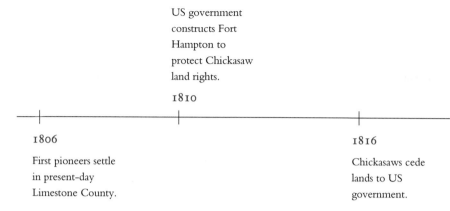

US government
constructs Fort
Hampton to
protect Chickasaw
land rights.

1810

1806

First pioneers settle
in present-day
Limestone County.

1816

Chickasaws cede
lands to US
government.

set aside $1,000 of his own money, hand lettered a sign that read "Future home of the East Limestone Fire Department," and stood it up in an empty lot. Donations poured in. Scates recalls one man who gave him a check for $100 and told him, "The community needs this. Don't ever let it go back the way it was. If you ever get into trouble, come see me." But Scates never had to. The community has fully supported the East Limestone Volunteer Fire Department ever since.

For decades, chicken stew sales were the department's major fundraiser, held monthly during the winter. But in recent years, the department has added other fundraisers, including barbecues, raffles, and singings, that bring in more money than chicken stew. They also have new funding sources, including a cigarette tax and an annual household fire protection fee. In fact, they don't really need the chicken stew sale anymore, which is now held annually and raises about $1,000. But firefighter Jonathan Hinton doubts the department will ever stop making chicken stew. He explains, "The community expects it. After the holidays are over, they start asking about chicken stew. Anytime they see you around town, they'll ask. They call the fire department. They leave notes on the door. That's all you hear is 'When y'all havin' chicken stew?'"[1]

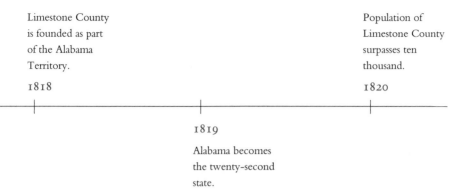

Limestone County
is founded as part
of the Alabama
Territory.

1818

1819

Alabama becomes
the twenty-second
state.

Population of
Limestone County
surpasses ten
thousand.

1820

If you mention goat stew or chicken stew in this pocket of the Tennessee Valley that includes a handful of counties in southern Tennessee and north Alabama, natives will know you mean a very particular and popular type of stew unknown outside this small, rural region.[2] The main ingredients include goat or chicken meat, potatoes, onions, corn, and tomatoes. The simplicity of ingredients and the use of long-simmered potatoes as a thickener (instead of flour or milk) make these stews unique among southern stew traditions.

Originally made on farms as a family meal (and possibly as the centerpiece of community gatherings), most families now consider the stews too labor intensive and time consuming to make for home consumption. Today, the stews are usually made in large quantities (twenty to one hundred gallons at a time) as annual fundraisers for a variety of organizations including volunteer fire departments, sports teams, churches, and civic clubs. Stews are also made for large family gatherings, church events, political rallies, and social events. Because of the labor involved in killing and preparing goats for stew, chicken stews are far more common today than goat stews.

Chicken stew recipes are handed down through generations in families or organizations. Though the core ingredients remain the same, individual cooks season the stew to suit personal preferences, using salt, pepper,

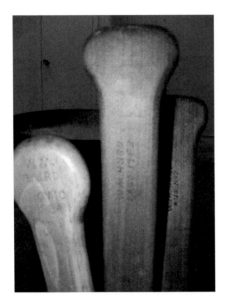

Stew paddles (photo by Emily Blejwas)

red pepper, and hot sauce. Originally cooked over wood fires, stews are now cooked in large cast-iron pots (often family heirlooms formerly used for doing laundry or making soap) over gas burners. When all of the ingredients have been added, the stew simmers over low heat for several hours, with constant stirring required to keep it from sticking to the bottom of the pot. A large wooden paddle is the favored stirring implement, rotated between multiple stirrers during the cooking process.[3]

Local researcher Bill Allen, who attended numerous stews in the region, notes that stew cooks are often middle-aged men who have served long apprenticeships in stew making: "Many of these head cooks had begun their participation as teens, carrying supplies, running errands, and scrubbing the pots after use. The next step up for them would be as young men grasping canoe paddles and keeping the stew stirred. They finally became designated as cooks when older men retired from active participation. Because the recipes used for making the stews are more often passed on orally than in writing, it was during this apprenticeship period that they learned what they would need to know to make a good stew."[4]

Though commonly held in the winter months, stew sales occur year-round in counties with particularly strong stew traditions. As Allen notes, it is "a rare week that passes without an announcement in one of the area newspapers about a chicken stew sale."[5] Stew patrons line up as early as six in the morning at their favorite organization's annual sale. They bring their own containers, most often gallon size glass jars, and usually buy one or two gallons of stew to freeze and eat year-round.

Though no one is completely sure of its origins, Tennessee Valley chicken stew was likely created by Scotch-Irish pioneers who immigrated to America in large numbers between 1710 and 1775, settling the Tennessee Valley region in the late 1700s and early 1800s. Most stew makers today are descendants of these Scotch-Irish settlers.[6] The chicken stew tradition seems to have emerged from a pioneer culture and ethos and is still rooted in rural communities today.

In Limestone County, Alabama, which claims one of the strongest stew traditions, frontier life was hardscrabble and uncertain from the start. Beginning in 1806, a handful of pioneers (98 percent of whom were Scotch-Irish) traveled by flatboat from east Tennessee down the Tennessee River and up the Elk River to settle on Chickasaw land in present-day Limestone County. Clashes between settlers and Chickasaw were frequent. The US government viewed the settlers as intruders, and soldiers frequently removed large groups of them from the land. When the settlers kept returning, Fort Hampton was installed in 1810 to completely rid the area of intruders, a rare example of the federal government protecting Natives from white settlers.

The Simms (or Sims) settlement, the first and largest settlement in present-day Limestone County, consisted of 450 families who pleaded with President James Madison in 1810 to allow them to stay on the land. They defined themselves as law-abiding people who believed the land had already been purchased from the Chickasaw when they settled on it, stating, "a great many of us solde our possessions and Came and settled in the winter and spring of 1807 without any knoledg or intention of violating the laws of government."[7] If removed, they contended, "we cannot take our produce with

Us and a great many not in a circumstance to purchase more will in consequence of this be brought to a deplorable situation."[8]

But the president rejected their plea and Fort Hampton soldiers removed the Simms settlers, burned their cabins and fences, and regularly sent out parties to make sure they did not return. Tennessee historian James McCallum relates that, in North Georgia, Fort Hampton soldiers "acted very rascally; cut down the corn with large butcher knives, threw down and burned fences and houses, and forced the settlers back over the line. In some localities the settlers soon returned, and the villainous work of removal and destruction of improvements was repeated." McCallum continues, "In Alabama, those who settled Simms' settlement were driven off and they went back over the line and built camps and shanties which they covered with bark which they stripped from the trees. A considerable number of these camps were together and the place was called Barksville for a long time."[9]

In 1816, the Chickasaw ceded their land to the US government. In 1818, Limestone County was founded as part of the Alabama Territory, less than a year old at the time. Named for the limestone naturally found in its creek beds, Limestone County was home to a few thousand settlers, but emigrants soon arrived in droves. Local historian Robert Walker Jr. writes, "At the beginning of 1817, the area . . . was a wilderness. By the end of 1818 there appeared to be a continuous farming settlement along the north banks of the Tennessee River in Alabama. The great highway from Virginia was thronged in 1818 and 1819 with crowds of settlers that more resembled an army on the march than home-seekers." By 1820, the population of Limestone County had surpassed ten thousand.[10]

Primarily of Scotch-Irish descent, settlers had traveled from Tennessee, Georgia, the Carolinas, and Virginia, eager to buy property in this fertile valley in the Great Bend of the Tennessee River. Many were "disillusioned with worn-out fields and poor economic conditions in the East and were attracted by cheap land from the Indian cessions, high cotton prices, and dreams of wealth."[11] As Alabama historian Wayne Flynt writes, "the forces that drove men and women to the Alabama frontier were not unlike the ones that brought them to America in the first place. They wanted land, a better living, and more freedom, . . . but the key to all their expectations was land. . . . The ownership of land seemed a magical elixir that promised to cure what ailed them."[12]

Though the land was fertile, settlers did not find an easy life in Alabama. With so many pouring into the state, food became scarce and many families soon hovered on the brink of starvation. Still, "Alabama Fever" raged, with hundreds of settlers arriving daily.[13] In north Alabama, 90 percent of the pioneers were white, more than 50 percent were squatters on federally owned land, and more than two-thirds were yeoman farmers.[14] Most arrived in Alabama carrying few possessions and little food, depending on the streams and forests for sustenance until the first harvest. "These families owned no slaves and had little chance of acquiring any," notes Alabama historian Leah Rawls Atkins. "They would not gain vast lands or build grand mansions or accumulate the wealth that brought prestige and power. They were the yeoman farmers of Alabama whose lives were stories of survival and endurance."[15]

Alabama derives from a Choctaw word meaning "clearers of the thicket," which precisely describes the state's early pioneers. The heavily timbered land in north Alabama, which served as Chickasaw hunting ground, was full of dangerous wild animals including rattlesnakes, bears, panthers, and wolves. Clearing land to plant the corn needed for survival required removing thick stands of timber "with simple tools, under danger from Indian attack, in time for a spring planting, and with no equipment heavier than an axe and grubbing hoe."[16]

Corn's high yield enabled pioneer families to survive on just a few acres of land.[17] They subsisted mainly on cornbread, vegetables from the garden, and wild game from the woods, including elk, deer, and turkey. They also trapped smaller animals and gathered wild peas and nuts. Coffee was ground from okra, rye, or parched corn. Tea was brewed from bohea or sassafras leaves. Sweetener came from cane or sorghum grass.[18] Life in Limestone County reflected the rest of the Alabama frontier. As Walker writes, "the life of these earliest settlers, both as intruders and then as landowners . . . was of

Mural of early Alabama settlers, by John Augustus Walker, 1939 (Auburn University Libraries)

a most primitive type. From the wilderness and surrounding fields they drew both the necessities and comforts."[19]

Frontier life "consisted of grinding and unremitting labor," writes Atkins.[20] Corn cultivation required the whole family's participation. Men, women, and children hoed, planted, cut tops, pulled fodder for livestock feed, fertilized, harvested, shucked, shelled, and ground corn, as well as mended fences and tended animals.[21] Tools were minimal and "in the early years, there were no gristmills, sawmills, tanyards, or blacksmiths. If one wanted or needed something, self-labor was the unit of production."[22]

Settlers lived in one-room log cabins with stick chimneys and spaces sometimes divided by buckskin curtains. Younger children slept on pallets and older children slept in the loft of the cabin (if it had one) or in the loft of the barn. Furniture, dishes, and utensils were fashioned from the bark of

Picnic party in Limestone County, early 1900s (Limestone County Archives)

hickory or oak trees. Door hinges were made from leather. Buckhorns were used for gun racks, clothing racks, and as handles for knives and other small tools. Light inside the cabins came from a wide fireplace or from candles.

Women made cloth using a spinning wheel, flax wheel, and loom, which were sometimes set outside to save indoor space. They dyed thread and wool with homegrown indigo or with the barks and roots of various trees. Pioneers tanned their own leather, and boys' and men's clothing was fashioned from the skins of deer, bears, panthers, wildcats, and wolves. Leather was also used to make shoes, harnesses, and bridles.[23]

North Alabama pioneers faced intense isolation, with homesteads so widely spaced that smoke from another chimney was rarely visible. The solitude of everyday life coupled with the tenuous quality of the frontier gave community events a critical importance. A spirit of cooperation and mutual help prevailed, with house raisings often held for new arrivals. Communities

Feeding chickens in Limestone County, 1927 (Auburn University Libraries)

also gathered for mutual work and camaraderie at log rollings, corn shucking parties, camp meetings, and quilting sessions.[24]

Though it is unclear whether Tennessee Valley stews emerged during pioneer days, it seems probable. Early cookbooks indicate that Scotch-Irish in the Southeast made chicken stew before immigrating to the Tennessee Valley, where they likely sustained their stew traditions while incorporating locally available ingredients. All of the components of Tennessee Valley stew were present in colonial America, used by Scotch-Irish populations, affordable and accessible on the Alabama frontier, and easy to grow or maintain. Stew was also a particularly useful dish on the frontier, as it stretched expensive ingredients like meat and could be prepared in a single cooking pot set in the fireplace.

Chicken stew sales are still a hallmark of rural communities today. Stew cooks are largely from Scotch-Irish farm families and stew sales are far less common in counties containing bigger cities. Stew sales also function as a vital social outlet and form of mutual help in the lives of rural residents, much like house raisings and quilting sessions of years past. They are a primary venue for rural fundraising and fellowship, with many patrons attending the same stews each year to socialize with the same community members. As Allen notes, "the social aspect is as important in the enjoyment of the stew gatherings as the stews themselves."[25]

Regardless of when they emerged, Tennessee Valley stews remained in a small geographic area due to extremely limited travel and communication. As Allen points out, "it wasn't until after World War I that people really began moving about to other areas. Food traditions developed early on in specific areas of the state and tended to stay there."[26] Today, chicken stew is still known in only a handful of counties hugging the Tennessee-Alabama border. Yet in these counties, chicken stew is deeply sown into local culture and a major element of the region's social life and identity.

The East Limestone Volunteer Fire Department has always cooked sixty gallons of stew using four pots at their annual chicken stew sale, but they plan to cook eighty gallons in two pots today. They begin filling the pots with water using five-gallon buckets but immediately run into trouble. The pots are brand new, and as the water starts to boil, bits of black sealant flake off the interior and float on the water's surface. For a while, the firefighters scrape spatulas down the insides of the pot and strain out the pieces, but it's no good. They start over with the smaller pots, almost an hour behind schedule.

Around five thirty in the morning, a few more firefighters trickle in, stretching off sleep. Boyd's twenty-one-year-old daughter, Carma, is among them. She was raised coming to the chicken stew sales and appears as a young girl in a photograph inside the fire department's award case. She is now a certified firefighter, making her the fourth generation of firefighters in her family, after both of her parents, her grandfather, and her great-grandfather.

Once the water boils, 240 pounds of chicken are dropped into the pots. An emergency call comes in over the radio, a motor vehicle crash. Everyone except Boyd, Carma, and me goes on the call. The change in pace is dizzying, from slow and languorous with country music on a tinny radio in the background to a full rush. The firefighters have grabbed their equipment and boarded the trucks before I even realize what happened. The department has forty members now, and I ask Boyd how they keep track of who responds to the calls. "You hear a call," he tells me, "you go." Then he adds, "Of course, they all jumped on this one because it's time to debone the chicken."

The chicken is removed and laid on two long tables. By now, a dozen firefighters have arrived to help. Under blue rubber gloves, they don thick cotton gloves to protect their hands from the heat. Some fire departments skip this step and use precooked chicken and canned broth, but Boyd insists it doesn't taste as good. It's about eight o'clock now, and the first customers of the day arrive toting gallon jars, asking if the department takes advanced orders, but here stew is sold on a first-come, first-served basis. The early birds are asked to come back at ten.

Once all of the skin, bones, and fat are removed from the chicken, the meat is returned to the pots along with 120 pounds of potatoes, 12 gallons of tomatoes, 36 pounds of onions, and 3 pounds of butter. Six gallons of corn will be added later, along with salt, pepper, red pepper, and tomato paste. Though some of the firefighters had gathered the night before to cut potatoes and on-ions, somehow they wound up twenty pounds short of onions, and more are cut in a hurry. Boyd cuts them holding unlit matches between his teeth to pre-vent his eyes from watering. It's an old wives tale, and he says it works.

More firefighters amble in. Someone makes biscuits, sausage, and bacon for breakfast. The firefighters take turns constantly stirring the stew using small wooden oars that resemble canoe paddles, made by a firefighter for the sole purpose of stirring chicken stew. His name, W. M. Hurd, is engraved on the handles, along with the dates they were made: Aug '82 and Nov '84. (Real canoe paddles are not used because they have a layer of wax on the sur-face that would melt off.)

By now, close to twenty firefighters (men and women) have arrived. They take turns stirring while spouses hold babies, or the firefighters hold babies while spouses stir. Several emergency calls come in throughout the morning, giving the event a surreal quality. Each time a call comes in, half

Chicken Stew

East Limestone Volunteer Fire Department, Carolyn Scates, 1974

2½ gallons water	½ gallon corn
20 lbs. chicken	¼ lb. butter
10½ lbs. potatoes	Salt and pepper to taste
3 lbs. onions	Red pepper
1 gallon tomatoes	Tomato paste to taste

Boil water. Cook chicken in water. Remove chicken from water and remove all skin, bones, and fat from chicken. Return chicken to pot. Add potatoes, tomatoes, onions, and butter. Simmer over low heat, stirring constantly. When stew thickens, add corn, salt, pepper, red pepper, and tomato paste. When wooden spoon (or paddle) sticks straight up in the pot, the stew is done.

Yields 5 gallons of stew.

of the firefighters dash to their trucks and peel out of the station, leaving the other half to slowly stir the stew. Or spouses and friends automatically move in to take their places stirring, collecting money, pouring stew into containers.

The scene speaks to the constancy of firefighting, the commitment that is required. Boyd tells me it can be hard on a firefighter unless his or her whole family is involved and supportive. It's clear that he is passing on the firefighting tradition to his daughter, along with the chicken stew tradition that is automatically a part of it. He makes sure she tests every batch multiple times to gauge what the stew needs.

To determine whether the stew is thick enough, a paddle is stuck straight into the middle of the pot. If the paddle doesn't tip over, the stew is done. And despite the late start, the stew is ready exactly on time, at ten o'clock,

Three generations of firefighters: Joey Boyd, Carma Boyd, and David Scates (photo by Emily Blejwas)

though customers have been lining up their jars since nine. Most have brought one or two glass gallon jars. Many have their names already written on the lids, but if they don't, the firefighters have a permanent marker on hand. As the jars are filled, patrons slide empty jars down a line that spans three long tables set end to end. Some customers have brought boxes or laundry baskets to carry several full jars back to their cars.

The firefighters fill jars continuously from ten until eleven thirty, when three-fourths of the stew has been sold. David Scates arrives and tells me about an old firefighter who used to come in and sample stew from every pot. One year, Scates told him that the next year, they would weigh him when he arrived and weigh him when he left and that way they'd know how much to charge. When the pace slows down and I take the opportunity to leave my jar filling post to down two Styrofoam cupfuls of stew in quick succession, Scates says, "We might have to weigh you too."

Lining up for stew at East Lime-stone Volunteer Fire Department's annual chicken stew sale (photo by Emily Blejwas)

By twelve thirty, the stew has sold out. About seventy gallons of stew were sold at $15 per gallon, earning the department just over $1,000 (before subtracting the cost of ingredients). Jonathan Hinton is already hosing down the pots and greasing them with Crisco to prevent them from rusting. The new pots will have to be set on fire to burn the tar off before the department tries to use them again. I still have black sludge under my fingernails from the tar, and Hinton warns me my clothes will smell like chicken stew for a week.

As I say my goodbyes, I'm given a Styrofoam cooler that Cricket bought at the dollar store and Joey filled with ice and a glass gallon jar of stew for me to take home to Mobile. One of the women firefighters insists on carrying it to my car. As we leave the station, the firetrucks return from a call, carrying Ashley and several other firefighters. Ashley's three-year-old son, Caden, has been playing with fire hoses and stomping around in his rubber boots. He watches his mother pull up and calls to her that he's going to be a firefighter too.[27]

FOUR

||||||||||||||||||||||||||||||||||||||||||||||||||||||||||||||||||||||||||||

Fried Green Tomatoes

Emblem of the Alabama Rural Table

When I think about the southern larder of favored ingredients,
I first think about vegetables.

—Frank Stitt, *Frank Stitt's Southern Table*

THE TOWN OF SLOCOMB, known statewide for its tomatoes, is tucked into Alabama's southeastern corner, nine miles from the Florida border. In the early 1950s, a handful of Slocomb farmers began growing tomatoes as an alternative to cotton and peanuts, then standard in the region. The local acidic soil gave the tomatoes a vibrant flavor and they became an instant favorite at farmers' markets statewide. In the 1960s, Slocomb tomato farmers formed a cooperative and built a market and warehouse. The surrounding county soon held one thousand acres in tomatoes.

In the late 1970s, however, the tomato market shifted as growing seasons lengthened, competition from growers in other states increased, and

Green tomatoes in batter at
the Slocomb Tomato Festival
(photo by Emily Blejwas)

large agribusinesses took hold. Most Slocomb tomato growers retired, dwindling the county's tomato holdings to one hundred acres. Yet, though tomatoes no longer drive the Slocomb economy, the town is still famous for them. In 1988, Slocomb held its first tomato festival to celebrate its heritage. The annual festival now features a parade, Miss Tomato Pageant, live music, vendors, children's activities, and the signature festival dish: fried green tomatoes.

The Slocomb Tomato Festival is held on the third Saturday in June, when tomatoes are green and the heat is striking. Today, local politicians pass around cardboard fans to festival-goers, who wear sun hats and walk unhurriedly among the vendors, but Eddy, Susan, and Forrest Morris move unceasingly between slicer, batter, deep fryer, and counter to keep up with demand

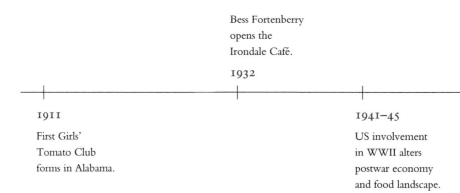

Bess Fortenberry
opens the
Irondale Café.

1932

1911

First Girls'
Tomato Club
forms in Alabama.

1941–45

US involvement
in WWII alters
postwar economy
and food landscape.

for the festival's most popular dish. In the past, local seniors operated the fried green tomatoes stand, but the task became too taxing. So this year, the Morris family of Eufaula, Alabama, is making the festival's fried green tomatoes for the first time, using bushels of green tomatoes from Aplin Farms, one of Slocomb's founding growers.

During the week, Eddy works in an antenna manufacturing factory and Susan as a nurse, but every weekend for the past year and a half, the husband-and-wife team have traveled the festival circuit in Alabama, Georgia, and Florida, selling deep-fried funnel cakes and blooming onions. Their eldest son, Forrest, age twenty-two, sometimes accompanies them. Although this is the family's first time making fried green tomatoes at a festival, they all grew up eating them.

Eddy uses his mother's batter recipe, a mixture of cornmeal, flour, garlic powder, red pepper, black pepper, and salt. He cuts green (unripe) tomatoes in thick slices and coats them with batter, dips them in buttermilk, then coats them with batter again before dropping them into the deep fryer. He uses buttermilk because it has a higher oil content, which helps the batter stick and gives it crunch. He claims it sticks best if you let the tomatoes set for five

Slocomb tomato
farmers form
cooperative.

Slocomb holds
inaugural tomato
festival.

1960s

1988

1987

*Fried Green
Tomatoes at the
Whistle Stop Café*
by Fannie Flagg is
published.

1991

*Fried Green
Tomatoes* film
premieres in
Birmingham.

Eddy and Forrest Morris at the Slocomb Tomato Festival (photo by Emily Blejwas)

minutes before frying them, but there's no time for that today. They are sold as soon as they are lifted from the fryer, lined up in a paper tray, and served alongside ranch dressing.

Eddy is quick to point out, however, that serving fried green tomatoes alongside dipping sauces is a new phenomenon. He tells me fried green tomatoes traditionally appeared as one of many vegetables in a rural midday meal or as a breakfast dish.[1] Eddy's mother, Lucille (known to her family as Big Mama), raised her children and grandchildren on vegetables from her garden and often served fried green tomatoes. Even after downsizing to an apartment, Forrest tells me, she always kept a small garden filled with peppers and tomatoes.[2]

From the rise of corn cultivation in early history until well into the twentieth century, agriculture remained the essential industry of the South. Though antebellum Alabama may evoke images of endless cotton plantations and wealthy slave owners, a very small minority ever lived that reality. Most white settlers entered Alabama as subsistence farmers, and most remained as such even after commercial planting developed. When the Civil War erupted in 1861, much of the state was still a frontier, and small family farms would define it for another eighty years.

As southern historian Thomas D. Clark writes,

> As the southern agricultural frontiers advanced, plain dirt farmers laid claim to modest landholdings, peopled the emigrant trails, opened fields and pastures in the virgin forests, built simple dwellings and barns, and established rural communities. All across new regions these yeomen established subsistence farming, created an uncomplicated economy, held fast to family ties and folkways, personified the image of much of the antebellum South, and formed the bulk of the population. . . . Whatever role the larger plantation and its more affluent owners may have played in regional commerce, politics, and social and cultural life, it was the yeoman farmer who opened large areas of the land, helped create counties and towns, "lived largely at home," and gave body and soul to southern rural life.[3]

In every generation before World War II, the vast majority of southerners (black and white) spent most of their waking hours in association with food. Rural families subsisted on the foods they could grow, gather, and hunt, supplemented by a few store-bought rations. Slaves often grew vegetables on small patches of land to augment their meager diets, and most African Americans remaining in the South postslavery continued to live by subsistence farming.[4] Fresh, seasonal vegetables (notably turnips, cowpeas, and sweet potatoes) paired with cornbread and occasionally hog meat defined the Alabama diet well into the twentieth century.[5]

From the woods and streams, rural southerners harvested fish, small game, fruits, nuts, berries, wild mushrooms, and greens. They kept chickens for eggs and cows or goats for milk. Meat was rarely consumed and was almost always pork, smoked or dried. Honey was obtained from bees and syrup from sugarcane or sweet sorghum. Desserts were based on wild fruits: peaches, apples, pears, figs, strawberries, and blackberries that were also canned, dried, or preserved. Cobblers were popular, made from fruit and simple ingredients, as were white cakes, custards, and cookies. Homemade peanut brittle and popcorn balls were holiday favorites.

Above all, vegetables lived at the heart of the rural, southern diet. Cultivated year-round in Alabama, vegetables were eaten fresh upon harvest or canned and stored in root cellars. Peas arrived first in the spring, then summer squashes, followed by tomatoes, corn, okra, many types of beans, peppers, and beets. Fall brought sweet potatoes, winter squashes, and a wide variety of greens (collard, turnip, kale, and mustard). Grown in abundance, sweet potatoes were banked for the winter in mounds of dirt and leaves and, when paired with collard greens, provided several essential nutrients.

Dinner, the largest meal of the day served at noontime, consisted of an array of vegetables from the garden and cornbread. And vegetables still make up the soul of southern meals today. As chef Bill Neal writes, "the variety of fresh vegetables on the Southern table is staggering. Any one meal may present fried okra, corn, butter beans, sweet potatoes, sliced tomatoes, cucumbers and onions, coleslaw, cantaloupe . . . by mid-summer, all vegetable meals (with biscuits or cornbread) are common."[6]

Working in the garden, Gee's Bend, Alabama, 1939 (photo by Marion Post Wolcott, Library of Congress, LC-USF33-030351-M3)

With vegetables at its core, southern food necessarily followed the seasons, making fresh and seasonal ingredients an essential quality of southern cooking that still holds true. "There's an old saying that what grows together goes together," writes Alabama native and chef Scott Peacock, "and the dishes we put on our tables have that natural seasonal affinity."[7] Food writer and Mobile native Eugene Walter insists that "if you want to be a good cook, you have to be a good gardener; it all works together."[8] Walter cites his grandparents as prime examples: "They took their greatest pleasure in fresh things in season rushed from plant to dinner table. The corn was never picked until the water was put on the stove to boil it in. Fresh radishes were plunged into ice water an hour before the meal and served with crusty bread, fresh country butter, and a little pile of salt on each plate. To eat one of those radishes was to experience the truth of the radish, and I remember that 'as sad as a store bought radish' was one of Ma-Ma's favorite similes."[9]

Homemade Syrup

From the early nineteenth to mid-twentieth centuries, homemade syrup was a staple of southern life. Because sugar was expensive, rural families often relied on syrup as a sweetener in cooking and baking and for pouring over biscuits and cornbread at breakfast. Many families cultivated small patches of sugarcane or sweet sorghum to use for making syrup. Alabama native and chef Scott Peacock, who traversed Alabama for several years interviewing elderly residents about food traditions of days past, confirms that "it doesn't matter where you grew up or whether you're black or white, everybody talks about syrup making." *

In Alabama, cane syrup was popular in the southern half of the state, and sorghum in the north. Sorghum is said to possess a distinctive, tangy flavor, stronger than sugarcane. Both were harvested in the fall, during "the narrow window after the cane has reached sufficient maturity for high-quality syrup and before freezing weather."† Because the sweetest reserves lie at the bottom of the stalk, the cane was cut as close to the ground as possible, then stripped of sharp leaves to ready it for the mill. The remaining stubs were covered with dirt to protect them from the cold, in hopes they would sprout again in the spring.

Most families did not own mills and made arrangements with a local miller to process their cane, often paying with a percentage of the syrup. Mill owners only needed and could afford small mills, most of which were vertical and powered by animals (usually mules). Once the cane was milled, the extracted juice was boiled over wood fires in enormous cauldrons made from cast iron or copper. Foam and other impurities were skimmed from the surface to render clear syrup with a pure flavor. After it cooked down to the desired consistency, the syrup was poured into gallon-sized metal buckets.

It took six hours to boil a pot of juice into syrup, and cooking two

Cane mill in Marshall County, Alabama, 1925 (Auburn University Libraries, 70.30.6.2)

pots every day for one week yielded a year's supply of syrup for one family. Thus, cane mills ran all day long during harvesting season, and in many rural communities, syrup making became a social gathering. "Occurring at an otherwise idle time," notes local historian Bill Outlaw, "cane grindings became a social focal point, bringing family and friends together with perhaps more dawdling the hours away than working. These gatherings ranged from simple visits to real occasions, with dances, candy making, and general jollification." A native of Calhoun County, Alabama, recalls that in the 1920s "girls and boys would come from miles around to gather at the syrup mill at night, as it would run a lot of nights until midnight. They had a lot of fun. We would dig a hole in the ground near the syrup pan and cover it with pummies [the squeezed-out cane stalks]. . . . Then we would try to get somebody to step into it. They would think they had fallen into the skimming hole, and everyone would laugh. We'd drink the cane juice and sop some of the hot syrup. I'd put apples into the pan where the syrup was cooking. They would be really sweet when they cooked."[‡]

A Works Progress Administration (WPA) narrative gives this description of a community cane grinding in Barbour County, Alabama, in the 1930s: "Everyone goes dressed for the occasion, in clothing that will stand a tubbing or may be discarded. Standing around the smoking and steaming fumes, one is covered with both the smoke and sweet vapor of cooking juice. To drink the juice as it comes from the mill is a pleasant pastime. Then to cook candy and have an old-fashioned 'candy pull' with all doing their best to get it off their hands, is an amusing sight."[§]

Syrup making reached its heyday in the 1920s but by the 1950s had begun a steady decline. The increasing industrialization of food had created plenty of affordable store-bought syrups and drastically cut the demand for homemade syrup. Further, the massive population shift from rural areas to cities between 1940 and 1960 diminished the available land and labor pool for syrup making. "When syrup production declined" writes Outlaw, "an era passed."[**]

Yet, a cane syrup company in Montgomery, Alabama, managed not only to weather the changing food landscape but to profit from it. The Alaga Syrup Company, founded in 1906, has been making cane syrup in the same downtown location for over one hundred years. It is now the oldest food company in Alabama and is run by the fourth generation of the founding Whitfield family. Alaga is a combination of Alabama and Georgia, the Whitfields' native states. Its logo features hands clasped in marital union, a sheaf of wheat representing all of the products the syrup can accompany, and a blue background signifying blue-ribbon quality.

Alaga syrup emerged in a wide-open market, since most families still made syrup at home in 1906. It quickly became the breakfast syrup of choice for families across the Deep South, especially once southerners began leaving rural areas and syrup making declined. As culinary historian Jessica Harris recalls of her grandmother, "breakfasts at her house were always occasions for beaten biscuits served dripping

Joe Todd, a fifth-generation syrup maker, in his cane field outside Dothan, Alabama (Alabama Farmers Federation)

with Alaga syrup (none of that thin maple syrup nonsense!) into which bits of butter had been mixed, streaky bacon, and grits."[††]

Alaga syrup grew to become a southern institution. Today, 95 percent of Alabama grocery chains carry Alaga syrup, which is sold throughout the Southeast. The syrup also sells well in Chicago and Detroit, where black families carried food traditions from the rural South to the urban north in the early decades of the twentieth century. "I'm amazed at the brand loyalty," states co-owner Virginia Whitfield. "Even now, in times of economic challenge, we have retained our market share. Alaga syrup gets passed down through the generations as a southern tradition."[‡‡]

Inspired by the devotion of Alaga customers, Whitfield launched a "Buy Alabama's Best" campaign in 2004 to identify and promote Alabama products among Alabama consumers. The program fosters partnerships among Alabama companies to boost shared marketing and highlights Alabama goods on grocery shelves. Whitfield has increased program visibility by televising a cooking session in the governor's mansion using all Alabama products, serving all Alabama products at press banquets, and organizing a syrup sop at a Montgomery Biscuits minor league baseball game. The program now includes over thirty companies who produce everything from cheese straws to pecans to sweet tea—and, of course, biscuits and cane syrup.[§§]

* Peacock 2011.

† Outlaw 2008:2.

‡ Description of making cane syrup drawn from Lewis and Peacock 2003:222–23; Outlaw 2008:2 (quotation); http://www.norrisc.com/syrup.html (quotation).

§ Couric 2009:186.

** D. H. Dean 2008; Outlaw 2008:2 (quotaton).

†† Harris 1989: xxii.

‡‡ Personal interview with Virginia Whitfield, 2010, Montgomery, AL.

§§ Ibid.

Though vegetables always made up a large part of the southern diet, the variety of vegetables on the southern table greatly expanded during the Civil War due to widespread poverty and food shortages. With no salt to cure pork, southerners of all classes began eating anything they could grow or find wild. For many, foods harvested from the woods and rivers marked the difference between hunger and starvation. These conditions cemented the concept of "southern food" as traditions fused across racial and economic lines.[10]

It remains unclear who brought the first tomatoes to America: it could have been Spanish colonists, British colonists, West African slaves from the Caribbean, or all three. Regardless, most Americans remained wary of tomatoes into the nineteenth century. Some believed they were poisonous. Others were simply unfamiliar with the fruit or did not care for its smell, appearance, flavor, or acidity. But the tomato experienced early success in the South, due in part to Spanish and French influences. Cultivated throughout the coastal South by the late eighteenth century, tomatoes were often used in gumbo and paired with okra. South Alabamians also used tomatoes to make ketchup.

Tomatoes flourished in the South, where they enjoyed a long growing season and thrived regardless of climate and soil conditions. In parts of the South, writes culinary historian Andrew Smith, "tomatoes grew almost spontaneously," sprouting up in weed beds, ditches, and garbage dumps.[11] In the garden, tomatoes grew easily and rapidly, without frames for support and using little space. They also produced in abundance: "Six tomato plants, occupying no more than 32 square feet" produced enough for a whole family.[12]

By the 1830s, tomatoes had become a treasure of the southern table, used extensively throughout the region. A decade later, they were consumed nationwide and had become fully integrated into American cookbooks and cooking traditions, thanks to hundreds of tomato recipes published by agricultural periodicals and newspapers that "disseminated tomato cookery to a rural audience and boosted its legitimacy throughout America."[13] Mary Randolph's seminal 1824 cookbook, *The Virginia House-Wife*, featured seventeen tomato recipes that "demonstrated the wide range of the tomato's culinary usage from soup to sweets and from breakfast to dinner dishes."[14]

Tomatoes received another boost in the early twentieth century, when southern county extension agents began encouraging the tomato's growth on a widespread basis, spawning a heyday for tomato cookery nationwide. Both farm and home demonstration agents touted the tomato's nutritional value and its potential as an alternative crop for rural families. Home demonstration agents made tomatoes the focus of girls' tomato clubs, founded to provide girls with income, confidence, canning skills, new farming techniques, scientific knowledge, and business sense.

From the founding of the first club in South Carolina in 1910 through 1917, girls' tomato clubs "swept the southern United States."[15] By 1915, thirty-two thousand girls (black and white) hailing from every southern state had joined. The girls, ages twelve through eighteen, planted tomatoes in small, individual plots, worked together to can their harvests, and marketed their final products. They received prizes based on quantity, quality, variety, and profit. "To be successful," writes culinary historian Elizabeth Engelhardt, "girls had to research their markets, price their goods, brand their lines, . . . standardize their products, . . . and become confident sales negotiators."[16]

Girls' tomato clubs also encouraged older generations to embrace crop diversification and local production at a time when the Alabama soil, economy, and rural family desperately needed them. It was a grassroots method for agricultural reform, from the girls up. As one Alabama tomato club member reported, "after the agent came to our home and actually gave a demonstration in making a hotbed and it proved successful, Papa was convinced there was something to demonstration work. Now, instead of only collards and cockleburs in our winter garden, we have turnips, cabbage, lettuce, spinach and beets."[17]

Despite the widespread use and versatility of tomatoes, attention from girls' clubs, and profusion of tomato recipes, fried green tomatoes are strikingly absent from most southern cookbooks.[18] That is, until 1987, when *Fried Green Tomatoes at the Whistle Stop Café*, a novel written by Alabama native Fannie Flagg, captivated readers across the country and catapulted fried green tomatoes into the national food spotlight. The dish became an instant emblem

Girls' Tomato Club, Calhoun County, Alabama, 1915 (Alabama Department of Archives and History, Montgomery, Alabama, Q9664)

of southern home cooking and was served in restaurants nationwide as an essential southern food.

Flagg, who was raised eating fried green tomatoes, suggests that they became popular in the South during the Great Depression, when "people would fry up most anything and pretend it was meat or fish, and . . . a pitcher of sweet iced tea and a plate of fried green tomatoes turned out to be . . . delightfully tasty."[19] Many southerners do recall, as Flagg does, eating fried green tomatoes in the 1940s and 1950s. But the dish was unknown to others until Flagg's novel, followed by the 1991 film *Fried Green Tomatoes*, made it popular.

Regardless of the universality of fried green tomatoes prior to Flagg's novel, the dish is certainly a symbol of southern cooking now. Moreover, fried green tomatoes have come to represent the classic rural, southern restaurant on which Flagg's novel is based. Flagg drew her inspiration for the Whistle Stop Café from the Irondale Café, owned by her aunt, Bess Fortenberry, and located in the small town of Irondale, Alabama, nestled between the freight yards of the Alabama Great Southern Railroad and the Georgia Pacific

Company, six miles east of Birmingham. It was in the café, wrote Flagg, that she "first learned about good food and kindness."[20]

Bess Fortenberry purchased the former hot dog and hamburger stand next to the railroad tracks and transformed it into the Irondale Café in 1932. "Bess, who came from a prominent Irondale family, was single and had a great enthusiasm for life. She was free-hearted, loved practical jokes, and built a successful business," writes one of her successors.[21] In the early 1940s, Fortenberry teamed with Sue Lovelace and Lizzie Cunningham, and the three women ran the café together for thirty years.

Housed in a small frame building with pale green siding, white trim, and a large Coca-Cola sign above the awning, the Irondale Café held an assortment of booths, tables, and stools, an old Rock-Ola jukebox, and floors that "sprang with you when you walked." Open weekdays, the café offered up traditional southern fare: one meat, three vegetables, cornbread, and coleslaw for a fixed price. Customers ordered a small or regular lunch; the difference was portion size and twenty-five cents in price. Beverages included tea, coffee, colas, and beer. There were no regular desserts, though pies were occasionally offered. If customers didn't care for the meat of the day, there was a to-go sandwich option and "always baked ham or barbecue in the cooler."[22]

The Irondale Café represents a crossroads in southern food history. In the early 1940s, the war industries that brought America out of the Great Depression transformed the way southerners grew, cooked, and ate food. Urbanization, increased travel on new highways, radio and television advertising, and the rising popularity of fast food all dramatically changed the agricultural landscape. Women entered the workforce in droves and families increasingly relied on new industrialized and convenience foods, including factory made bread and cake mixes, frozen foods, and canned goods. In most southern families, labor-intensive cooking was relegated to Sundays and holidays.

Further, from 1940 to 1960, the southern farm population decreased by almost 60 percent. The mechanization of agriculture caused labor decline and changes in government farm policy that created large tracts of land, paving the way for big agribusiness and discouraging small farming. By the 1960s, millions of southern small farmers and their families had left rural areas and

Fried Tomatoes

LETTICE BRYAN, 1841[*]

Select tomatoes large and ripe, take off the peelings, cut them in thick slices, and season them with salt and pepper. Have ready a plate of finely grated bread, dip each side of the sliced tomatoes in it, taking care to make as much of the bread adhere to them as possible, and fry them brown in butter, which should be hot when they are put in. Serve them warm; mince very fine an onion or two, fry them in the gravy, and transfuse the whole over the tomatoes.

[*] Smith 1994.

relocated in cities or suburbs. The era of widespread subsistence farming that had dominated the South for a thousand years had come to an end.

To fill the void, cafés, diners, and "meat and threes" sprang up offering the same food southerners had cooked for generations. As Flagg writes, "café cooking . . . is nothing more than good, old-fashioned home cooking not done at home."[23] In small, rural communities, downtown cafés became beloved gathering places where cooks made the food southerners had grown up eating on a daily basis, helping to preserve and sustain nearly two hundred years of southern culture. The Irondale Café played this role, which Flagg explains: "These little cafés were not always grand but they were the very heart of the town, with personalities of their own. And when one closed down it was mourned for generations. For weeks afterward, you could see lost old men still peering inside the boarded up windows, hoping that maybe, somehow, it could come back to life, . . . and none of the new, cold, operating room sterile, orange plastic fast food joints can ever take the place of the old café, where the silverware never matched and more often than not was bent and covered with water spots. . . . It was silverware with a past. That spoon

Fried Green Tomatoes

Lucille Morris, early 1940s[*]

Keep to a 3 to 1 ratio of corn flour and plain white flour. (If you cannot find corn flour, use the finest ground cornmeal you can find.) For small batches, blend together ¾ cup corn flour and ¼ cup plain white flour. Add 1 teaspoon each of salt, black pepper, ground red pepper, and garlic or onion powder. Slice a green tomato about ¼ inch thick and dredge in the dry batter, then in the buttermilk, then back in the dry batter. It is best to let the tomatoes set for about 5 minutes so the batter can absorb the milk and the juice of the tomato. Fry at about 350 degrees until golden brown.

[*] Her son Eddy Morris gave me the recipe.

you are stirring your coffee with may have been used by your grandmother thirty years ago and that knife by your first cousin just yesterday."[24]

The success of Flagg's novel and the subsequent film sparked national interest in the Irondale Café. *Fried Green Tomatoes* premiered in Birmingham in January 1992, and on February 5, a lengthy article in the *Birmingham News* identified the Irondale Café as the original Whistle Stop Café. The headline read, "Seen the movie? Now taste the title!" Soon afterward, three women begged to enter the Irondale Café after it had closed one Friday afternoon. "They wanted to be able to say that they had come to the original Whistle Stop Café," recalls Mary Jo McMichael, who owned the café at the time along with her husband, Billy. "And I was absolutely floored. We didn't have any national publicity, so I don't know how people found out about us, but they did. They started coming in droves. Tour groups would call us. Buses would come by. . . . We couldn't have imagined the huge impact the movie would have on our business."[25]

Fried green tomatoes at the Irondale Café (photo by Michelle Campbell,
Birmingham News)

Irondale Café owner Jim Dolan with a plate of fried green tomatoes (photo by
Michelle Campbell, *Birmingham News*)

At the time, fried green tomatoes were one of many vegetable options on the menu, but today, the Irondale Café never opens without them. By 1995, café cooks were frying sixty to seventy pounds of fried green tomatoes every day. Though the film clearly turned fried green tomatoes into an icon, some southerners are quick to point out the dish's longevity on the rural table. As cookbook author Damon Lee Fowler recalls, shortly after the film's release, "a Southern so-called social historian asserted that fried green tomatoes were merely apocryphal, that nobody really ate them, at least, not anymore. Poor thing; she's never been to my house . . . or she would've known better."[26]

FIVE

‖‖

Lane Cake

Alabama Women in the Progressive Era

Lane cake, coconut cake, and red velvet cake not only conjure tastes
but also stories of the ladies who bake them.
—Angie Mosier, "Cakes"

AS THE LOCAL STORY GOES, sometime in the late 1800s, Emma Rylander Lane left her native city of Americus, Georgia, and moved with her husband, a Central of Georgia Railway agent, to the town of Clayton, Alabama.[1] Here, she struck up a friendship with Lucy Walker Parish, whose large downtown Victorian home hummed with activity. Its massive front porch hosted numerous social events including tea parties, wedding receptions, and youth dances, and one of the first paved sidewalks in town, popular with roller skaters in the 1890s, circled out front. Because Lucy had planted a magnolia tree on a side lawn, a friend dubbed the Parish home Magnolia Manor.[2]

Lane Cake

Emma Rylander Lane*

BATTER FOR CAKE
8 egg whites
1 cup butter
1 cup sweet milk
2 cups sifted sugar
3¼ cups sifted flour
2 teaspoons baking powder
1 tablespoon vanilla

FILLING
8 egg yolks
1 large cup sugar
½ cup butter
1 cup raisins, seeded and finely clipped
1 wine-glass good whiskey or brandy
1 teaspoon vanilla

Sift the flour and baking powder together three times, cream the butter and sugar until perfectly light, add to it alternately, little at a time, milk and flour, until all are used, beginning and ending with flour. Last, beat in the well whipped whites and vanilla. Bake in four layers, using medium sized pie tins, with one layer of ungreased brown paper in the bottom of each tin.

Filling—Beat well together eight egg yolks, one large cup of sugar, and half a cup of butter. Pour into a small, deep stew pan and cook on top of the stove until quite thick, stirring all the time, or it will be sure to burn. When done and while still hot, put in one cup of seeded and finely clipped raisins, one wine-glass of good whiskey or brandy and one teaspoon of vanilla. Spread thickly between the layers and ice. It is much better to be made a day or two before using.

My prize cake, and named not from my own conceit, but through the courtesy of Mrs. Janie McDowell Pruett of Eufaula, Ala.

* Lane 1898.

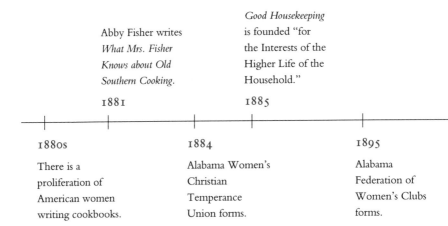

Abby Fisher writes *What Mrs. Fisher Knows about Old Southern Cooking.*

1881

Good Housekeeping is founded "for the Interests of the Higher Life of the Household."

1885

1880s

There is a proliferation of American women writing cookbooks.

1884

Alabama Women's Christian Temperance Union forms.

1895

Alabama Federation of Women's Clubs forms.

The Parish family relates that Lucy Parish and Emma Lane experimented with new recipes in Magnolia Manor's large kitchen. The modern cake had recently made its debut, thanks to the widespread availability of white flour and the invention of baking powder: a quick, easy, and reliable alternative to yeast. Baking powder revolutionized cake making, which took on a particular fervor in the South, where for centuries "a Southern cook's reputation was judged more by her baking than any other culinary endeavor," writes food historian Damon Lee Fowler, who notes that "even women who had an accomplished cook in the kitchen took particular care with the baking, often to the point of doing it themselves."[3]

Baking powder rendered cake layers airy and fine textured, so to avoid losing the richness of the old English-style cakes, southern bakers added dense fillings of fruit and nuts between the cake layers instead of directly into the batter. The whole cake was then enveloped in a light, white icing. Southern women invented a number of these extravagant cakes around the turn of the century, including the Lady Baltimore, Moss Rose, Robert E. Lee, and Japanese Fruitcake.[4]

At Magnolia Manor, Emma Lane created a four-layer white cake made with flour, baking powder, butter, sugar, egg whites, and vanilla. She spread

Emma Rylander
Lane authors *Some
Good Things to Eat.*

1898

Alabama Women's
Christian
Temperance
Union endorses
women's suffrage.

1914

Women make up
one-third of voters
in Alabama.

1920

1900

American women
have an average
of 3.5 children
(half of the 1800
average).

1920

The Nineteenth
Amendment gives
women the right
to vote.

Lane Cake (photo by Meredith Bell Foltynowicz)

a heated mixture of egg yolks, butter, sugar, raisins, whiskey, and vanilla between the layers and frosted the whole cake with a boiled, fluffy white icing. When she entered it in a baking competition at a county fair in Columbus, Georgia, the cake took first prize, and so Lane named it Prize Cake. But a friend later convinced her to lend her own name to the dessert, and so the cake appeared as Lane Cake in Lane's cookbook, *Some Good Things to Eat*, which was self-published in 1898.[5]

Lane Cake was an immediate hit in Alabama. Because it was so labor intensive, it was usually reserved for birthdays, anniversaries, and other special occasions. As Appalachian food writer Fred Sauceman notes, "in Alabama, and throughout the South, the presentation of an elegant, scratch-made, laborious Lane cake is a sign that a noteworthy life event is about to be celebrated."[6] In *To Kill a Mockingbird*, a novel by Alabama native Harper Lee, a Lane Cake is baked to welcome Aunt Alexandra to Maycomb. Describing it, Scout states, "Miss Maudie Atkinson baked a Lane cake so loaded with shinny it made me tight."[7]

Indeed, the Lane Cake's alcoholic edge gives it a slightly wild reputation, especially in Alabama's dry counties. It was nicknamed the Ha Ha Cake for this reason and became popular at Alabama eggnog parties held at Christmastime. Churchgoers often substituted grape juice for the whiskey, as did mothers making children's birthday cakes. "Being members of the Baptist church, having a cake which included whiskey was considered a bit 'naughty' for us," notes a Georgia native. "But it sure tasted good."[8]

Over the years, the Lane Cake saw many modifications, including the addition of coconut, dried fruit, and nuts to the filling. Some bakers ice the entire cake with the filling mixture. And as a relic of bygone eggnog parties, Lane Cake is still tightly wed to the Christmas season in Alabama. Lane suggested the cake is best if made a day or two before serving, to allow the flavors to blend. Some Alabamians recall their grandmothers making the cake during Thanksgiving weekend and letting it stand until Christmastime.[9] In 2016, the Lane Cake became the official state cake of Alabama.

But Emma Rylander Lane's countless hours experimenting in the Parish kitchen and the time and resources she took to publish *Some Good Things to*

Eat were not solely about personal satisfaction or sharing good recipes. As she explains in the cookbook's preface: "The object of this book is to meet some of the most imperative needs of the Southern housekeepers. . . . The first thought of every woman when she assumes the duties of a home should be her kitchen, as the health, happiness, and prosperity of a family depend largely upon the wisdom and economy of the housewife."[10]

Lane was actually part of a national wave of women writing cookbooks with the express purpose of helping homemakers run economical and healthy households. The second half of the nineteenth century saw an explosion of American cookbooks, written mostly by women. "The subject of cookery has never received so much and so intelligent attention as at the present time," claims an 1890 cookbook. "There are . . . Cook Books of all sizes, shapes, claims and pretentions—Cook Books everywhere."[11]

The cookbook revolution was spawned by a growing dissatisfaction with European recipes that were viewed as expensive, complicated, vague, and incomplete. As an alternative, American women began creating cookbooks geared specifically for homemakers that took a common sense approach to cooking. These methodical, direct, easy-to-follow, economical, and comprehensive cookbooks often contained several hundred recipes. They were also intended to be universal: useful for beginners or experts, rich or poor. The *White House Cook Book*, published in 1887, aimed to meet "completely. . . the requirements of housekeepers of all classes."[12] Many cookbooks focused on economy, discussing ways to manage the family table and household to save both time and money. Authors encouraged readers not to waste anything, to recycle and repurpose, and to use ingredients found in nature.

Like Lane, cookbook authors revered the homemaker's work as the foundation of family health and happiness. One author compared the government of a family to that of a nation. Another likened cooking to building a house. As a result, the cookbooks they created extended far beyond recipes and cooking advice to include instruction in every facet of household management, including food preparation, family health, nutrition, home maintenance, sickness, child rearing, kitchen organization and equipment, mishaps and emergency situations, rules of etiquette and hospitality, and kitchen gardens.[13]

Alabama Eggnog Parties

Eggnog traces its roots to posset, a medieval English drink that blended eggs, alcohol, cream, cinnamon, and nutmeg. Because eggs and milk were expensive and uncommon for most citizens, posset was a drink for the aristocracy. The word eggnog *first appears in the early seventeenth century to indicate a beverage used to toast one's health, but its origins are debatable. Nog could refer to the seventeenth-century English ale with origins in east Anglia or could derive from* noggin, *a small, wooden mug used to serve alcohol in English taverns.*

Eggnog appeared in America in the eighteenth century, where a variety of alcohol was used to make it, depending on what was cheapest and most widely available: when brandy and wine were heavily taxed, Americans substituted Caribbean rum; when the Revolutionary War cut off access to rum, whiskey or bourbon was used. Even Prohibition could not stop the flow of eggnog. Americans simply substituted moonshine (corn whiskey).

Throughout the nineteenth century, American eggnog was commonly made in large quantities as a social drink and served mainly during the holiday season alongside cake. As a visitor to South Carolina in 1842 noted, "before breakfast, at Christmas time, everyone takes a glass of egg-nog and a slice of cake. It is the universal custom and was not on this occasion omitted by anyone. As Christmas was kept during four days, egg-nog was drank regularly every morning."*

Eggnog was at the center of holiday parties given by wealthy Alabama planters, known as eggnog parties. In antebellum years, "when Southern affluence reached its zenith," Alabama eggnog parties were particularly lavish.† Male slaves were charged with making the eggnog by blending hundreds of gathered eggs with well-aged whiskey ordered from far-off distilleries. Dressed in their finery, guests began

Couric-Smith House in Eufaula, Alabama (photo by Jana Chapman)

*arriving on Christmas Eve morning and the parties continued until
nightfall on Christmas Day. Though intended for the elite planter
class, some plantation owners provided farm cabins and slave quarters
with eggnog, extending the celebrations throughout the countryside.*

*The town of Eufaula, Alabama, awash in historic plantation homes
and located twenty miles east of the Lane Cake's birthplace, was
particularly known for its eggnog parties. A 1930s account describes
great log fires in marble-trimmed fireplaces, spacious living rooms,
candles gleaming in shiny chandeliers, and holly wreaths adorning
every entrance. In the living room, huge crystal bowls brimming with
eggnog lined broad central tables. Every visitor was given plenty of
eggnog to drink, which was always served alongside salted nuts and
holiday cakes, including fruitcakes, coconut cakes, and Lane Cakes.[‡]*

* Neal 1985:188.

† Kytle 2009:188.

‡ History of Alabama eggnog parties drawn from ibid.

Eggnog
MRS. CHARLES A. BLONDHEIM JR.*

1 egg per person

1 tablespoon whiskey per egg, plus 1

1 tablespoon sugar per egg

½ pint whipping cream for each 6–8 eggs

Whip the cream. Separate eggs. Whip whites until stiff. Whip yolks until very thick, about 10 minutes, longer for large amounts. Add sugar and whiskey, mix with egg whites and whipped cream.

* Smith 1976:24.

Cookbook titles from the 1880s include *The Appledore Cook Book: Containing Practical Receipts for Plain and Rich Cooking, Common Sense in the Household: A Manual of Practical Housewifery, The Cottage Kitchen: A Collection of Practical and Inexpensive Receipts, Cookery for Beginners: A Series of Familiar Lessons for Young Housekeepers, Hand-book of Practical Cookery, for Ladies and Professional Cooks: Containing the Whole Science and Art of Preparing Human Food, The Universal Household Assistant, Miss Corson's Practical American Cookery and Household Management*, and *Miss Parloa's Kitchen Companion: A Guide for All Who Would Be Good Housekeepers.*

Further, nineteenth-century cookbook writing was not confined to white women. In 1881, Abby Fisher authored the oldest-known cookbook written by a former American slave.[14] Fisher was born in South Carolina, likely in 1832, and likely of a union between a slave and her owner. She grew up in plantation kitchens, where she learned to cook, and eventually moved to Alabama. In 1870, Fisher was married with ten children and working as a cook in Mobile. Sometime in the next decade, the Fisher family relocated

David Walker Lupton
African American Cookbook Collection

Housed at the University of Alabama in Tuscaloosa, the David Walker Lupton African American Cookbook Collection is "one of the largest and best-documented collections of African American cookbooks in the United States."* Containing 450 volumes spanning from 1827 to 2000, the collection includes many "community cookbooks" compiled by churches, sororities, and a range of women's organizations. These cookbooks offer a window not only into the food traditions of African Americans in Alabama but into "ethnic identity, family and community life, social history, the roles of women and men, values, religion, and economics. . . . Almost every title in the Lupton Collection suggests more than recipes," notes curator Jessica Lacher-Feldman. "Food is linked with music, humor, social satire . . . cultural and religious celebrations . . . and almost every other aspect of life."†

* Lacher-Feldman 2011:84.

† http://www.lib.ua.edu/libraries/hoole/collections/luptoncollection.htm.

to San Francisco (an eleventh child was born en route), where Abby began a pickling and preserves business and worked as a caterer for the upper class.

Abby Fisher flourished in San Francisco, winning medals for her pickles, preserves, and sauces at state fairs in San Francisco and Sacramento. She was often asked to compile her recipes in a cookbook, and though unable to read or write, she acquiesced, dictating her recipes to several prominent white patrons. In the preface to *What Mrs. Fisher Knows about Old Southern Cooking*, Fisher states that the book is "based on an experience of upwards of thirty-five years" and is intended to be "a complete instructor, so that a child can understand it and learn the art of cooking."[15]

During the Progressive Era (1890–1920), when women were churning out cookbooks in record numbers, their status in society was transforming dramatically. Women were increasingly claiming roles outside the home, which began to dissolve the division between the public sphere of business (belonging to men) and the private sphere of home (belonging to women) that had dominated the nineteenth century.

In Alabama, the Civil War had disrupted conventional gender roles by giving southern women the opportunity to perform traditionally male work. Many had managed family farms while their husbands were away at the front. Others began working outside the home for the first time at steel mills and defense centers. Post–Civil War economic conditions extended the trend, drawing many young women to work in the textile mills to help support their families.

Technological advances of the 1890s—including central heating, electricity, indoor plumbing, cooking stoves, electric refrigerators and appliances, ready-to-wear clothing, commercially baked bread, canned goods, and baking powder—further untethered women from the home by freeing them from some of the hardest work associated with housekeeping. Public education emerged, releasing mothers from their roles as teachers and allowing some to hold respected positions as educators. And finally, women had an average of 3.5 children in 1900, which was half the 1800 average.

Taken together, these trends enabled women to be far more active outside the home, resulting in a proliferation of women's organizations in the late nineteenth century. Though art and literary clubs were founded first, women soon moved beyond goals of self-improvement to societal improvement. As American cookbook expert Jan Longone notes, women "started with helping themselves and each other and moved into helping all of society."[16] In the 1890s, women created a large number of organizations to address a range of problems, many of which stemmed from rapid industrialization.

In Alabama, church organizations, teachers' associations, and temperance groups comprised the bulk of clubs formed by women in the nineteenth century. The Alabama Women's Christian Temperance Union, founded in 1884,

Women and men attending a teachers' institute in Pickens County, Alabama, circa 1900 (Alabama Department of Archives and History, Montgomery, Alabama, Q8872)

addressed a range of social issues including alcoholism, women's education, poverty, child labor, prison reform, and homes for abandoned women and children. In 1895, the literary clubs of major Alabama cities merged to form the Alabama Federation of Women's Clubs. The initial 130 members soon shifted the federation's focus to civic affairs, tackling a wide variety of issues including illiteracy, public education reform, juvenile delinquency, and treatment of juvenile offenders. It would eventually become the largest women's organization in Alabama.[17]

The growing presence of women in the public sphere ignited a national debate over a woman's proper place in society, including disputes over whether she should work outside the home and whether she should vote. Cookbooks served a dual purpose in the whole affair: they had enabled women to help each other, sparking a desire to aid all of society and leading women into the public sphere. Yet, cookbooks also affirmed a woman's traditional role by emphasizing her importance as the keeper of family health and happiness.

Progressive Era cookbooks were increasingly shaped by a national domestic reform movement that elevated "traditional household responsibilities to the status of a profession, in which all the new resources of science and technology were applied to the improvement and more efficient management of the home."[18] The field of domestic science was born, and the latest information on nutrition, diet, and health reached women at Expos nationwide.

Cooking schools emerged, often founded and directed by women who preached the principles of domestic science to millions through classes, articles, and books. Through these outlets, they explained the chemistry, physiology, and philosophy of food and how to employ it toward a better existence. Sarah Tyson Rorer, founder of the Philadelphia Cooking School, believed "the teacher or cook book (an ever present teacher) that does not teach health, body building, and economy in time and money, is short lived."[19] Fannie Farmer, founder of the Boston Cooking School, wrote that once "a knowledge of the principles of diet [is] an essential part of one's education, . . . mankind will eat to live, will be able to do better mental and physical work, and disease will be less frequent."[20]

Yet, while domestic science provided vital information on nutrition and health, it also affirmed a woman's place as being in the home. Women's magazines burst on the scene, lauding and reinforcing women's traditional roles. In 1885, *Good Housekeeping* was founded for the "Interests of the Higher Life of the Household" and offered articles on household management, home decor, childcare, fashion, and beauty.[21] Within a decade, fifty-five thousand women subscribed. In 1889, a new editor expanded the *Ladies Home Journal* to include house plans, tips on home decorating, and stories in which unhappy working women find love and marriage as the solution to their woes. Circulation doubled in a decade to reach eight hundred thousand.

Ironically, domestic science was intended to streamline housework, freeing women to pursue other interests, but wound up elevating home life and encouraging women to devote more time to it than ever before. Women were caught in a curious mix of time-saving devices and expanding home duties. Baking powder allowed for quicker, easier baking, but women used it to create extravagant, laborious cakes.

Alabama "club women" managed to skirt gender debates by defining their public activities as family centered. All of their work, like promoting temperance and education, was purposed to improve home life. Entering the public sphere as homemakers, club women brought their domestic ideals, values, and concerns to the political arena to benefit Alabama families.[22] As one woman explained, the Alabama club woman was "a homemaker in the broadest sense, her labors not confined to brightening merely her own fireside circle, but reaching Statewide to countless homes where wretchedness and poverty sit side by side with ignorance and crime."[23]

Because they accessed the public sphere in the name of home and family, Alabama club women believed they operated within traditional gender constructs and were in fact "fearful of being identified with the objectionable 'new woman'" of the Progressive Era, notes Alabama historian Mary Martha Thomas.[24] Writing in Selma in 1895, Mary LaFayette Robbins, the first president of the Alabama Federation of Women's Clubs, rejected the notion of the new woman and urged fellow women to pursue activities that fit within traditional gender boundaries: "The idea, that greater privileges, and graver responsibilities have evolved a new woman, radically different from the original one, is altogether a mistake. An error, which has tempted woman into paths, for which she is by nature unfitted. . . . The one, wholesome truth, embodied in the so-called woman problem, is the fact that idleness is subversive of the well-being of every individual. Out of this truth arises a query worthy of every thoughtful woman's consideration. The question, what may she do without stepping outside of her proper environment."[25]

Significantly, Alabama women's clubs did not belong only to white women. From the inception of the club movement, African American women formed their own clubs for the betterment of society. The earliest of these included the Ten Times One Is Ten Club (1888) and the Anna

Henrietta Gibbs, president
of the Alabama Federation
of Colored Women's Clubs
(1936–43) and the Anna M.
Duncan Club. In 1921, Gibbs
became the first African American woman registered to vote
in Montgomery (Alabama
Women's Hall of Fame)

M. Duncan Club (1897) of Montgomery and the Tuskegee Women's Club
(1895). In 1899, several of the early clubs united to create the Alabama Federation of Colored Women's Clubs. By 1904, more than twenty-six African
American women's clubs existed throughout Alabama and worked on a range
of issues, with a focus on juvenile justice and prison reform.

Women's rights and women's suffrage were not part of the typical club
woman's agenda. As Thomas writes, "such overt political participation was in-
compatible with their more cautious approach to obtaining influence through
the invocation of women's traditional domestic qualities."[26] Though a statewide suffrage organization had formed in Alabama in 1893, the movement

Women's suffrage booth at the state fair, Birmingham, Alabama, 1914 (Alabama Department of Archives and History, Montgomery, Alabama, Q4096)

floundered for nearly two decades because early advocates urged women to reject traditional gender divisions to obtain equality with men. But many Alabama women found their power and identity in the home, they took pride in it, and most had no interest in reconstructing their identity and relinquishing their power.

Beginning in 1910, however, "a new generation of leaders" revitalized the Alabama suffrage movement by touting the vote as a venue for enhancing family health and prosperity.[27] Support for the movement swelled, gaining endorsements from two major Alabama women's clubs in 1914 and 1918. By this time, Alabama women had already developed speaking and writing skills, expertise, connections, confidence, and a bond of sisterhood through club membership. As Thomas notes, by 1910, Alabama club women "had learned how to organize, how to lobby the legislature, how to hold conventions, and how to achieve their goals," skills they now used to advocate for the right to vote.[28] In this way, women's clubs proved vital to the suffrage movement in Alabama and throughout the nation. Longone calls the club movement "one of the most important sociological phenomena of the century" and "the foundation of feminism."[29]

The Nineteenth Amendment, giving American women the right to vote, was ratified on August 18, 1920. By November, the newly formed Alabama League of Women Voters had registered nearly 124,000 women who made up one-third of the statewide vote that year. "By the end of the Progressive period in 1920," writes Thomas, "Alabama women had undergone significant changes in roles, life-styles, values, and expectations."[30]

Throughout the Progressive Era, cookbooks had played an evolving and complex role in these values and expectations. In one sense, cookbooks reinforced the status quo, but in quite another, they encouraged women to esteem their vital role in family health and to improve the lives around them. Cookbooks were a sister to the club movement that laid the foundation for women's suffrage, and some cookbooks even supported suffrage itself. Titles including *The Woman Suffrage Cookbook* (1886) and *Washington Women's Cook Book* (1909) aimed to recruit readers to the cause as well as support it through cookbook sales.

More than one hundred years after the Lane Cake debuted in *Some Good Things to Eat* and nearly ninety years after women secured the right to vote, I stand at the front door of Magnolia Manor, in Clayton, still surrounded by its vast front porch and the magnolia, oak, and pecan trees that Lucy Parish planted as a young wife. It is a Saturday in March, the first warm day after an unusually cold Alabama winter, and since leaving the highway eighty-seven miles ago, I passed few cars moving through a landscape of rolling hills, red clay, budding trees, and blue sky.

Lane Cake ingredients
(photo by Valerie Downes)

Lucy and her husband, Joseph, moved into this house shortly after it was built in 1890 and raised four children here. The bed where Lucy birthed their fourth child still stands in the front bedroom and Joseph's ledger books from his days of managing the dry goods department of the family mercantile store sit stacked on a low shelf in the foyer, next to a winding staircase. In fact, all of Magnolia Manor brims with antiques, colorful glass windows, and old Parish family photographs.

Today, three generations of Parish women have gathered to make a Lane Cake in the kitchen in which it was invented. It is the first Lane Cake any of them has ever made. We work from a copy of *Some Good Things to Eat*, reprinted by Lucy Parish's granddaughter, Rebecca Beasley, in 1976. Beasley owned only half of her grandmother's copy of the original book but was able to pair it with another half owned by Emma Lane's great-granddaughter. She retyped the book on a typewriter, and the 1976 copies have since sold out. To reprint it, Beasley will have to retype it again on a computer. She is considering it. Of late, there has been a flurry of interest in the Lane Cake.

Adele Kahn Weil: An Alabama Club Woman

In 1898, the same year Emma Rylander Lane published Some Good Things to Eat, *Adele Kahn coauthored* The Twentieth Century Cookbook *with friend Lena Moritz. In the book's preface, the authors note their intent to create a cookbook that would "commend itself to every housekeeper." Further, they "endeavored to bring our recipes within the scope of the most moderate income, and in many cases where elaborateness is called for, we have given another simpler and less expensive recipe for the same dish."**

A lifelong resident of Montgomery, Adele Kahn Weil is an archetype of the Progressive Era woman in Alabama. Born in 1873 to German Jewish parents, Weil became active in all manner of clubs, civic matters, social reform, and art and literature societies from a young age. As an adult, she was highly regarded as an authority on economics and chaired the economics and home demonstration committees of the City Federation of Montgomery Women's Clubs and the living cost committee of the Montgomery County League of Women Voters. Weil once gave an address on living costs that had "the charm of the personal touch, the humorous common sense, and the wide sweep of intimate knowledge," reported the Montgomery Advertiser.[†]

Typical of club women, Weil used her expertise to improve lives, launching several projects aimed at helping women, families, and farmers save money, access economical goods, gain skills, and increase earning power. She was a key organizer of the Montgomery Curb Market, where farmers could earn capital and avoid shipping costs by selling and trading products locally and housewives could find reasonable food prices. At the market, farmers were allowed to sell anything they raised, "be it wool or willows, pecans or potatoes." In 1927, nineteen farmers and nine hundred buyers attended

Adele Kahn Weil (photo by
Emily Blejwas, from Alabama
Department of Archives and
History collection)

Young woman weighing a cake at a curb market in Montgomery, Alabama,
circa 1920–40 (Alabama Department of Archives and History, Montgomery,
Alabama, Q5557)

the Curb Market's opening day. Today, the Curb Market runs as it always has, every Tuesday, Thursday, and Saturday morning.

The Montgomery Canning Club, another of Weil's pursuits, used volunteer labor to can food for the needy. After the Red Cross approached Weil about the feasibility of the idea, she organized a mass meeting of Montgomery women to launch the project, then organized and directed it. The Red Cross donated the equipment, the food was donated by farmers or purchased from cash donations, and the labor came from women volunteers who canned thirty-five thousand cans of vegetables, fruits, and soup in one summer. The club also promoted food conservation and provided canning demonstrations to homemakers.

Weil was passionate about economic development and chaired two separate committees determined to enlarge Montgomery's city limits to boost its population in hopes of attracting industry. In the early 1930s in a letter to the editor of the Montgomery Advertiser, Weil remarked on the need to attract large businesses, enlarge the tax base, and show the city was growing and progressive.

Her letter demonstrates a comprehensive knowledge of Alabama. After citing the state's yearly rainfall, she asserts that Alabama rivers possess one-fourth of the potential electrical waterpower of the entire United States: "Enough energy to turn every factory wheel in the Southern States and plenty to spare."‡ She also cites the yearly value of Alabama crops and outlines the resources in every section of the state, including northern minerals, Black Belt soil, and the port of Mobile with its market access to Central and South America. In fact, to engender this type of knowledge and passion in others, Weil coordinated a citywide Alabama Day in which all Montgomery students participated in Alabama history and resources programming.

Newspaper articles describe Weil as an "outstanding figure" with "a wealth of experience combined with unusual executive

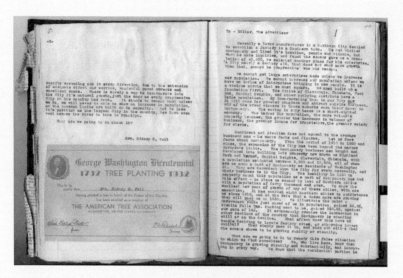

Letter from Adele Kahn Weil to the editor of the *Montgomery Advertiser,* circa 1932. (Alabama Department of Archives and History, Montgomery, Alabama, Q15158)

ability." Her daughter notes that Weil "was known as a clever woman, always ahead of her time." And Weil herself posted a horoscope from November 1935 on the first page of her personal scrapbook that allows a glimpse of how she may have viewed herself. The horoscope defines Sagittarians as strong minded, dominating, proud, reserved, diplomatic, kind, generous, and loyal, and as having a commanding manner and natural executive ability.§

* Moritz and Kahn 1898:1.

† *Montgomery Advertiser* article, clipping from page 10 of the Weil scrapbook, SPR207, Alabama Department of Archives and History, Montgomery.

‡ Alabama Department of Archives and History, Montgomery, Q15158.

§ Sternberg 2009:131 (quotations); Biography of Weil based on ibid. and from files at the Alabama Department of Archives and History.

Rebecca Beasley and granddaughter Lucy (photo by
Valerie Downes)

We follow Lane's instructions as best we can: sifting flour and baking powder together three times and beginning and ending with flour when mixing it alternately with milk. We use real vanilla and real whiskey. But there are things we have to guess about. There is no temperature given for the oven, since Lane would have baked the cake on a wood stove. She gives no cooking time instructions. She specifies "a wine glass" of whiskey, so we put in seven ounces, though a restaurant pour is only five. We find no recipe for the boiled frosting that is supposed to coat the entire cake (perhaps this was such common knowledge in 1898 that Lane did not bother to include it), so we go without.

As we move about the kitchen, Beasley recalls that her grandmother Lucy was kind to all, regardless of their station in life, and that she hated to have a vacant place at her table. Beasley's daughter, Rebecca, listens quietly and helps with the preparation while her daughters play around the kitchen table. Lucy is six and Victoria is three. At one point, their grandmother tells them in a serious voice, "Girls, the first Lane Cake was made here. In your great-great grandmother's kitchen." They listen wide-eyed, not sure what to make of it. They lick the batter from the beaters.

The cake is delicious and does, as advertised, pack a punch. As we eat, I consider how far women have come in the one hundred and some odd years since the first Lane Cake was baked here. Rebecca Beasley is the mayor of Clayton. And while I bake and Valerie, the photographer, shoots, the fathers of our sons are minding them. But then there are the things soaked in continuity. Little girls dancing around the kitchen. Women measuring and baking and wrapping cake slices in pieces of foil. And just before I leave, Beasley shows me a sweet, pale-pink dress smocked in the traditional southern style. She had it made in Montgomery for Lucy's first beauty pageant next weekend. "What does she have to do?" I ask. "For the pageant? Oh, probably just twirl around."[31]

Alabama historians William Warren Rogers and Robert David Ward write that "the female journey was not a straight line of progression that started with complete legal inferiority and culminated in the ratification of the Nineteenth Amendment in 1920." Rather, "it was a thing of twists and turns, of advances and retrogression that started long before and continued long after women acquired the right to vote."[32] Alabama women, I think, continue to walk that twisty line.

SIX

Banana Pudding

The Banana Docks at the Port of Mobile

> In all towns is something of difference, but in some towns it is
> more emphatic, it grows into the people themselves. Mobile,
> its streets, its trees, its parks, all are unique, and the people
> partake of that. It is in their speech, in their suspicions, gossip,
> accent, dialect. These things, you say, are universal, there is
> not really a fundamental difference in them. No—only enough
> to make a town itself stand out like a banner in the breeze.
>
> —Julian Rayford, *Cottonmouth*

BY 1890, THE CITY of Mobile had been languishing in an economic
depression for twenty-five years, brought on by the market collapse of cotton,
its primary export commodity. At the dawn of the Civil War, Mobile had
been the third-largest exporting city in the country and a major cultural
center in the South, akin to Charleston or New Orleans. But after the war,
cotton claimed half of its prewar worth. To revive the city, its leaders turned

Unloading a banana steamer, Mobile, Alabama, circa 1906 (photo by Detroit Publishing Company, Library of Congress, LC-D4-19455)

to imports, which would both diversify the economy and make use of existing harbor infrastructure that went unused during cotton's off-season, when the docks stood empty and workers went jobless for weeks on end.[1]

Imports were part of a larger plan to transform Mobile into a "thriving deep-water port" at a time when "foreign trade was a symbol of national power" and "many Americans believed that selling, buying, and investing in foreign markets was critical to the economic health and development of the country."[2] City leaders also had another reason for improving Mobile's harbor. With its French and Spanish heritage and laissez-faire lifestyle, Mobile had always been different from the rest of Alabama. But in the 1890s,

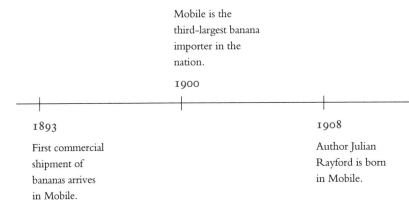

Mobile is the
third-largest banana
importer in the
nation.

1900

1893

First commercial
shipment of
bananas arrives
in Mobile.

1908

Author Julian
Rayford is born
in Mobile.

following the long economic downturn, Mobile had earned a reputation as a loose city known for horse racing, gambling, drinking, and prostitution. City leaders aimed to clean up Mobile, push it forward, and brand it with a new identity in the twentieth century.[3]

With this in mind, the Mobile Chamber of Commerce offered an incentive of $1,500 to the first company to operate regular fruit ships from Central America to Mobile for one year. In 1893, the first commercial shipment of bananas arrived in Mobile on the ship *Sala*, consigned for the Mobile Fruit and Trading Company. The Snyder Banana Company soon entered the trade as well, making Central American bananas Mobile's first regular import.[4]

Mobile joined the banana trade just as bananas were poised to become an American staple. The first US banana import allegedly arrived in 1804, when a schooner brought thirty stalks of red bananas from Cuba to New York. During the next fifty years, a handful of importers regularly brought bananas and other tropical fruits from Cuba to port cities along the East Coast, including New York, Philadelphia, and Baltimore. The shipments were small, consisted primarily of Cuban red bananas, and were purchased by pushcart peddlers who bought a few bunches at a time off the docks.[5]

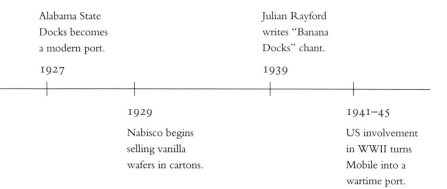

Alabama State Docks becomes a modern port.
1927

Julian Rayford writes "Banana Docks" chant.
1939

1929
Nabisco begins selling vanilla wafers in cartons.

1941–45
US involvement in WWII turns Mobile into a wartime port.

Bananas emerged in American popular culture as an icon of the tropics, symbolic of "romantic adventure and associated with palm trees, warm weather, and perpetual vacation."[6] Through the 1840s, bananas remained exotic and expensive. "A single Cuban Red banana sold for 25 cents," notes historian John Soluri, equivalent to $6.40 today.[7] Midcentury, however, "the dynamics of the post-emancipation period in the Caribbean" prompted a boom in banana exports, when jobless descendants of Caribbean slaves began selling bananas to North American schooner captains.[8]

In the second half of the nineteenth century, bananas entering the United States arrived from several Latin and Caribbean countries including Honduras, Costa Rica, Guatemala, Nicaragua, Panama, Colombia, and Jamaica. In 1877, the Honduran national government passed a new Agrarian Law to provide "tax and other financial incentives for cultivators to grow crops for international markets."[9] Honduras quickly became the leading Central American exporter of bananas and remained so until 1970.

Europeans and Americans began creating large commercial banana plantations in the tropics, where much of the arable land existed in "sparsely populated Caribbean lowland," requiring export companies to build the land, infrastructure, and workforce from scratch.[10] They cleared jungles, drained

Banana plantation in Costa Rica, circa 1910 (Library of Congress, LC-F81-2652)

swampy coastal regions, and constructed roads, railroads, stores, hospitals, and schools. They established steamship lines, built communication facilities, and invented new radio technologies, some of which are still in use today. They hired natives, displaced from their land and way of life, as laborers who toiled for low wages spent in company stores.[11]

The economic benefits of the banana trade were negligible for these workers and for local populations at large, but dramatic for delegates of the governments in power. Scholar Virginia Scott Jenkins explains: "Often the United States companies had managed to acquire so many concessions in taxes and importing rights that very little banana revenue remained in the country where the fruit was grown. The term 'banana republic' was coined around 1935 to describe a corrupt and hopeless puppet dictatorship in a country whose government was unduly influenced by United Fruit and other American fruit exporting companies."[12]

In 1876, Americans still considered bananas exotic. Most Americans had never even seen one. Wrapped in foil, bananas sold for a dime (roughly two dollars today) at the Philadelphia Centennial Expo that year. The banana plant, located in the Expo's forty-acre display of tropical plants, "was so popular that a guard had to be posted near it so that visitors would not pull it apart for souvenirs."[13] But by the 1890s, the combination of faster steamships and locomotives, an extensive railway system, and refrigerated boxcars brought more bananas to more regions of the country. In Alabama, new steamships rapidly crossed the Gulf of Mexico to Mobile Bay and rail connections took bananas directly to St. Louis and Chicago.[14]

By 1900, the banana trade was a thriving enterprise and a linchpin in Mobile's economy. The third-largest US importer of bananas (behind New York and New Orleans), Mobile was known throughout the nation as a banana port. And the banana trade continued to grow. In 1900, fifteen million bunches of bananas passed through US ports. By 1910, that figure had reached forty million.[15] Expanded production yielded lower prices, making bananas affordable and accessible year-round. They became "the first seasonless fresh fruit available for mass consumption" in the United States.[16]

By 1910, bananas had transformed from novelty into common household commodity, found in grocery stores nationwide. They were "an integral part of the American diet in all parts of the country" and "were offered to immigrants who came through Ellis Island in New York as their first taste of America. Even though the fruit itself was imported," notes Jenkins, "European immigrants equated it with the United States and with what real Americans ate."[17] By 1915, Mobile's city leaders had secured $3 million in federal funds for harbor improvements, allowing for extensive waterfront and harbor development in the 1920s. The Alabama State Docks had become a modern port by 1927, and bananas remained one of the city's most important exports throughout the 1930s.[18]

The Mobile banana docks sat at the foot of Dauphin and Government Streets, in the heart of the downtown waterfront. Here, the United Fruit Company docked their signature white banana boats, "the Great White Fleet," painted to reflect the Caribbean sun. When the boats arrived,

Banana dockworker, Mobile, Alabama, 1937 (photo by Arthur Rothstein, Library of Congress, LC-USF33-002424-M1)

longshoremen hefted the banana stems, weighing forty to eighty pounds each, onto their backs and carried them down the gangplank. The stems then passed down a long line of men extending from boat to warehouse, where they were weighed, checked, and loaded onto refrigerated boxcars.[19] The trains that carried bananas north would return to Mobile with Jonathan apples and concord grapes grown in colder climates.

In 1903, with the banana trade booming, the United Fruit Company invested in conveyors to unload bananas onto the docks in Mobile.[20] The conveyors were fixed in orange-brown houses with narrow roofs that sloped away from the water's edge. They were operated by lowering a belt device

Unloading of bananas via steam conveyors at the Mobile, Alabama, docks (Alabama Department of Archives and History, Mobile, Alabama, Q8662)

with steel rods holding canvas pockets into the hold of the banana boat. As the chains rolled, dockworkers on the boat plunged a stalk of bananas into each pocket, "golden shining yellow against the dirty gray of the canvas" recalls Mobile native and folklorist Julian Rayford.[21] At the bottom of the conveyor, inside the train shed, dockworkers pulled the stalks from the pockets and heaved them onto tables, where they were weighed and checked. At last, two dockworkers lifted each stalk onto the shoulders of a third, who carried it to an orange boxcar.[22]

Banana dockworkers were predominantly black men. As Rayford recalls, "that was a black man's job. White men were bosses or checkers or spectators."[23] In fact, from 1890 to 1900, when the banana trade took root in Mobile, the city experienced its largest influx yet of black migrants from rural Alabama, Florida, and Mississippi. Many fell into the informal banana docks trade: picking up work when they could and collecting pay at the end of the day. It was not steady or unionized work, and it was certainly difficult, hot, backbreaking labor.[24]

Loading bananas onto a boxcar, Mobile, Alabama (Erik Overbey Collection, Doy Leale McCall Rare Book and Manuscript Library, University of South Alabama, G7)

The banana docks eventually spread along the Mobile waterfront, occupying the equivalent of four city blocks. A hub of activity and noise, the docks were popular with local children who came after school and on the weekends to watch the commotion, eat free bananas, search for tropical spiders, and fish from the docks. Rayford, who grew up in Mobile during the 1910s and 1920s, describes the scene in his novel, *Cottonmouth*: "White kids stood hopefully watching for ripe fruit to drop off the bunches. They darted quickly under the guard lines and grabbed a fallen ripe banana and ran, or, kids with steadier nerves artfully gathered ripe ones and hoarded them inside their shirts, and, with a bulging shirt and bulging pockets, said to any kid who might ask for one, 'To hell wit' you! Go git your own!' Kids

Loading bananas onto a boxcar, Mobile, Alabama, 1932 (Erik Overbey Collection, Doy Leale McCall Rare Book and Manuscript Library, University of South Alabama, N242)

with a shirt full of ripe ones, rich, lush bananas, walked off proudly. If they shared them at all, it was done magnanimously, with a buddy. Only with a buddy."[25]

Rayford's "Banana Docks" chant is one of the few descriptions of Mobile's banana docks in existence. He first wrote the chant in 1939, continued to modify it until 1974, and always performed it with the changes in volume, pitch, tone, and speed that he heard at the banana docks as a child. Performing some sections rapidly and drawing out others, Rayford created a rhythm that alternately lulled and startled the listener, mirroring his descriptions of the scene, like the images of water lilies riding the waves against the sharp orders of the checkers.[26]

Checking and weighing bananas, Mobile, Alabama (Eric Overbey Collection, Doy Leale Mc-Call Rare Book and Manuscript Library, University of South Alabama)

In the opening stanza, Rayford sets out to describe "the confusion and excitement, the great hurly-burly of happiness, the noise, the singing and chanting on the banana docks in Mobile." He details the landscape: the ocean backdrop, the docks, and the noise of workers singing and chanting, machines running, foghorns, bells, train whistles, and boat whistles. He describes "the ching of tabulating machines, the hum and the click and the roll and the bumpity-thumpity clanking of the conveyors. The chanting of the checkers and the steady hum of the men totin' bananas and occasionally, a fragment of a song:—a long time, sweet daddy! a long time, sweet momma!"

At the docks, Rayford recalls the "waves that slap-slap-slapped against the pilings, the whine of ropes tightening as they were strained around pilings, the groan of pilings as a ship's weight nudged them, the creak of planking in the wharf, the short echo of a violent gust of sound when a tug captain yanked the whistle cord." He describes seagulls crying, mewling, wheeling, diving, ascending, and the "soft splash of their clean forms on waves." He recalls water lilies riding the waves and "the smell of blackstrap molasses drifting down from Beauregard Street."

Rayford describes the hundreds of riverboats moored at the docks, along with a cluster of tugboats and many small, white banana boats. He recalls some of the banana boats' names: the *Musa*, *Herman Winter*, *Mexico Trader*, *Vera*, *Gansgourd*, and *Liasgourd*. And "all along the docks, gangs of men loading and unloading ships" including "hundreds of men toting bananas, burdened like Atlas with monstrous stems of bananas" to the warehouse, with bosses yelling and chanting "in a vast hum-shuffle-roar come on move along, move along—pick 'em up! pick 'em up! pick 'em up! come along there, now!, step along there, now, step along!"

Rayford once referred to the banana docks voices as "the most exciting thing you ever heard in your life."[27] He performed them in rapid succession so that they blended into a cacophony, giving listeners the impression of hearing all of the voices at once.

There is the yelling of the bosses:

Come on here, boy. Pick it up! Pick it up! Git that lead out'n you' ass and pick it up! Tote 'em on down, son! Come on, move along, pick 'em up, pick 'em up! Speed it up! Speed it up! Come along there, now! Take 'em on down! Step along there, now! Step along!

The cries of the checkers:

Yellow 23! Yellow 23! Yellow 23! Red car 19! Green car 21! Green 21! Green 21! Hey you, god damn it, green 21! Where you going! Yellow 23! Yellow 23!

And the mellow hum of the singing dockworkers:

Tell Louise I see her in the mornin'
Tell Louise I see her in the mornin'
Tell Louise I see her in the mornin'
When the daylight come[28]

Julian Rayford

Born and raised in Mobile, Julian Rayford became many things: writer, journalist, artist, historian, sculptor, poet, and entertainer. But, above all, Rayford was a folklorist. He made the collection of folklore his life's work, traveling the country, listening to street vendors, talking to average people, and collecting stories in notebooks. He studied and sculpted American folk heroes. He read extensively and amassed a great knowledge of American history. He became, as one reporter called him, "a living national monument of American folksong, legend, and poetry."*

In 1953, one admirer called Rayford "the most interesting authority on American folklore that I know, largely because, for him, this is no dry subject of academic research in pursuit of which he collects specimens, but a way of life in which he earnestly and enthusiastically believes. In pursuit of American folklore, he has traveled back and forth across the country, voyaged up and down its rivers, listened to the chants, songs, and stories of the people at work and at play, made friends of everybody from roughnecks to academicians, combed the literature of the subject in more than one library, and then embodied it in painting, sculpture, poems, stories, popular and learned articles, and in his own performances."†

Julian Lee Rayford, known to friends as Judy, was born in 1908 on Adams Street in Mobile. He was the youngest of seven boys. His interest in folklore is perhaps unsurprising, considering that his mother was the daughter of Dick Ogletree, a well-known antebellum minstrel singer, and his father was an engineer for the Mobile and Ohio Railroad who allegedly worked with Casey Jones. Rayford's father died when he was a toddler, and Rayford came up as a self-described "typical small town hoodlum," scrappy and fighting.

Rayford made sketches all his life. At the age of ten, his art teacher

Julian Rayford (History Museum of Mobile Collection, Doy Leale McCall Rare Book and Manuscript Library, University of South Alabama)

discovered Rayford was colorblind and suggested he pursue sculpture, which he did, as well as poetry. In 1926, he enrolled at a private high school in Birmingham, working as a janitor to pay his tuition. He enrolled at Duke University in 1927 and paid his way by painting stage screens and doing odd jobs. In 1928, Rayford became an apprentice to the sculptor Gutzon Borglum, who called him "the boy with soul." At the time, Borglum was working on the presidential faces for Mount Rushmore. Rayford was present at the dedication of the first face, George Washington's, in the summer of 1930.

He spent the next seven years traversing America by train, studying and producing art, writing poetry, working odd jobs, and collecting stories. Fellow Mobilian Eugene Walter, who knew Rayford at the time, called him "a piece of impudence" and "a live wire" with "a wicked sense of humor." Rayford used to fling copies of his poems out of trains and truck windows. He would boldly enter small-town restaurants and offer to chant in exchange for a sandwich, and it usually worked.

In 1937, Rayford returned to Mobile and became a journalist at the Mobile Register. He began work on his first novel, Cottonmouth, which was fictional but largely autobiographical. The narrative, set in the years 1910–30, portrayed both the life of a boy coming up in Mobile and the life of the city itself. The book was published in March 1941, the same month Rayford was drafted into the army.

Discharged in December 1941 due to narcolepsy, Rayford continued to support the war effort by making recruitment posters, painting camouflage on warships, and performing a one-man singing and storytelling show at military hospitals in the Pacific. In the fall of 1945, he returned to Mobile permanently and turned his eye for folklore toward his hometown, compiling Gulf Coast stories and researching the history of Mardi Gras in Mobile.

In the 1960s and 1970s, Rayford performed his folklore repertoire at universities and libraries across the country. He recited the cries of street vendors peddling brooms, peanuts, ice, pencils, oysters, crabs, rags, okra, charcoal, and pine straw that he had heard in Mobile in his youth. He chanted the voices of banana dockworkers, riverboat men, and railroad conductors. Audiences were spellbound. A Kansas City reporter claimed that Rayford came "close to being an American Chaucer," stating, "he has that same precise ear for the spoken language and dialects, the easy rhythmic sense and the same passion for collecting the poetic, funny, and mythical tales that people invent for themselves."[‡]

Rayford was known as a natural and vibrant performer who took on the expressions and mannerisms of each character he portrayed with an intense realism. Archibald Rutledge, who attended one of Rayford's *performances, wrote to him: "You have the rare gift of being able to electrify an audience. I do not believe I ever heard another speaker capable of holding his hearers so constantly on the verge of laughter and of tears. I have heard many speakers on folklore, and many singers. You far surpass them all; for to your profound knowledge you add the passion and the imagination of a genuine creative artist. To hear you has been one of the rarest and most delightful privileges of my whole life."*§

Rayford's chants, however, were not confined to scheduled performances. Folklore was his constant companion, and he often related stories "at the first pause in conversation, regardless of the occasion," recalls Mobile archivist Jay Higginbotham, who adds that "sometimes during a card game, or at some social gathering, [Rayford] would startle those around him by suddenly breaking into a chant he'd learned from a black man selling newspapers. Some found his impulsive performances odd or eccentric, but no one could stop him. Judy, it was obvious, saw folklore as something which is more alive when it is beyond print. 'Alive and kicking,' is how he phrased it." Folklorist Studs Terkel relates, "From the moment I met [Rayford] till the moment we parted I was able to get in only two or three words."**

Rayford died in 1980 and was buried, per his request, in Mobile's Church Street Cemetery next to his idol: the reviver of Mobile Mardi Gras, Joe Cain.††

* Ritter 1975:19.

† From files at the Mobile Public Library, Local History and Genealogy Branch.

‡ Ritter 1975.

§ From files at the Mobile Public Library, Local History and Genealogy Branch.

** Higginbotham 1991; Terkel 2005:263.

†† Biographical information on Julian Rayford drawn from B. Williams 2011 and from files at the Mobile Public Library, Local History and Genealogy Branch.

Rolling Stores

Rolling stores, first made from horse-drawn wagons and later from trucks, once carried supplies to rural families throughout Alabama. Abundant in the state until World War II, at least twenty-five rolling stores operated in Pike County alone. As Alabama folklife expert Stephen Grauberger notes, "while most people still made periodic trips to town for supplies, the rolling store was an added convenience to them and a necessity for those who were not able to get in to town to shop."* The stores ran regular, weekly routes, and merchants often bartered with customers, trading commercial items for farm goods like eggs, chickens, pecans, and vegetables.

* Description of rolling stores in Alabama based on Grauberger 1996.

When massive amounts of bananas began arriving in Mobile, locals were intrigued by the foreign fruit and tried them in many existing recipes, including pudding. And just as bananas transformed from luxury to staple, banana pudding began as an extravagance before becoming a classic southern dessert. Before the 1880s, bananas "were served only on important occasions and used in small quantities to display wealth and sophistication."[29] They were primarily used in desserts, and banana pudding was found at highbrow social events and on the menus of fashionable hotels.

When bananas became more affordable and available, more cookbooks began including recipes for banana pudding, made by combining homemade custard, bananas, cake, and sometimes rum. Hester Poole's *Fruits, and How to Use Them*, published in 1890, featured a dozen banana recipes, including banana pudding. Her recipe instructs: "Line a glass dish with thin slices of

Banana pudding at
Sisters' Restaurant
in Troy, Alabama
(Alabama Tourism
Department)

plain cake and cover them with thin slices of banana. Have a second layer of cake and banana then pour over them a very thin boiled custard. Serve with whipped cream piled on the top."[30] In 1902, Sarah Tyson Rorer's *Mrs. Rorer's New Cook Book* included a "Hawaiian Recipes" section that featured fried bananas, baked bananas, banana cake, and banana pudding. The following year, *The Kentucky Receipt Book* by Mary Harris Frazer also featured a banana pudding recipe.

In the 1910s and 1920s, as banana imports to the United States continued to increase, a torrent of discoveries was made about health and nutrition. Newly minted women's magazines, cookbooks, and home economics manuals marketed new information about calories, germs, and vitamins to women. In fact, women were "deluged with articles in newspapers and magazines about the relationship of nutrition and diet to health."[31] Fresh fruit was

Adelaide's "Famous" Original Banana Pudding
BUD'S BEST COOKIES*

⅔ cup sugar + ¼ cup

¼ tsp. salt

2 eggs separated

Bud's Best Vanilla Wafers

¼ cup flour

2 cups milk

1 tsp. vanilla flavor

6 ripe bananas, sliced (thin)

Combine sugar, flour, and salt in the top of a double boiler, stir in milk. Cook over boiling water, stirring until thickened. Beat egg yolks and gradually stir into hot mixture. Return to double boiler; cook 5 minutes, stirring constantly. Remove from heat, add vanilla. Line one quart casserole with Bud's Best Vanilla Wafers and top with sliced bananas. Pour portion of custard over bananas.

Repeat, ending with custard on top.

Beat egg whites stiff but not dry. Gradually add ¼ cup sugar and beat until mixture forms stiff peaks. Pile on top of pudding. Bake in preheated 425 degree oven for 5 minutes. Serve warm or chilled. Makes 7 servings.

* Courtesy of Bud's Best Cookies.

widely promoted, and bananas were touted as nutritious, filling, affordable, and germ-free due to their protective peel.

To capitalize on the trend, the United Fruit Company, one of the largest US enterprises, created marketing divisions and educational programs to convince Americans to eat bananas every day. The advertising campaign was "directed at the middle class with emphasis on style, quality, and the health benefits of eating bananas."[32] It particularly targeted children, providing classroom teachers with banana coloring sheets and geography lessons. Magazines nationwide carried advertisements for a new "banana book," replete with recipes.[33]

Banana pudding became a dessert for all classes. Often made with leftover cake, it provided a way to use stale or extra ingredients by combining them with something fresh and affordable. Alabama native and chef Scott Peacock recalls his grandmother making banana pudding by combining bananas, eggs, and milk "with whatever she had on hand—leftover cake, toasted white bread [or] stale biscuits."[34] More affluent southerners used vanilla wafers, cookies that originated in southern homes and local bakeries. In 1929, Nabisco became the first company to distribute the wafers in cartons to preserve freshness, and their popularity soared.

But for rural families, banana pudding made with vanilla wafers was an extravagance. Bettye Kimbrell, raised on a farm in Fayette County, Alabama, in the 1940s and 1950s, recalls her mother making banana pudding only for special visitors and cemetery Decoration Days. Most rural desserts were made from ingredients at hand, including homegrown fruits and homemade syrup. Banana pudding with vanilla wafers was "a real rarity" for Kimbrell's family since both ingredients had to be purchased from the rolling store that came by the house each week.[35]

Likewise, Cora Berry's mother made banana pudding only for Sunday dinners. Berry's mother, Mary, was born in 1944 and raised seven children in Mobile. She made banana pudding using bananas, vanilla wafers, and custard made from eggs, flour, sugar, vanilla, and milk. The dish was topped with meringue, baked until the meringue browned on top, and served following a fried chicken dinner, a tradition Cora continues for her own daughters and grandchildren today.

But when I ask if she makes her mother's version of banana pudding, Cora shakes her head. "I tried it once, but something went wrong. I think maybe I left it in the oven too long." She laughs. "So now I just do it the easy way." Like most southerners, Cora makes banana pudding by layering bananas and vanilla wafers in a dish and pouring pudding over them. (In most

Alabama grocery stores, vanilla wafers are stocked next to the bananas.) Cora also adds vanilla flavor and banana flavor (extract) to give the pudding an extra kick and tops it with whipped cream and crushed vanilla wafers once it cools and sets.[36]

With the outbreak of World War II, Mobile's economy changed dramatically. As the port of the nation's second-largest interior river system with rail connections stretching into the Midwest, river connections to Birmingham's steel and iron industries, and a long shipbuilding tradition, Mobile became the ideal wartime port. Shipyards churned out ships in record numbers, and the demand for weapons, munitions, war materials, and supplies kept the Alabama State Docks operating at full capacity. In 1940, Mobile's entire workforce numbered seventeen thousand. By 1943, the city was home to forty thousand ship workers alone.[37] Though still the city's leading import in 1939, bananas were soon replaced by bauxite, raw wool, and manganese ore.[38]

Banana imports resumed prewar levels by 1953 and continued to increase yearly until 1963, when the United Fruit Company cut operations in Mobile. Del Monte shipped bananas through Mobile from 1974 to 1985 but then shifted to Biloxi/Gulfport, Mississippi, in the late 1980s. Though bananas had played a pivotal role in Mobile's economy, identity, and industry for over fifty years, the banana docks were razed in the late 1980s and early 1990s to make way for a new convention center.

At the time, Chris Raley, a native of Lexington, Kentucky, was in his twenties, a new arrival to Mobile, working at a downtown hotel across from the banana docks. One afternoon, as Raley sat across from the demolition site drinking a cold beer, he decided that if they could tear the docks down, he could build them back. Once occupying the shoreline along four city blocks, the docks included large warehouses, cranes, and floating barges. "Those warehouses were gorgeous," Raley recalls. "Brick, with twelve-foot windows and beautiful architecture. They could have converted them into shops and loft apartments. They could have made a whole historic waterfront area like they did in Charleston."

Instead, despite protest by some Mobilians, the demolition went forward. Until it closed in 2010, Raley's restaurant, the Banana Docks Café, which opened across from the former site of the banana docks in 1991, was the lone reminder of Mobile's banana industry in the entire city. Raley pulled historic banana docks photographs from the University of South Alabama archives to hang on the walls, infused the restaurant with a tropical décor, and put banana pudding on the menu.[39]

SEVEN

Fried Chicken

Decoration Day on Sand Mountain

Fried chicken, so simple, so golden, so savory and pristine, yet
in every way elegant, in its flawless conception and its simple
execution encapsulating both a Southerner's attitude about
food and everything that is good about a Southern kitchen, . . .
always special and festive, yet ever comfortable and familiar.

—Damon Lee Fowler, *Classical Southern Cooking*

IN THE FRIED CHICKEN recipe that appeared in the popular 1828 cookbook *The Virginia Housewife*, Mary Randolph wrote "practically everything that needs to be said about the fine art of frying chicken," claims journalist John Egerton. "Cut them up, dredge them in flour, sprinkle with a little salt, put the pieces in a skillet with hot fat, fry them a golden brown, and then make gravy in the leavings." However, notes Egerton, "millions of words have been written since then in a vain attempt to improve upon her method. There are all sorts of little refinements and special touches and personal tricks of the trade that

Fried chicken at Martin's Restaurant in Montgomery, Alabama (Alabama Tourism Department)

make good pan-fried or skillet-fried chicken a topic for endless discussion, but in the end they are simply minor variations on Mrs. Randolph's original theme. Southern fried chicken in all its manifestations derives from that base."[1]

Most southern cooks do agree on a handful of common denominators in making fried chicken. The chicken should be battered and fried in a heavy pan or skillet. The quality of the raw chicken is important, as is taking the time to fry it properly. Fried chicken should ideally be served hot from the skillet, "with a crust that snaps and breaks with fragility—a contrast to the tender, moist meat," writes southern chef Bill Neal.[2] And of course, it should be eaten with the fingers.[3]

Decoration Day
traditions emerge
in Appalachia.

EARLY 1800s

|

1800s

Fried chicken is
a luxury for most
Alabama farm
families.

1817

Inaugural
Decoration Day
at Whitehall
Cemetery in Sand
Mountain region
is held.

Recipes for fried chicken abound, arriving in a constant stream via southern magazines, cookbooks, and blogs. "Perhaps the most amusing department of all southern kitchen studies is the endless array of chicken recipes," writes Mobile native Eugene Walter, "and the debates, discussions, disagreements, and family feuds on just what is really the true southern fried chicken."[4] The batter can be flour or cornmeal or both in any number of proportions. Older recipes use cracker crumbs. Some cooks add milk, egg, salt, pepper, red pepper, hot sauce, lemon, or garlic to the batter. Some insist on frying young birds weighing less than two pounds. Some say less than one and a half. Some say it doesn't matter. Some cooks dip the chicken in milk or buttermilk and some do not. Some insist on a double dip.

Chicken can be fried in vegetable oil, canola oil, melted butter, or lard, sometimes with the additions of bacon drippings, milk, or lemon juice. Or, as Neal writes, "some poor birds are saturated with all sorts of foreign elements, from Worcestershire sauce to soy sauce."[5] The amount of oil is up for debate, along with whether to remove the skin before cooking and whether to cover the chicken while frying. Fried chicken is usually served with gravy, made with chicken juices, milk, or wine, served on the side or poured over the chicken.

The disputes over fried chicken reflect its status as one of the most em-

Classic fried chicken
recipe appears in *The
Virginia Housewife*.

1828

Warren G. Harding
and Calvin Coolidge
presidential campaign
uses "A Chicken in
Every Pot" slogan.

1928

1920S

Fried chicken is the
staple Decoration
Day food on Sand
Mountain.

1940–60

Poultry becomes
big agribusiness,
making fried
chicken affordable
for all.

Fried Chicken

Cut them up as for the fricassee, dredge them well with flour, sprinkle them
with salt, put them into a good quantity of boiling lard, and fry them a light
brown, fry small pieces of mush and a quantity of parsley nicely picked to be
served in the dish with the chickens, take half a pint of rich milk, add to it a
small bit of butter with pepper, salt, and chopped parsley, stew it a little, and
pour it over the chickens, and then garnish with the fried parsley.*

* Randolph 1828.

blematic and pervasive dishes of the South. Fried chicken occupies a pivotal
place on the table for all kinds of southerners and is served at every type of
function, from picnics to funerals. Egerton contends fried chicken is "probably the single most popular and universally consumed food ever to come from
this region" and is "generally recognized as the South's gift to the world of
food."[6] Walter believes it "comes as close to being the ideal all-purpose, all
occasion dish as anything in this country."[7]

The Southern Skillet

Despite the myriad disagreements over how to cook fried chicken, every southern cook will attest to the importance of the cast-iron skillet, "the only authentic implement" for cooking fried chicken. As food writer Juliana Gray explains, "there are several items, tools and tricks of the trade, without which any Southern kitchen is incomplete. A good paring knife. Mason jars and fresh canning lids. A big iced tea pitcher. Bacon fat. And, perhaps most essential, a cast-iron skillet. As any Southern grandmother will tell you, this last item is an absolute must. . . . With proper care—and they do require extra attention, even obsession—an iron skillet can last over a century, longer than the grandmother singing its praises, possibly longer than the child receiving the lecture."*

New skillets are washed in hot water (without soap) only once, after which they are cleaned only when necessary and only with a small amount of salt or sand. Using water or cleaning agents would destroy the blackened crust of seasoning that develops on the skillet after years of use. In fact, food writer John T. Edge contends that the reason southerners always refuse help in the kitchen following a meal

Yet, despite its present ubiquity, fried chicken was long considered a luxury in the South. Well into the twentieth century, southern farmers maintained flocks of chickens mainly for their eggs, a source of year-round food and supplementary income for farm families. Especially crucial during the Depression, egg money shielded many families from hunger. Chickens themselves were rarely consumed, usually killed only after they were too old to produce eggs. They were often put into stews, as only a long, slow simmer could tenderize the tough meat of older birds.[8]

is due as much to fear that "some well-meaning outlander will scrub out Momma's skillet in the sink" as it is to southern hospitality.[†]

Cast iron is preferred because it evenly distributes heat over the cooking surface and (after seasoning) is practically nonstick. The porous nature of cast iron also continually absorbs the flavor of the food, and once this seasoning occurs, it imparts the flavor onto every dish prepared in it, making the skillet crucial to producing a well-seasoned fried chicken. Further, because the seasoning on every skillet is different, the flavor of the fried chicken prepared in it is original to the cook. This unique blend gets passed down through the generations every time the skillet changes hands. As Edge writes, "each time a Southern cook hefts a skillet to the stovetop, he or she is not alone. Trapped within the iron confines of these skillets and stewpots are the scents and secrets of a family's culinary history. Burnished black by countless batches of fried chicken and catfish, embossed in an inky ebony by the crusts of cracklin' cornbread past, cast-iron cooking utensils are meal memories in and of themselves."[‡]

[*] Neal 1985:121; Gray 2004:146.

[†] Edge 1999:127.

[‡] Ibid.:126–27 (quotation at 126).

Tasty fried chicken demands a young bird, and so it was considered a supreme delicacy reserved for Sunday dinners and special occasions. In fact, chicken on Sunday came to symbolize a "widely desired level of economic well-being" among southerners, as reflected in a 1928 Republican campaign ad that lauded President Harding and Vice President Coolidge for putting "the proverbial 'chicken in every pot.'"[9] Until the mid-1900s, chicken remained more expensive than beef or veal and was eaten regularly only by wealthy farmers.

Dinner on the ground at Antioch Baptist Church, Marion County, Alabama, circa 1914 (photo courtesy of Roger L. Howard)

Further, as detailed in Psyche Williams-Forson's *Building Houses out of Chicken Legs: Black Women, Food, and Power*, fried chicken has deep connections to African Americans in the South, who cooked it in plantation kitchens, sold it at railroad stations, consumed it as travel food during Jim Crow years, and eventually prepared it for social, fundraising, and family functions.

Its luxury status earned fried chicken a place as the centerpiece of southern "dinners on the ground." A hallmark of Appalachian culture, dinner on the ground is served on the grounds of a church or cemetery and accompanies the most important Appalachian events, including church homecomings, all-day singings, and Decoration Days. Drawing participants from great distances, these daylong events make a large meal necessary. Each family brings a few dishes to share. The meal was traditionally consumed at noontime on the actual ground, as the name reflects; over time, it has become more common to eat on the tailgates of cars or at long tables fashioned from sawhorses and plywood and set under shade trees.

To reflect the significance of the events, participants traditionally brought the most impressive, expensive, and laborious dishes they could make to dinners on the ground, which were often set on white linen tablecloths. As food writer John T. Edge writes, "then and only then did cousin Effie's buttermilk-dipped, corn flour–crusted fried chicken make an appearance. Then and only then did Aunt Ellen take the time to bake both a chess pie and a pecan pie, not to mention convince Uncle Jimmy to lug along the ice cream churn and a bushel of freshly picked peaches."[10]

Fried chicken, still a delicacy for most Appalachian families, was the core dish of dinners on the ground in the nineteenth and early twentieth centuries. In the 1920s, novelist Carl Carmer attended a dinner on the ground on Sand Mountain in northeast Alabama to which residents carried food in shoeboxes, all of which contained fried chicken. Common sides included beaten biscuits, cornbread, pickles, preserves, and white frosted cakes for dessert.[11] Northeast Alabama native and journalist Rick Bragg recalls a dinner on the ground he attended in the late 1960s: "Imagine a hundred church ladies, all schooled in the culinary genius of generations, unloading trunkloads of potato salad, homemade pickles, barbecued pork chops, beans (butter, green, pole, lima, pinto, baked, navy and snap), deviled eggs dusted with cayenne pepper, pones of cornbread cooked with cracklin's, fried chicken, squash casserole, a million biscuits, a bathtub-sized vat of banana pudding, pies (lemon, cherry, apple, peach, fig, pecan, chocolate-walnut), cakes (you name it), and enough iced tea and RC Colas to drown a normal man."[12]

In fact, dinners on the ground often became an unspoken contest between cooks, with all of the women trying to outdo each other. Sand Mountain native Jerry Smith recalls that "each of these proud and worthy matrons had some kind of special dish, and you'd always see folks jockeying for starting positions nearest their favorites just before the blessing was given."[13] In pockets of Appalachia, the competition continues. "It is not an anonymous buffet," wrote Alan and Karen Jabbour in 2010. "Women from each family sit or stand by their offerings, describe them to others, and invite people to try them."[14] Edge describes a similar scene: "In a clutch near the tallest tree stand the elder cooks, proud and haughty. As they unveil their specialties to the accustomed 'oohs' and 'ahhs' of the assembled throng, the younger women work the crowd, soliciting a promise to taste their sweet potato pie or take a nibble of their deviled eggs. . . . The preacher steps forward to offer thanks. For the briefest of moments, all is still and quiet. But as soon as he utters amen, the rush is on. Savvy diners, secure in their knowledge of last year's best and worst, make a beeline for their favorites, while the cooks sit back to savor the praise."[15]

Dinner on the ground almost always accompanies Decoration Day, a prime holiday in Appalachia. Held annually in the spring, families gather at cemeteries to adorn graves, reconnect with relatives and friends, reminisce about times past, and honor the departed. Throughout the nineteenth and early twentieth centuries, Decoration Day remained one of the most important events in Appalachian Alabama, "the highlight of the church year," as one native called it.[16] In fact, girls were more likely to receive a new dress for Decoration Day than for Easter.[17]

The origins of Decoration Day are unclear, as little has been recorded about the tradition. It likely began as a ritual in family cemeteries (possibly carried to America by Scotch-Irish settlers) before expanding into a community ritual as populations increased and cemeteries grew to include multiple families. Folklorists Alan and Karen Jabbour believe Decoration Day has existed since at least the early 1800s. Noting the strong Decoration Day tradition in Liberia (a nation settled by former American slaves between 1820 and 1850), they posit that Decoration Day was central to Appalachian culture prior to 1820 and was carried to Liberia by former slaves who had lived in the region. But regardless of its early history, Decoration Day traditions were certainly formalized and intensified in the decades following the Civil War to honor the roughly 260,000 Confederate soldiers who perished in it.[18]

Though the tradition is waning in some areas, Decoration Days are still celebrated throughout central and southern Appalachia. In Alabama, they are

Decoration Day at Old Blue Creek Cemetery in Jefferson County, Alabama, circa 1904 (photo courtesy of Joey Brackner)

particularly common on Sand Mountain, one of the southernmost reaches of the Appalachians. A sandy plateau twenty-five miles across and seventy-five miles long, Sand Mountain begins in the northeastern corner of the state and aims toward Mobile. In the 1920s, Carmer described it as a land of loblolly pines with straight, thin trunks and narrow roads.[19] Journalist Dennis Covington describes the people of Sand Mountain as those who traditionally "prided themselves on their independence and self-sufficiency. They grew what they ate, bartered for what they couldn't grow, and did without those conveniences they couldn't fashion out of the materials at hand."[20] Today, many Sand Mountain natives still adhere to an Appalachian culture that includes Decoration Day observances.

Alabama Decoration Days are held in the late spring and early summer when blossoming flowers can be used to beautify the cemetery. Most are held in May, with a few spilling into late April and early June. Each cemetery designates a particular Sunday of a particular month as its annual Decoration Day and sometimes posts the chosen day on a sign in the cemetery. As most people have family buried in various cemeteries, Appalachian residents commonly attend several Decoration Days each season.

Because the mountains made settlement sparse and travel slow, Decoration Day was formerly one of the only times of year that whole families would assemble. Today, distant relatives often return home for Decoration Day, giving the event the quality of a family reunion. For most, connecting with family and friends is as important as honoring the dead. As one Sand Mountain native notes, "being a big, rural family, we didn't go a lot of places, so we loved going to the cemetery to see all the cousins. It was the highlight of the year."[21] Native Billie Crumly writes, "eating, hugging, laughing, trading stories and memories, oohing and aahing over new babies, etc. is how it was done (and in some cases still is) on Decoration Day."[22]

Though Decoration Day refers to the day families gather at the cemetery for fellowship and flower decoration, the event actually begins with a prior cleanup day. Traditionally, Appalachian cemeteries were covered in sand, featuring mounds roughly a foot wide and several inches high that ran the length of each grave, stopping "short of the headstone to prevent clay and mud from splashing, staining, or etching the headstone face."[23] Cleaning the mounds required ridding them of grass and weeds, then reshaping and smoothing them. If a mound had sunk during the year, more sand was added to build it back.[24] Headstones were also treated with a special blend of cleaning agents that commonly included white vinegar, baking soda, and Ajax.

As the final task, the cemetery was swept clean with brush brooms, made from several saplings (often dogwood) tied together with twine or baling wire saved from spent hay bales. "Sweeping was the last thing you did because you didn't want anyone's footprints on the clean ground," explains Crumly, "just like when your mother swept the yard."[25] This tradition reflects the notion that the cemetery is a home for the dead and, as such, "should feel like home in its outward appearance and should be managed the same way a home's yard is managed."[26]

The practice of sweeping and mounding sand graveyards flourished well into the twentieth century but retreated as grass cemeteries became more common. Cleanup days now involve trimming grass, pulling weeds, planting, and pruning. Many cemeteries now have paid groundskeepers, however, making the cleanup day unnecessary.

Traditionally, any flower in bloom was used to adorn the graves on Decoration Day. Seasonal flowers on Sand Mountain include rhododendrons, honeysuckle, and roses, which bear an especially deep connection to Decoration Day and were once planted in dooryards and along fences solely for this purpose. In sand cemeteries, flower stems were stuck straight into the mounds so the graves appeared blanketed in flowers. Shells were sometimes added, as well as crepe paper flowers.

Fashioned by stretching paper into petals and twisting them around wire stems, crepe paper flowers were made several weeks prior to Decoration Day, mostly by women and girls, and stored in shoeboxes. Made to resemble real flowers, they were set in the sand in natural formations, with some standing singly and others in clusters, some close to the ground and others standing tall. Some families dipped crepe paper flowers in paraffin to make them rain resistant, but Crumly recalls those at her family cemetery bleeding in the first rain, turning the sand beneath them shades of red, purple, and blue. The craft declined rapidly in the 1950s and 1960s as artificial flowers made from plastic, then cloth, became available.[27] Today, families usually bring fresh flower arrangements.

Decoration Day tradition requires the decoration of every grave in the cemetery, and so it becomes the cemetery community's responsibility to decorate any graves left bare. As the Jabbours note, letting graves "lie undecorated seems to reveal a certain lack of respect. Ideally, respect must be shown for the entire community of the dead."[28] Once the flowers have been laid, families cluster around the graves, recalling the histories and stories of the people buried there, reflecting on the past, reconnecting with each other, and passing down family lore to younger generations. Decoration Day provides a key opportunity to share family knowledge, and attendees often bring along old family photographs and genealogy lists.[29]

Making crepe paper flowers in
Grovespring, Missouri, 1982
(photo by Allen Gage, courtesy
of Bittersweet, Inc.)

The Decoration Day service is traditionally held outside, often under a shade tree, though today some cemeteries have small buildings. Music is essential: everyone sings hymns, and special music is provided by community members who play instruments and sing gospel songs. Because most cemeteries are not affiliated with a particular church, guest preachers from the community give the message, which often likens cleaning the cemetery to preparing oneself for the Lord's coming. A blessing for the meal concludes the service, followed by dinner on the ground.[30]

During Decoration Day services on Sand Mountain in the 1950s, native Jerry Smith recalls that most of the men stayed outside the church, "gathered around the newest car on the lot, telling war stories and whittling and spitting and kicking the sand with the toes of their shoes and smoking roll-your-owns and looking at the car's engine." Meanwhile, the boys were busy enticing ant-lions to the surface of the sand, whittling pipe bowls from acorns "the size of our fathers' thumbs," and turning green from smoking them.[31] Dinner on the ground featured fried chicken, river catfish, green beans, turnip greens, collards, okra, field peas, corn on the cob, baked beans, potato salad, coleslaw, deviled eggs, macaroni and cheese, biscuits, cornbread, sweet tea, and an unending variety of desserts. Over the years, Smith relates, people became accustomed to bringing certain dishes, so there were rarely any duplicates.

By the 1950s, chickens were in the middle of a revolution in America, birthed by a fascination with amateur science and breeding, a substantial increase in farmers' flocks, advances in technology, and railroad expansion. Between the 1940s and 1960s, the poultry industry morphed into a large agribusiness, making chickens affordable for mainstream Americans for the first time. No longer confined to Sunday dinners, fried chicken became daily fare in the South.[32] Regardless of its newfound popularity, fried chicken remained a staple of Decoration Day dinners on the ground.

At Whitehall Cemetery, built into a hill in the Sand Mountain region of northeast Alabama, locals believe Decoration Day has been observed since 1817, when white settlers obtained the Native American burial ground and began burying their kin here. The wooden markers have long since rotted away, but the graves of Native Americans and early settlers still lie beneath a flat space at the foot of the cemetery. Though no one knows exactly who is buried there, the area is kept grassy and free out of respect for the graves below.

In the past, community members gathered on the Wednesday before Decoration Day to clean the cemetery. It was an all-day affair of hard labor, with dinner on the ground held afterward. But since a groundskeeping fund was established in the 1960s, the community now gathers only on Decoration Day, held on the Saturday after the first Sunday in May. When I ask if this was done to avoid conflicting with Mother's Day, native Ruthie Smith replies, "Oh, no. This has been going on since long before Mother's Day." (Indeed, Mother's Day did not become an official American holiday until

1914.) Whitehall community members suspect Saturday was chosen to avoid conflicting with all the other Decoration Days in the region, to allow people to attend as many as possible.[33]

The kin of roughly one hundred families are buried at Whitehall, and the descendants of six of those families comprise the core of the Decoration Day participants. Together, they form a makeshift family with a surprisingly tight bond. As Mia Etchberger explains, "some of these people that come to Decoration Day you never see anywhere else. You only see them once a year, but they're still so important to your life. You don't always even know their names, but you know their faces."

Etchberger serves as secretary for the Whitehall Cemetery Board, which met in 1991 to discuss Decoration Day's dwindling attendance. She was charged with sending out yearly invitations, and attendance rebounded to around eighty yearly participants. Later, Etchberger decided to send out newsletters after Decoration Day as well, to summarize the day's events and entice people to attend the following year. Her letters detail the weather, those in attendance (especially new visitors), the music, the food, and the Bible message. They also include cemetery updates and photographs.

Etchberger is the first person to arrive on Decoration Day this year, a sunny, windy day, and hands me a stack of invitations and newsletters from years past. "What do they call that when you get something directly?" she asks me.

"Um. A primary source?"

"Right. Well, this is a primary source, honey."

At Whitehall, children are the ones who lay fresh flowers on any undecorated graves. As a child in the 1930s, Ruthie Smith used to pick roadside wildflowers on the way to the cemetery for this purpose. Today, she and Marie Clayton clip blossoms from pink petunias and drop them in a handful of baskets for the children to carry. Roses also bear a special significance at Whitehall: in years past, Decoration Day participants wore a red rose if their mother was living and white if she had passed.

Etchberger points out a man I should talk to sitting under a large tree in

Decoration Day at Whitehall Cemetery (photo by Emily Blejwas)

the center of the cemetery that offers the only shade, though today the breeze is strong and cool. I walk up the grassy slope and meet Dave Raley, who sits in a camp chair next to his wife, Mary Lynn, with another empty camp chair beside him, as if he were expecting me. Raley pulls out his laptop and shows me exactly where we are on a quadrangle map of Alabama.

The couple has traveled here from North Carolina, a twelve-hour drive, but Raley thinks nothing of it. Plenty of people travel from Tennessee, Florida, Georgia, North Carolina, even as far away as Virginia, to attend Decoration Days on Sand Mountain, which Raley calls "one of the main holidays in this area. People come home for Decoration Day more than any other holiday," he says. We walk through the cemetery, and he points out the backward headstones for those who committed suicide (supposedly to keep them out of heaven) and the pairs of stones with heads facing opposite directions: brothers who fought for opposing sides during the Civil War.

As we walk, more cars fill the edges of the cemetery. People sit in camp chairs around the graves, visiting, pulling weeds, and laying down flowers. Many conversations center on departed family members, and more than a few people speak about their parents with tears in their eyes. At eleven, the service begins with singing that travels up the hill. Some walk down to join it while others remain at the graves with their loved ones.

The service is held in a simple concrete block building, painted white, with a green gabled roof, unpainted concrete floors, and paneless windows that allow the air to blow through in occasional gusts. Before this building was constructed, the service was held in a wooden structure containing backless pews made from large, halved logs and a podium at one end fashioned from a large black gum log. Before the wooden building, the service took place under a giant old oak tree that was later struck by lightning. Locals say the agreement with Native Americans giving white residents this land was signed under that tree.

A couple dozen people have gathered for the service. They sit in rows of folding chairs singing a hymn without accompaniment or musical notation. Only the lyrics are printed in the program, since everyone knows the tune. I note that the hymn was written in 1868, another tradition that postdates Decoration Day. The service usually includes special music as well, but the family that provides it is attending a college graduation in Birmingham today. In the past, music at Whitehall also included shape note singing.

Following the hymn, the preacher gives his Bible message, titled "What Do Our Stones Mean?" He speaks of the continuity of generations through the past, present, and future, and the importance of telling children about family members who have gone before. He cites biblical notions that the dead will rise again and that we will all live together eternally. He reminds us the Earth is only temporary and we must prepare for our departure from it. The final hymn reflects his message:

> There's a land that is fairer than day
> And by faith we can see it afar
> For the Father waits over the way

To prepare us a dwelling place there.
In the sweet by and by
We shall meet on that beautiful shore.
In the sweet by and by
We shall meet on that beautiful shore.

The service concludes with a closing prayer, brief business session, and an offering for cemetery upkeep. As soon as it ends, the folding chairs are set along the walls and the men carry in long tables, set end to end in the center of the room to form a buffet. As the women smooth out red-and-white-checked tablecloths, there is a flurry of activity outside as car trunks pop open to reveal Tupperware containers full of fried chicken, pulled pork, ham, squash casserole, sweet potatoes, baked beans, corn, okra, scalloped potatoes, broccoli casserole, green beans, deviled eggs, green salad, seven-layer salad, potato salad, fruit salad, cornbread, rolls, sweet tea, and many desserts, including banana pudding, coconut cake, chocolate pie, brownies, and strawberry cake. All of the dishes are set out, and everyone files through.

Dinner is spent visiting and recollecting. One woman busily writes names on the backs of old family photographs as her great aunt identifies the people in them. Another man recalls the egg custard pies and fried apple pies (typical of Appalachia) that his mother used to bring to Decoration Days. Raley remembers when they used to buy a block of ice from the train and make lemonade with it in a washtub. "That was the only time you had ice all summer, on Decoration Day," he says. "Another interesting anecdote about the train tracks: one time a cow got run over on the tracks and the company paid the owner for her loss, so then everyone started tying cows to the tracks."

As the meal drifts to a close, people begin to pack up their things and say their goodbyes. Though Etchberger's invitations and newsletters have revived Decoration Day at Whitehall, other Sand Mountain Decoration Days have dwindled down or faded out completely. Some communities no longer include dinner on the ground, and when they do, it's often not a homemade meal. "This one is still intact," one Whitehall member tells me. "Still quaint."

But some are concerned about the fate of Decoration Day at Whitehall.

A few contend that the younger generation is uninterested, and one woman is certain that her children, now in their forties, will not decorate her grave on Decoration Day. Her son once asked her why Decoration Day is so important. She shakes her head, repeating his question. "Why? It's about respect." With tears in her eyes, she nods toward the grave she is tending. "That's my mama."

EIGHT

‖‖

Boiled Peanuts

George Washington Carver, the Wiregrass,
and Macon County Farmers

A POPULAR SOUTHERN SNACK, boiled peanuts are sold in the late summer and fall at roadside stands and farmers' markets across the Deep South. They're a favorite at fall football games, on long drives, or anywhere you can eat them outside. To make them, peanuts are boiled (in the shell) in salted water for hours, then soaked until reaching the desired degree of saltiness. The boiling process softens the legumes and gives them a bright flavor and a strong, salty taste. Cookbook author John Martin Taylor asserts that "perfectly boiled southern-style peanuts are always salty, but not overly so [and] should perfectly accompany a beer, iced tea, or soft drink."[1]

Al Hooks, a produce grower in Macon County, Alabama, makes boiled peanuts year-round to sell at farmers' markets across middle Alabama. A few times weekly, he boils twenty-five pounds of peanuts in a large black kettle behind his house, next to a cooler full of vegetables, a wooden work shed, and an emergency vehicle Hooks transformed into a delivery van. He boils

National peanut
production triples
from previous year.

George Washington
Carver launches a
movable school.

1866

1906

1861–65

Peanuts are an
essential food
for Confederate
soldiers.

1896

George Washington
Carver heads the
new Agriculture
Department at
Tuskegee Institute
in Alabama.

1910

Alabama has
second-highest
number of tenant
plantations in the
South.

Truck selling boiled peanuts in south Alabama (photo by Charlotte Strode)

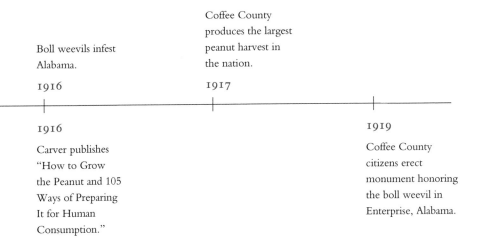

Boll weevils infest
Alabama.

1916

Coffee County
produces the largest
peanut harvest in
the nation.

1917

1916

Carver publishes
"How to Grow
the Peanut and 105
Ways of Preparing
It for Human
Consumption."

1919

Coffee County
citizens erect
monument honoring
the boll weevil in
Enterprise, Alabama.

both green (freshly picked) and dry peanuts. The dry peanuts boil for three to four hours and retain some of their crunch, but the green peanuts boil for five to six hours, becoming so soft that some customers eat the whole peanut, shell and all.

Peanuts have long-standing connections to African Americans in the South. As detailed by culinary historian Andrew Smith in *Peanuts: The Illustrious History of the Goober Pea*, peanuts were introduced to Africans in the early 1500s when Portuguese traders established peanut enclaves along the West African coast to supply fleets traveling to Asian ports. Peanuts spread quickly throughout Africa, where the cultivation of a similar groundnut was already widespread. Africans substituted the peanut for the groundnut in established cooking methods (including boiling), and peanuts soon eclipsed groundnuts in popularity as they were more prolific, had more oil, and were easier to grow.

On the coast of West Africa and in the Caribbean, slave traders planted peanuts as an inexpensive and nourishing food for captive slaves awaiting ships for their journey to America. Peanuts quickly became a staple of the slave diet. The peanut's American nicknames trace their origins to West African words: *goober* comes from *nguba*, the word for peanut in the Kimbundu language of Congo, and *pindal* and *pinder* derive from the Angolan *mpinda*.

In America, African slaves planted peanuts in their small, personal gardens throughout the South. They were an ideal food, as slaves were given little time to cultivate their own crops. Peanuts could be grown in marginal soil; were easily harvested, stored, and prepared; and produced in abundance. They were also a rich source of protein and magnesium, a nourishing part of the slave diet.

American slaves consumed peanuts in a multitude of ways, including raw, roasted, and boiled, and in soups, sauces, savory dishes, and sweets. As in Africa, peanuts were a central component of cooking, often used as a thickener for soups and stews. Further, since African slaves did the cooking in both rural and urban settings, they were the ones to inject peanuts into southern food culture. In fact, boiled peanuts are still most common in areas that once held the largest slave populations, including Alabama, Georgia, Mississippi, South Carolina, and the Florida panhandle.[2]

Slaves and free black people also became America's first peanut vendors. From mule drawn carts, they sold peanuts and produce raised in their gardens in southern towns and cities. Wealthy southerners, however, shunned the peanut. For centuries, Europeans had used peanuts only as animal fodder, and affluent southerners considered the peanut "fit only for slaves and the poor." The practice of cracking open the shells and tossing them on the ground also gave the peanut "an unrefined air."[3] Thus, peanut consumption was relegated to the working classes, who bought peanuts at fairs and circuses and from vendors on urban street corners, in local markets, and in train stations.

The Civil War brought a massive change in peanut consumption in America. Union and Confederate soldiers alike carried peanuts as a lightweight and nourishing snack, consuming them raw, ground as a coffee substitute, roasted, and boiled (often over a campfire as cooking facilities were scarce). Boiled peanuts were particularly popular because the salt acted as a preservative, allowing soldiers to carry them in their kits for up to a week.

When Union blockades cut off supplies to the South in the final years of the war, Confederate soldiers had little to eat but peanuts, which often served as an emergency ration. The tune "Goober Peas" became a popular Confederate camp song and later, a classic southern folksong.

Following the Civil War, soldiers returned home with a "newfound affinity" for the peanut and it surged in popularity, becoming a favorite American snack.[4] Peanut production soared, and by the turn of the century, peanuts had become a major commercial crop and an elemental American food.[5] Boiled peanuts, once a mainstay of the Confederate soldier's diet, became a southern institution. Peanut boils emerged as a core social gathering throughout the Deep South. Held in late August during cotton picking and ginning season, peanut boils gave family, friends, and neighbors a chance to gather and celebrate the harvest. Peanuts were boiled in large iron wash pots at outdoor parties that sometimes drew several hundred people. Today, the Crenshaw County Shrine Club preserves the tradition every Labor Day weekend at the World's Largest Peanut Boil in Luverne, Alabama, where they boil and sell fourteen tons of peanuts.

In Alabama, the lives of African Americans changed very little after the Civil War. White plantation owners retained economic control over African Americans in part through an unspoken, collective agreement not to sell land to them, forcing many to become sharecroppers. In the tenancy system (which also included many poor white farmers), the landowner furnished land, some supplies, and a house for the tenant. The owner made all of the decisions about crops and farming practices, and the tenant did all of the work, often remaining in the fields from early morning until nightfall. When the crops were harvested, the tenant received one-third to one-half of the profits.

Most sharecropping contracts lasted just one year, giving tenants little stability. Further, because they lacked income until the crops were harvested, tenants were forced to borrow money for basic needs, including food, clothing, and household supplies. These items were purchased on credit from white merchants who inflated prices and loaned at extortionate interest rates (sometimes exceeding 50 percent), making the loans nearly impossible to

Alabama tenant farmers hoeing cotton, 1936 (photo by Dorothea Lange, Library of Congress, LC-DIG-fsa-8b29688)

repay. The profits from the crops usually failed to cover tenants' debts, so they kept borrowing and harvesting, locked in a system of debt and rural isolation that was little better than slavery and offered no real economic independence.

Southern historian Thomas D. Clark calls sharecropping "an economic straightjacket."[6] As historian Kenneth Phillips notes, the daily lives of Alabama sharecroppers were more primitive than those of medieval Europeans: "Housing consisted of primitive log cabins or clapboard shotgun houses. . . . Indoor plumbing was nonexistent; water was provided from open wells or nearby springs and creeks, and bathrooms were outdoor privies located a few yards behind the house, creating serious sanitation problems. . . . The tenant family's diet consisted mainly of cornbread, corn mush, fatback pork, and

Window in a sharecropper's
cabin, Walker County,
Alabama, 1937 (photo by
Arthur Rothstein, Library
of Congress, LC-USF33-
T01–002390-M4)

molasses. . . . Poor diet, lack of sanitation, and substandard housing led to widespread health concerns, such as hookworms, pellagra, and rickets."[7]

By the 1890s, "tenant farming dominated Alabama agriculture" and by 1910, Alabama had the second-highest number of tenant plantations in the South.[8] Some former slaves, however, did manage to purchase their own land. From 1865 to 1915, black farmers purchased fifteen million acres of land nationwide, most of it in the rural South. By 1920, black farmers owned 14 percent of the nation's farms. Yet in Alabama's Black Belt, home to the cotton plantations that were once the heartbeat of the state's economy, black

Tenant farmer near Anniston, Alabama, 1936 (photo by Dorothea Lange, Library of Congress, LC-USZ62-70695)

sharecroppers and black landowners alike lived a meager existence. Black Belt soil was eroded and overworked, cotton prices had plummeted, and widespread absentee landownership exacerbated both poverty and land deterioration.[9]

Into this bleak scene stepped George Washington Carver. In 1896, Carver became head of the new agriculture department at Tuskegee Institute in Macon County, Alabama. Macon was a typical Black Belt county, suffering from widespread tenant farming, parched soil, and poverty. Yet Carver made it his mission to help poor farmers sustain themselves and make a living, stating that "the primary idea in all of my work was to help the farmer and fill the poor man's empty dinner pail."[10]

He produced hundreds of farming bulletins that were practical, comprehensible, and free, and kept his processes simple and accessible. In 1906,

Carver designed and helped launch a movable school to bring the latest farming techniques from Tuskegee Institute to rural Alabama. Called the Jesup Wagon, the horse-drawn wagon featured charts, agricultural products, seed samples, and equipment to teach farmers how to improve their practices and harvests.[11] In its inaugural summer, the Jesup Wagon reached two thousand people every month.

Carver encouraged Macon County farmers to plant crops that would give nitrogen back to the soil, like peanuts, sweet potatoes, soybeans, and black-eyed peas. Unlike cotton, these crops had a high nutritional content and could be used for personal consumption.[12] Peanuts were also a viable cash crop for Alabama farmers as their rising national popularity yielded a larger market and high prices.[13] Extension agents from Tuskegee Institute (now Tuskegee University) and Alabama Polytechnic Institute (now Auburn University) joined Carver in his mission, becoming "major voices for crop diversification" throughout the state.[14]

Though some Alabama farmers were receptive to the extension service's ideas, they often found it impossible to heed the advice. Small farmers could only secure loans by growing cotton, which made producing other crops financially impractical even though most farmers were trapped in a spiral of debt. Crop diversification was even less viable for tenant farmers, who were told by landowners what to plant and depended on them for access to credit. As southern historian James Giesen writes, "true crop diversification was a noble plan, but it was hard to imagine a place in the South that could realistically pull it off."[15]

There was one place in Alabama, however, that was uniquely positioned to pull it off, after receiving the push it needed from a new arrival in the fields: the boll weevil. A Mexican beetle with a voracious appetite for cotton, the boll weevil had infested the entire state of Alabama by 1916. Its effect on the cotton crop was horrific, with some areas seeing 60 percent losses in the initial years of infestation. At the time, Alabama's economy was almost entirely based in agriculture, and cotton was its primary cash crop. Economic losses were devastating.[16]

George Washington Carver

Although his exact birthdate is unknown, George Washington Carver was likely born in 1864 or 1865 to enslaved (or recently emancipated) parents in rural southwest Missouri. He was raised on the farm of his parents' former owners, Moses and Susan Carver. As a young boy, Carver was often excused from hard labor and allowed to wander the woods, where he became curious about the natural world. He spent much of his childhood collecting rocks and flowers and developed such a keen eye for nature that he became known as "the plant doctor" in his youth, with people bringing him sick plants from all over the county.

Carver's only book as a child was a thin Webster speller. Eager for more, he left the farm around age twelve to pursue his education. In Fort Scott, Kansas, he worked odd jobs that included taking in laundry, typing telegrams, teaching guitar, cooking, and working as a blacksmith to support himself while he attended school. After seeing a black man lynched by a white mob, however, Carver left Fort Scott and wound up in Minneapolis, Kansas, where he built his own sod house and finished high school. He was then accepted to Highland College in Kansas but was rejected when it was discovered he was black.

Several years later, following work as a homesteader in western Kansas, Carver enrolled at Simpson College in Iowa, where he spent a year as an art student before deciding he could better improve the lives of poor African Americans by pursuing an agricultural degree. He transferred to Iowa Agricultural College (now Iowa State University), where he became the college's first black graduate. After earning a master's degree in agriculture, Carver became the university's first black faculty member. He worked as an assistant botanist at the college's experiment station from 1894 to 1896.

In 1896, Carver left Iowa to head the new agriculture department

George Washington Carver studying plant disease in his lab at
Tuskegee Institute (photo by P. H. Polk, Alabama Department
of Archives and History, Montgomery, Alabama, Q4843)

at Tuskegee Institute in Alabama. His work addressed the entire nat-
ural system: the water supply, insects, soil, and plants. He believed
everything in nature had a purpose, and once remarked that weeds were
only vegetables growing in the wrong field. Carver taught his students
that nothing in nature could be disturbed or removed without harming
the system as a whole. He used only natural fertilizers like compost
and swamp muck and managed insects through crop rotation and plant
selection. His ideas and methods made substantial contributions to
conservation, ecology, sustainable agriculture, and organic farming.

Carver also taught his students to waste nothing, instruct-
ing them to "save everything. From what you have, make what
you want." Indeed, Carver built his Tuskegee laboratory by
scavenging local trash yards. He believed that even the poorest
farmers could improve their living conditions through the proper
use of natural resources, and he made it his life's work to ap-
ply the principles of science and nature to benefit humanity.

He created a school farm to demonstrate his ideas to students
and a movable school to demonstrate his ideas to farmers. Called
the Jesup Wagon, the movable school evolved from a horse-drawn
wagon to a mechanized truck and featured a variety of demon-
stration equipment including a milk tester, butter churn, and cot-
ton chopper. Carver used the school to teach farmers how to in-
crease cows' milk production, fatten hogs faster, enrich the soil to
grow better crops, and improve their homes and health through
better sanitation. The Jesup Wagon laid the foundation for Tus-
kegee's agricultural extension program, and Carver became well-
known for his promotion of alternative crops and crop rotation.

Carver encouraged farmers to plant soil-building crops like pea-
nuts and sweet potatoes, and he is best known for the products he
created from them: over 285 from the peanut, 118 from the sweet

Farmers in Alabama's Wiregrass region, however, were prepared for the
boll weevil and ready to diversify. The Wiregrass, which includes southeast
Alabama, parts of south Georgia, and the Florida panhandle, is named for the
grass species *Aristida stricta* that once covered the floor of its longleaf pine forests. With its sandy soil, cotton farming in the Wiregrass was always tenuous,
and farmers had been experimenting with alternative crops for years. Peanuts were well suited to the sandy soil and subtropical climate, and Wiregrass

potato (including molasses, vinegar, and shoe blacking), and 75 from the pecan. He also discovered medicinal uses in plants and used local clay to develop an array of house paint colors to enable poor farmers to beautify their homesteads. A painter himself, Carver used these clays along with peanut oil in hundreds of paintings.

Measuring his success in terms of public good rather than personal wealth, Carver put no stake in material possessions and always wore the same old baggy suit, though with a fresh flower in his lapel. He was unconcerned with money and often only cashed his paychecks to help a student in need. He refused raises and offers to work in private industry and patented almost none of his products, insisting that "God gave them to me. How can I sell them to someone else?"

Although his annual salary was never greater than $1,500 per year, Carver amassed a life savings of $60,000 that he gifted to the George Washington Carver Foundation and Museum at Tuskegee University. On January 5, 1943, Carver passed away without any known relatives. Yet for three days, thousands poured into Tuskegee to pay their respects.*

* Information on George Washington Carver based on exhibits at the George Washington Carver Museum in Tuskegee and the Museum of Mobile in Mobile and also from email exchanges with Carver expert Mark Hersey.

farmers had been planting them long before the boll weevil arrived. The area actually led the state in peanut production.[17]

So in 1916, when Wiregrass farmers in Coffee County faced bankruptcy after the boll weevil destroyed more than two-thirds of the cotton crop, they readily changed thousands of acres from cotton to peanuts and were rewarded with a bumper crop. In 1917, the county produced one million bushels of peanuts: the largest peanut harvest in the nation.[18] "In no county was there more swift a change from cotton to peanuts," notes Giesen. "For all of the years that a chorus of progressive voices, including extension agents, scientists, businesspeople, newspaper editors, and politicians, had called for immediate diversification of Alabama's cotton fields, Coffee County's move to peanuts happened almost overnight."[19]

A 1917 article in the *People's Ledger* of Enterprise, the county seat, describes the transformation: "Nearly every vacant building in the town of Enterprise is being used to store peanuts, hay and corn. Nothing like it has ever been known here before. . . . Tons upon tons of hay is being saved from the peanuts and it is said to be gaining in favor with stockmen as a food article for the horses and cattle. The price has been fairly good and it is claimed that the hay more than pays for the picking of the nuts. . . . If the produce coming to this town from the farms were not shipped as fast as it arrived the whole town would be flooded with peanuts and blocked with hay."[20]

With an easy source of animal fodder, many Coffee County farmers began raising hogs alongside peanuts, adding to both income and diversification. Peanut oil and peanut butter production facilities sprung up in the county. At the same time, World War I "disrupted both the demand for cotton and safe shipping routes across the Atlantic," making peanuts a "more secure investment than cotton."[21] War blockades also caused peanut shortages while demand soared, pushing prices higher and clinching peanut farmers' success in the Wiregrass. The rising peanut demand was driven by several factors. The National Emergency Food Garden Commission strongly encouraged Americans to grow peanuts to support the war effort, and peanuts soon became a symbol of patriotism. They were a common substitute for meat on "meatless days" and peanut flour was dubbed "Victory Peanut Flour."[22] At the same time, the field of nutrition exploded, with a stream of discoveries about vitamins and dietary needs. Doctors began endorsing peanuts as a health food and culinary experts inscrted peanuts into a wide variety of dishes. Scientists developed new uses for the peanut, including peanut oil, which soon replaced whale oil used for machinery and vegetable oil used in cooking.

But no one did more to boost peanut popularity than George Washington Carver, who brought peanut product development to unimaginable levels, awakening Americans to the possibilities of peanuts.[23] As the story goes, a woman who heeded Carver's advice to plant peanuts wound up with so many they were rotting in the fields. She sought help from Carver, who viewed nature as God's broadcasting system and rose early every morning to take long walks in the woods to commune with his Creator. On that particular day, he recalled, "I said to God, 'Mr. Creator, I would like to know all about the creation of the world.' And God answered, 'Little man, your mind is too small to take it in. Ask something more your size.' Then I said, 'Mr. Creator, I would like to know all about the peanut.'"[24]

Carver returned to his laboratory with a handful of peanuts, dissected them, and began inventing new uses for the peanut. In 1916, he published "How to Grow the Peanut and 105 Ways of Preparing It for Human Consumption," which became his most popular farming bulletin, seeing eight editions in thirty years.[25] Carver eventually designed over 285 products from the peanut, including milk, soft drinks, vinegar, pickles, chili sauce, mock oysters, cough syrup, skin creams, hair oil, shoe blacking, and inks.[26] He once demonstrated the peanut's versatility to a group of Alabama businessmen by serving a grand banquet based entirely on peanuts: peanut soup, ersatz "chicken" made of peanuts, peanuts used as a vegetable, salad with peanut oil dressing, a peanut "cheese," peanut ice cream and cookies, and coffee made of roasted peanuts.[27] The press dubbed him "The Peanut Man."

American farmers increased peanut acreage sevenfold between 1914 and 1918, with much of the new acreage in Alabama, Texas, and Georgia, on land formerly used for cotton. From 1909 to 1919, peanut acreage increased 577 percent in Coffee County, where, in 1919, peanut acreage actually surpassed cotton acreage.[28] High peanut prices brought unprecedented prosperity to Coffee County. In Enterprise, many farmers opened bank accounts for the first time. Telephones, screened windows, running water, automobiles, and musical instruments debuted on farms. The city raised teachers' salaries, paved streets and sidewalks, and built new schools and hospitals.[29]

Enterprise citizens raised $3,000 for a monument to honor the boll weevil: the pest that had brought them from despair to abundance. Proposed by city councilman Roscoe Owen "Bon" Fleming, the monument was dedicated

Boll Weevil Monument

The original boll weevil monument, built in Italy, featured a classical Greek female figure in a flowing gown standing atop a pedestal. A fountain surrounds her, and her arms hold a small fountain over her head. The figure is life sized, and the monument stands thirteen feet tall. Thirty years after it was dedicated, local artist Luther Baker decided that the boll weevil monument should have a boll weevil. In 1949, Baker fashioned a boll weevil out of linotype metal and attached it to the small fountain held aloft.

The monument has suffered various pranks over the years. Vandals have placed alligators and soap in the fountain. The boll weevil, and sometimes the entire monument, has been stolen several times, but the city of Enterprise always located and repaired it. In July 1998, however, vandals ripped the boll weevil out of the statue's hands and permanently damaged the statue. Because it was too difficult and costly to repair, a polymer-resin replica was erected in its place. The original statue is on display at the Enterprise Depot Museum. *

* Berntson 2011.

December 11, 1919, at the intersection of College and Main Streets, at the heart of the downtown business district. Some 5,000 people attended the ceremony, though the scheduled keynote speaker, George Washington Carver, was delayed by rain.[30] The inscription at the base of the monument reads,

> In profound appreciation of
> The Boll Weevil
> And What It Has Done
> As The Herald of Prosperity

Boll Weevil Monument in downtown Enterprise, Alabama, circa 1960s (Alabama Department of Archives and History, Montgomery, Alabama, Q7723)

This Monument Was Erected
By the Citizens of
Enterprise, Coffee County, Alabama

Yet, shockingly, this was "not the beginning of a broad crop diversification movement, but its brief apex." As Giesen explains in his seminal book, *Boll Weevil Blues: Cotton, Myth, and Power in the American South*, "in the years to come Coffee County farmers disregarded the statue's reminder to diversify. Despite the development of peanut and hog processors, which were supposed to have guaranteed a local market for the legumes, cotton quickly returned as the major economic force in Coffee County and the rest of southeast Alabama. . . . Only a couple of years after they had announced their allegiance to the peanut, farmers around Enterprise again planted more land in cotton than in the legumes. Ten years after the statue was erected, cotton acreage had risen to pre–boll weevil (and pre-statue) levels. Cotton returned to Coffee County almost as quickly as it had gone."[31]

Giesen gives several reasons for this surprising turnaround. First, "farmers had a hard time ignoring the lure of high prices." Even with the boll weevil, the high cost of insecticide, weather instability, an unreliable market, and sandy soil, there was still a chance that cotton could turn a profit. And "at the beginning of the season," Giesen reports, "most growers simply eyed the cotton price and decided what crops to plant."[32] The return to cotton was also bolstered by cotton's cultural hold in the South, and by racism and segregation, which permeated the extension service. Most white agents had little contact with black farmers, and some believed African Americans were incapable of embracing new technologies. Black agents did reach black farmers, but black tenants had no decision-making power over crops and black landowners could only access credit to plant cotton.[33]

Herein lies the reason for diversification's ultimate failure in Alabama. It collapsed, explains Giesen, "because it did not deal with the economic problems that forced farmers into cotton (and debt) season after season. . . . Without creating structural changes in the rural economy—credit, suppliers, and markets—there was no real hope of delivering crop diversification to the agricultural South. . . . Within the economic, social, and cultural system of agricultural production in the rural South there was little room for any kind of talk of true reform of systems."[34]

When diversification faded, poverty swelled. By 1930, the boll weevil "had made its way across the entire region and the South was actually growing more cotton than when the weevil set out; landowners still enjoyed great advantages over the majority African American labor force; and the region's credit system still forced thousands into debt and wedded the region to cotton production," writes Giesen.[35]

Plowing land in Macon County, 1937 (photo by Arthur Rothstein, Library of Congress, LC-USF33-002423-M2)

These truths were painfully evident in Macon County, where George Washington Carver had labored for years to improve the lives of local farmers. To avoid the boll weevil, cotton growers had relocated from the rich, black lands of lower Macon County to "the cutover lands of the hill country. A profit was made for a few years, but eventually the poorer soils gave out, hastened by the system of absentee management and tenant farming."[36] Though African Americans owned nearly half of Macon County farms in the early 1930s, limited credit options forced them to struggle alongside sharecroppers to grow cash crops, primarily cotton and corn, on the worn soil.

New Deal programs aimed to provide southern farmers with the necessary capital to transition to progressive farming strategies, including crop diversification. In Macon County, the Resettlement Administration purchased 10,000 acres from 133 impoverished families and relocated them to more fertile farmland. Thirty of the families moved to Macon County's Prairie Farms Settlement, where they were encouraged to grow a variety of new crops, including peanuts.

Most Macon County farmers, however, either continued to struggle or abandoned farming altogether. Across the South, black landholdings, which had peaked in 1910 at fifteen million acres, began a steady decline. Many black southerners headed to the urban North in search of better jobs and a better living, while those who remained in the South faced rising white violence, Jim Crow segregation, discrimination, and disenfranchisement, all of which contributed to black land loss. Black southerners were often prevented from buying land or were sold only the least desirable acreage. Black sharecroppers who participated in the civil rights movement were routinely fired and evicted. Black landholders were systematically denied credit, loans, and aid by local banks and the US Department of Agriculture. The loans they did secure often came with exorbitant interest rates.

In the 1960s and 1970s, federal farm policies emphasized expanded production. In Macon County, the federal government began paying small (predominantly black) farmers not to plant. Small farmers could earn higher incomes by renting their land to large (predominantly white) farmers who could plant more. As a result, most black farmers in Macon County quit farming in the 1960s and 1970s and never returned. By 1999, black landholdings nationwide had fallen to 2.3 million acres.[37] By 2010, Al Hooks was the only full-time black farmer in Macon County. Every full-time farmer producing large-scale crops like cotton, corn, and soybeans was white. Every black farmer produced fruits, vegetables, and hay, and all except Hooks did so part time.

Hooks is a third-generation farmer. His grandfather, Thomas, was a railroad cook who owned farmland. Hooks's father, Lonnie, owned a substantial amount of property in Macon County and was able to give each of his eleven children forty acres. Nine of the eleven children still live in Macon County. As the eldest son, Al spent a lot of time farming with his father until Lonnie quit farming in 1965, when Al was a teenager.

In the produce business since 2002, Hooks grows greens (turnip, collard, mustard), kale, rutabaga, red potatoes, beans (snap and butter), peas, squash (five varieties), cabbage, corn, okra, cucumbers, strawberries, blackberries, plums, and watermelons. He began by selling his goods at the Macon County Farmers Market in Tuskegee, but he quickly discovered that many Macon County residents could not afford fresh produce, so he was forced to expand to other markets catering to a mostly white middle-class clientele.

Hooks now travels to ten farmers' markets each week, spread across middle Alabama, to sell enough produce to sustain himself and his wife. He is up by five in the morning every day and often shells peas or boils peanuts until eleven or twelve at night. But hard work and long hours are no strangers to Hooks. He spent twenty-five years as a logger and, before that, worked at a plastics plant in Montgomery, where it was so hot that workers regularly passed out walking through the plant. The handrail leading to the second floor was too hot to touch. "It felt like hell around a concrete wall," Hooks says. In nine years of work, he took one vacation day.

Hooks's clients are mostly seniors. The farmers' markets are held during the day, making them popular with retirees, and Hooks also visits nutrition sites where seniors can use vouchers to buy fresh fruits and vegetables. Many of his customers confide in him about their lives, their health, and their concerns, and he enjoys that part of his work. He also enjoys selling a great product, taking pride in his work, and getting positive feedback. "It's a joy," he says, to produce something that benefits young and old alike.

Yet, Hooks took a large salary cut when he left logging for farming to care for his wife after she suffered a stroke in 2002. He also felt the strain of the economic downturn in 2009 but receives no financial assistance from state or federal sources. He draws no retirement from the plastics plant, which let him go just before he would have qualified.

Hooks, however, is not one to dwell on obstacles. Along with two other Macon County farmers, he worked with the mayor of Tuskegee and Tuskegee University to contract with local grocery stores, which now sell the farmers' produce during the height of the growing season. In June 2010, the farmers filled their first orders for the stores. Hooks is also working to get a processing plant located at his farm, which would enable Macon County farmers to sell canned items in stores during the off-season, providing them with year-round income. He also hopes to offer U Pick produce at his farm as soon as he can afford the insurance.

We walk out back, and Hooks ladles out some fresh boiled peanuts, still steaming, from the kettle into a plastic ziplock bag. He sells the quart bags for three dollars each, but they sell only at markets outside Macon County. Here, they are a luxury item. These boiled peanuts are dry, the way Hooks prefers them, and have been soaking for two hours in jalapeño peppers. They taste amazingly good. I buy the obligatory Coke at the gas station off the highway and eat the peanuts on the long drive home.[38]

Al Hooks (photo by Emily Blejwas)

NINE

Wild Turkey

Hunting and Wildlife Conservation in Alabama

Whereas the wild turkey is undoubtedly the most noble of all
game birds upon the North American Continent; and whereas
Alabama has one of the largest per acre populations of wild turkeys
of any state in the United States; and whereas the reputation of the
Alabama wild turkey for being crafty, wary, and difficult to kill is
legendary, and whereas the wild turkey is beyond any doubt the
wild game bird most fitting to be designated as the official state
game bird for the State of Alabama, now therefore be it enacted by
the legislature of Alabama: The wild turkey is hereby designated
and named the official state game bird for the State of Alabama.
—Alabama State Legislature, May 28, 1980

FOR A WHILE, it's only black dark and black coffee in Steve Barnett's Jeep,
which he would like to trade in for a pickup truck. The 180,000 miles across
rutted roads to remote turkey hunting camps have taken their toll. Barnett is
on his second bobblehead turkey mounted to the dashboard, after wearing
out the legs of the first. This one, a gift from his fifteen-year-old daughter, has

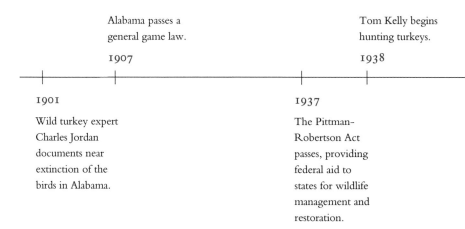

Alabama passes a
general game law.

1907

Tom Kelly begins
hunting turkeys.

1938

1901

Wild turkey expert
Charles Jordan
documents near
extinction of the
birds in Alabama.

1937

The Pittman-
Robertson Act
passes, providing
federal aid to
states for wildlife
management and
restoration.

a head that tilts to one side, flashing attitude. The Jeep also sports a National Wild Turkey Federation license plate that reads "wary." As Barnett says, it's "tricked out for turkeys."

As the dark eases its grip, we can make out silhouettes, then contours, and suddenly it's light enough to exit the Jeep and quietly shut the doors. The pale light and slight chill help me shake off the last remnants of sleep. I met up with Barnett, wildlife biologist and coauthor of *The Wild Turkey in Alabama*, at a twenty-four-hour gas station off the highway at four fifteen this morning, and when we signed into the club, there were three hunters ahead of us. During the spring turkey season, peak gobbling occurs thirty minutes before and thirty minutes after sunrise.

We walk to a high ridge, where sound carries best. At first, we hear only frogs, which are so unbelievably loud they sound like barking dogs. When the frogs quiet down, we hear birds and finally turkeys, which are among the last to join in. We hear two, both gobbling sporadically, maybe twice in twenty minutes. Barnett located two gobblers here last week and is pretty sure these are the same two. They do have distinct voices: one gobble is bright and clear like a ringing bell, the other low and gravelly.

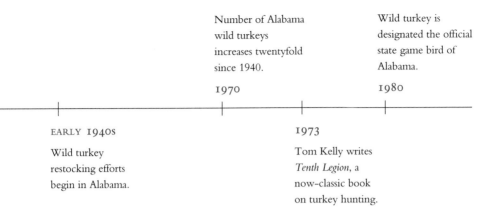

Number of Alabama wild turkeys increases twentyfold since 1940.

1970

Wild turkey is designated the official state game bird of Alabama.

1980

EARLY 1940S

Wild turkey restocking efforts begin in Alabama.

1973

Tom Kelly writes *Tenth Legion*, a now-classic book on turkey hunting.

One of the turkeys sounds as if he's in our designated area, so we return to the Jeep, park on a closer road, and walk in without speaking. We begin a pattern of listening, walking, calling, waiting, walking. It is incredibly quiet. Several times, I hear the snap of a single leaf as it breaks from its branch, clatters through tree limbs, and lands with a thud, as if making a purposeful plunge. My boots hammer the ground, and my stomach growls. Mercifully, when we reach the creek, the whole ground is covered in pine needles and our steps make no sound at all.

When we move, we move fast. I focus on keeping up, keeping quiet, and keeping out of the briars. Yet, there is time for Barnett to show me gnawed stumps along the creek bed where beavers chewed off trees to build their dams, a wild azalea in full pink bloom, coyote tracks, a matted place in the grass where a deer lay and the branches his antlers broke above it. He shows me turkey hen tracks, which he can differentiate from gobbler tracks by the distance and space between the toenails. He shows me strut patterns in the sand, where gobblers dug in and dragged their wings.

To Barnett, turkey hunting is "a nature study in addition to a hunt." He explains: "Turkeys like a mixed habitat: clear land, open fields, underbrush, young timber, old timber, pine, hardwood. They like to nest where the woods meet clear spaces. You have to know the area and know turkey behaviors, where a turkey wants to go, where he likes to walk. You have to strategize to get to the location before he does. And it helps to know what he eats and which trees produce nuts that he would eat."

At one point we hear two turkeys and both are responding to Barnett's calls. We track the closer one, and Barnett is constantly strategizing. He plans to circle out in front of him and wait for him to pass us. If we approach him directly, Barnett explains, he'll get scared and quit gobbling. But suddenly, both turkeys stop gobbling completely. It's typical for gobblers to cut off in the late morning, Barnett says. Though most hunters leave, he stays, hoping the turkeys will start up again after a rest.

Because wild turkeys often return to the same places to strut, we set up a few paces into the woods next to a sandy path full of hen tracks and strut marks. We spend over an hour, maybe closer to two, sitting with our backs against separate trees, unmoving, waiting to see if the turkey will walk past. I watch spiders crossing shiny webs and caterpillars clinging to single blades of grass, but having slept only a few hours the night before, I soon drift in and out of sleep. Every forty-five minutes or so, Barnett uses his box caller, but nobody answers.

Barnett warned me earlier that calling is just a small portion of turkey hunting, that knowing the lay of the land and turkey habits is far more important. "First, you can't make a turkey come somewhere he doesn't want to go," he said. "Secondly, calling too much increases the likelihood he'll figure out you're not a hen. Thirdly, because hens usually go to gobblers, calls often fail because you're asking him to do something he does not naturally do."

Close to noon we stand up and stretch, accepting that the turkeys have stopped gobbling. But it doesn't bother Barnett, as there are plenty of mornings he doesn't hear any turkeys at all. "I consider the hunt a successful experience if I hear a gobbler and can spend some time tracking him, calling, and setting up," he says. "It's icing on the cake if I get to see the gobbler strut and hear him drum. Shooting him is euphoric but anticlimatic. Hearing turkeys gobble and the challenge of the hunt are a better measure of the experience than the actual harvest."

He shows me some pictures of his turkey harvests this season, and I am stunned. In every one, the turkeys are laid out carefully on the forest floor. They appear peaceful against a backdrop of pine and foggy morning light. Killed with a single shot to the neck, they are unruffled and unbloodied. Even the word "harvest" seems soft. These are not the photos of grinning men holding up dejected kills. In fact, Barnett appears in none of them.

We walk back toward the Jeep, and I get a sense of the rhythm of it: pulling on camouflage in the dark, the early morning chill of the truck, watching the world wake up, listening, tracking, calling, setting up, waiting, and the inevitable packing up, with or without a gobbler strung across your back. There is only one hunter left in the club when we leave. On the ride out, I watch the turkey bobblehead nod with the furrows in the road and tell Barnett I think it's nice he has at least one compliant turkey in his life.

A love of turkey hunting often gets passed down through the generations. In Barnett's family, the sport began with Steve's great-grandfather, George Barnett, who hunted one of the last isolated groups of turkeys in Winston County, Alabama, in the early 1900s. Steve, who is now teaching his own son to hunt, began by tagging along with his father, initially without a gun of his own. His father pointed out tracks, trails, droppings, and wildlife as they walked together through the woods, talking and listening in what Barnett defines as "a naturalist experience."

"Turkey hunters definitely feel a connection with land and wildlife," Barnett says. "It's not only the harvest. It's the total nature experience. It's the thrill of hearing and then seeing wild turkeys, regardless of the hunting aspect. The main reason I hunt is to hear the turkey gobble. It's a wild sound, to hear an animal make that noise. I think hunters are natural conservationists because to think of a world without wildlife . . . it would be pretty bleak. And there are already species that are gone."[1]

Indeed, it was sportsmen who launched the nation's first conservation movement in the late 1800s in response to the destruction of wild turkey

Eastern wild turkey (courtesy of Larry Price, National Wild Turkey Federation)

populations and their habitats. Eastern wild turkeys, native to North America, had lived in abundance for thousands of years before Europeans arrived. Across what is now the southeastern United States, wild turkeys thrived in longleaf pine ecosystems that dominated the region, where they often wandered in flocks of up to five thousand birds.[2]

In Alabama, wild turkeys were almost as common as blackbirds. During his travels in neighboring Florida, explorer William Bartram wrote in 1773: "I was awakened in the morning early, by the cheering converse of the wild turkey-cocks (*Meleagris occidentalis*) saluting each other, from the sun-brightened tops of the lofty Cupressus disticha and Magnolia grandiflora. They begin at early dawn, and continue till sun rise, from March to the last of April. The high forests ring with the noise, like the crowing of the domestic cock, of these social centinels; the watch-word being caught and repeated, from one to another, for hundreds of miles around; insomuch that the whole country is for an hour or more in a universal shout."[3]

Native Americans relied on turkey eggs and flesh as a significant part of their diet and taught European settlers how to hunt and prepare wild turkey, which was often fried or put into stew. Until the Civil War, much of Alabama remained a frontier where domestic animals played a small role. Most meat was wild, and wild turkey was a mainstay of the frontier diet for Native Americans and Europeans alike.

But as Europeans moved across the American frontier, wild turkey populations rapidly diminished. Prizing Manifest Destiny, early settlers sought to subdue wild America, turning unruly forests into neat farms. Conquering and mastering the land was viewed with a sense of national pride. "Wild things were something to be overcome and forgotten," and "wild creatures were no match for the unchecked invasion by ax, plowshare, livestock, and gun."[4] As pioneers felled timber and plowed prairies to make way for farms and towns, turkey habitat vanished. Further, farmers often let hogs run loose in the woods, where they competed with turkeys and other wildlife for food. Market hunting, which began in the early 1800s, also posed a grave threat to wild turkey populations, but most states had limited (if any) game laws.

Between 1850 and 1900, entire wildlife populations were decimated in what became known as the Age of Extermination.[5] By 1900, large-scale agriculture boomed in Alabama, with four million acres planted in cotton and millions more in hay and corn. Wild turkey expert Charles Jordan, who grew up hunting turkeys with his father and brothers, wrote in 1901 that though Alabama was "once the paradise of hunters . . . the work of destruction goes on from year to year, and the birds are being greatly reduced in numbers in many localities. The extinction of them in some states has already been accomplished, and in others it is only a matter of time."[6] Indeed, only a few pockets of wild turkeys remained in Alabama. Squeezed into narrow bands of woods along the rivers, there were fewer than ten thousand birds statewide.

As American wildlife populations hung by a thread, hunting for sport continued to grow in popularity. At the turn of the century, American sportsmen expressed grave concern over the perpetual decline of wildlife and lobbied for

Wild Turkey

In 1901, Alabama native and wild turkey expert Charles Jordan wrote a twenty-one-article series for the magazine *Shooting and Fishing* that became the heart of *The Wild Turkey and Its Hunting*, America's first book devoted to the wild turkey. The book was published posthumously by Edward A. McIlhenny, who wrote of his friend and colleague: "A careful observer and lover of the wild turkey, . . . Mr. Jordan knew more of the ways of the wild turkey in the wilds than any man who ever lived. . . . For many years the study of this bird occupied almost his entire time."*

In *The Wild Turkey and Its Hunting*, Jordan explains "the secret of cooking the turkey." He asserts that "of matters with which the average sportsman has to do, there is none so little understood as that of cooking game, and especially the turkey. . . . In the solitude of the forest the hunter should not be at loss for methods of cooking even if he has but a frying pan; a log for a table; his plate, a section of bark or large leaf."† He writes:

> Imagine a gobbler dressed and lying on a log or piece of bark beside you. Take a sharp knife, run the blade down alongside the keel bone, removing the flesh from one end of that bone to the other. By this process each half breast can be taken off in two pieces. Lay this slab of white meat skin side down, then begin at the thick end and cut off steaks, transversely, one half inch thick, until all the slab is cut. Now sprinkle with salt and pepper and

game laws, including hunting seasons and bag limits. In 1907, Alabama passed a general game law that embodied the state's first real legislation for organized wildlife protection. The law provided for a state game commissioner, a licensing system, the prohibition of sale and shipment of game, season limits, landowner permission requirements, and protection of nongame birds. It also created the Alabama Department of Game and Fish.

pile the steaks up together; thus the salt will quickly penetrate. . . . Just as soon as the salt dissolves and the juice begins to flow, spread out the steaks in a pan, sprinkle dry flour lightly on both sides evenly. . . . Give the pan a shake and the flour will adjust itself. This flour at once mixes with the juices of the meat, forming a crust around the steak, like batter. Have the frying-pan on the fire with plenty of grease, and sizzling hot so the steak will fry the moment it touches the hot grease. Put the steaks in until the bottom of the pan is covered, but never have one steak lap another. If the grease is quite hot the steak will soon brown, and when brown on one side, turn, and the moment it is brown on both sides take out of the pan. By this method you retain almost every particle of the juice of the meat, and at the same time it is brown and crisp and will nearly melt in the mouth. The flour around the steak does not only prevent the escape of the juice, but also prevents any grease penetrating the meat. If you like gravy, have the frying-pan hot and about a teaspoonful of the grease in which the meat was fried left in it; take a half pint of cold water and pour into the pan. Let this boil about five minutes, when you will have a rich, brown gravy, which [should be] season[ed] with salt and pepper and pour[ed] hot over the steak. You don't want a thing else to eat except some good bread and a cup of creole coffee. Having eaten turkey thus cooked you would not care for baked or roast turkey again.[‡]

* McIlhenny, Jordan, and Shutfeldt 1914:x.
† Ibid.:233.
‡ Ibid.:234–36.

The real victory, however, came in 1937 with federal passage of the Pittman-Robertson Act. The most significant wildlife preservation legislation to date, the act impacted American wildlife in more ways than any other effort. It established the Federal Aid in Wildlife Restoration Program, which distributed funds from a new federal tax on hunting licenses and equipment to state agencies to hire trained wildlife professionals, purchase and manage

Hunter crouched in front of a tree with a turkey caller in his hand and a gun in his lap, circa 1930–59 (Alabama Department of Archives and History, Montgomery, Alabama, Q458)

millions of acres of critical habitat to rehabilitate wildlife, develop land to make it more suitable for wildlife, and finance wildlife research.[7]

The Pittman-Robertson Act had immediate effects in Alabama. Federal funds supported the creation of thirty-two wildlife management refuges totaling seven hundred thousand acres, a new graduate program in Game Management at Auburn University, and the purchase of four thousand acres in Clarke County to restock wild turkeys. This acreage became the Fred T. Stimpson Wildlife Sanctuary, named for an avid sportsman and outspoken conservationist with long-standing ties to the area. At the sanctuary, wildlife biologists used intensive management practices to establish a central reservoir of wild turkeys to trap and relocate to vacant ranges throughout the state.

Restocking efforts coupled with effective land management practices enabled Alabama's wild turkey population to grow from ten thousand birds in

Wild turkeys at Fred T. Stimpson Wildlife Sanctuary (photo by Carrie Threadgill)

1940 to two hundred thousand in 1970 to five hundred thousand in 2007. Wild turkeys now occupy most of the suitable range for turkeys in Alabama, prompting lifelong turkey hunter Tom Kelly to call their restoration "the single finest example of restoration of a species in the history of game management." In fact, most of the wild turkeys in Alabama today originated from birds relocated from the Fred T. Stimpson and Upper State Wildlife Sanctuaries in Clarke County.

Restored wildlife populations tripled the number of American hunters between 1937 and 1987. In 1944, only fourteen states had wild turkey seasons. Today, every state in the United States has a wild turkey season except Alaska (though they do have a National Wild Turkey Federation chapter). Alabama has one of the largest per acre populations of wild turkeys of any state and one of the highest rates of turkey harvests in the nation. Turkey hunting is a major source of recreation and revenue for the state. Hunters spend $45 million annually in Alabama on spring turkey hunting alone.[8]

When Tom Kelly began hunting turkeys in Alabama in 1938 at the age of ten, his grandfather told his father, "It's a pity to start him. There won't be any more turkeys by the time he grows up." In those days, Kelly relates, "hunting was pitiful. The only reason you did it was because you had a grandpa that would take you out and you liked it. You had to have a very low threshold of expectation. If you heard a turkey gobble, the hunt was a success. If you killed one a year, people would hang around you to see if you'd let any secrets drop. If you killed two a year, the Pope should be notified so he could canonize you. If you killed three a year, you were a cheating, dirty liar. Nobody could kill three a year."

Nowadays, however, Kelly estimates "hunters will see more turkeys in their first five years than I saw in my first twenty-five."[9] Further, Alabama turkey hunters remain critical partners in conservation, protecting turkey populations by hunting legally and ethically within season and bag limits, only harvesting males, and reporting poachers. They also provide harvest data that helps wildlife biologists monitor population trends and set appropriate season and bag limits to ensure a sustainable wild turkey population. Many Alabama turkey hunters belong to local chapters of the National Wild Turkey Federation, where, as Barnett says, they "unselfishly contribute large sums of money for habitat restoration."[10]

So what is it about turkey hunting that has driven sportsmen to ardently defend and rebuild wild turkey habitats (often by donating their own time and money) for 130 years? According to Barnett, "it's the challenge of it, the chase. You don't want to get too close and scare him off, so you get as close as you can without spooking him. . . . If he sees you move or if something just looks off about the landscape, he's gone, and usually you won't be able to track him again. So you're constantly moving, setting up, trying to figure out what the turkey might do next. It's a quick, active form of hunting. You're trying to think like a turkey, to outsmart him."[11]

Indeed, turkeys have long enjoyed a reputation as the most mysterious and evasive game species of the South. In the spring of 1991, naturalist Joe Hutto imprinted two broods of wild turkeys and spent nearly a year following them through the woods of north Florida. He found the birds to be secretive, elusive, and profoundly inconspicuous. Frequently, he encountered "people who have never observed a wild turkey even though they live in an area where these birds are considered to be abundant."[12] After many months spending fourteen-hour days with the turkeys, Hutto wrote, "I am beginning to suspect that no matter how much time I spend with these birds, they will always remain a mystery to me."[13]

The hallmark elusiveness of the wild turkey stems from several natural traits. Wild turkeys excel in their ability to detect movement, even at long distances. They possess 360-degree vision and a highly developed sense of hearing. They have powerful legs that enable them to run in excess of twelve miles per hour and can take flight instantly. They can differentiate colors and exhibit color preferences. They have a well-developed sense of place and memory and are excellent at gauging distance and direction.[14] As Hutto notes, "a spring gobbler who answers my call from a quarter of a mile away needs no other sound from me. If he chooses to come, he will know almost exactly from what bush or tree trunk the call came."[15]

Wild turkeys also possess an "extraordinary state of awareness" and attention to detail.[16] Hutto's turkeys exhibited "an awareness that at once includes the smallest crawling particle on a leaf and the red tailed hawk soaring a half mile up the field. They acknowledge, in some way, any sound or occurrence in the area. . . . They never fail to warn me of the slightest element of interest in our environment: a squirrel or bird in a nearby tree, a snake passing quietly nearby, or a hawk soaring at an altitude that is almost invisible to me. . . . Many times it is only with great difficulty that I locate some telescopic speck silently moving across the sky. . . . [Their] sensory ability clearly borders on the supernatural."[17]

Furthermore, wild turkeys have a comprehensive genetic program that allows them to distinguish a hawk from a vulture at a thousand feet, differentiate venomous and nonvenomous snakes, and discern if wild turkey feathers

Wild turkey in flight, Springville, Alabama (photo by Joe Songer, *Birmingham News*)

are from a different brood. They have complete insect recognition regarding palatability and danger. Wild turkeys build on this innate knowledge by constantly investigating their environment. As Hutto relates, "they are curious to a fault, they want a working understanding of every aspect of their surroundings, and their memory is impeccable. They gather specific information about a particular environment, conspicuously apply that information to a framework of general knowledge, and make appropriate choices in modifying their behavior. The apologies that precede discussions about wild turkey intelligence are definitely not warranted. I have never observed another animal making such a dedicated effort to know and to understand."[18]

Finally, wild turkeys exhibit personality variations that "could account for much of the unpredictable behavior that we observe in turkeys in the wild," writes Hutto. "As any turkey hunter will attest, only a small percentage of wild turkeys behave and respond in a predictable manner."[19] Barnett wholeheartedly agrees, stating that wild turkey hunting provides "infinite variety because every turkey is different. What works for one won't work for another. You have to tailor your movements to that specific turkey and that specific time." Turkeys on public land, for example, act and react differently from turkeys on private land. Further, recent research revealed genetic differences between turkey populations within the state of Alabama. Wild turkeys in north Alabama's Sipsey Wilderness bear a closer resemblance to turkeys in the Arkansas Ozarks than to Alabama Gulf Coast turkeys. These findings do not surprise Barnett, who unequivocally states that mountain turkeys are harder to hunt.

It was Tom Kelly, dubbed "the poet laureate" of wild turkey literature, who introduced me to Hutto's work. Kelly, a lifelong Alabamian, is easily considered America's favorite wild turkey storyteller. He is credited with creating and dominating the genre, after writing over a dozen books and scores of magazine articles on turkey hunting over the past thirty years. The National Wild Turkey Federation calls Kelly's first and most popular book, *Tenth Legion*, "the best and funniest book on the quest for the lonesome longbeard" and "the bible of turkey hunting."[20]

But Kelly is not one to glorify himself or the past. When asked about his naval service during World War II, he says he played a lot of baseball. He claims he attended Auburn University on the GI bill "to get my dad off my back" and chose a degree in forestry "because they offered it." His attitude toward turkey hunting is the same. He calls the early days of hunting "pitiful" and believes the best hunters are those learning right now. The last line of his book, *The Season*, reads: "The good old days are right this minute. *Sicut erat in principio, et nunc, et semper.*"[21]

Like Barnett, Kelly loves the sport for its challenge. "Turkey hunting is just like 1–0 ball games," he says. "It is not so much what is happening as what could be happening."[22] He defines the hunt as "an intellectual exercise driven by sound . . . a series of moves and countermoves. 90% of turkey hunting is done with the ear," he notes. "When turkeys don't talk, they are effectively invisible."[23]

Though Kelly has been hunting turkeys in Alabama for over seventy years, he puts his success rate at about 25 percent based on turkeys that he calls, sets up on, and hears gobble at least once after sitting down. Yet, there are many mornings when the turkeys don't gobble at all. Statistics confirm the difficulty of the sport. Though Alabama hunters are allowed to harvest five turkeys per year, it is not uncommon to hunt a whole season without bagging one. On average, Alabama spring turkey hunters spend seven days hunting and harvest only one turkey. "I admit freely that turkeys are smarter than I am," Kelly says. "They will make anybody look ridiculous." Yet, this doesn't bother him in the least. He believes that in turkey hunting, as in life, "it's better to travel than to arrive. True turkey hunters don't want guaranteed success and they don't take shortcuts. They know you win some and lose some. . . . Turkey hunting is not a game that needs a score or a scorekeeper and does not require the production of a dead turkey to qualify as a success. . . . Most of the really good [turkey hunters], most of the old timers, talk more about the ones that get away than they do about the ones in the back of the truck."[24]

Barnett and Kelly echo the sentiments of wild turkey hunters reaching back generations. In 1866, one sportsman dubbed turkey hunting "the best specimen of the wild forest sports—a trial of skill between the perfection of animal instinct, and the superior mental endowments of man."[25] He wrote, "The wild turkey seems filled with the instinct of self-preservation, being the shyest and wariest of all game found in the American continent. . . . Where the haunts of the turkey are surrounded by plantations, they become so wild, from being so frequently hunted, that it is almost impossible for the hunter to get within gunshot. Only a veteran in the art has any chance of success. It is recorded of an old hunter that he once chased a turkey regularly for three years, only catching sight of the bird twice."[26] A few decades later, Charles Jordan agreed: "There are times when the keenest sportsmen will be outwitted, often when success seems assured . . . many veteran turkey hunters have in mind some old gobbler who seemed invincible; some bird that had puzzled them for three or four years without their learning the tricks of the cunning fellow."[27]

The fairness of the fight is crucial to turkey hunters. They despise landowners who plant patches of chufa (a grass turkeys find irresistible) and simply wait for turkeys to show up. The 1866 hunter insisted "the only legitimate style of turkey-killing [is] to call up some crafty old gobbler and fool him."[28] Charles Jordan rejected "nefarious tricks" and validated only sportsmanlike hunting, stating, "I have too much respect for this glorious bird to see it killed in any but an honorable way."[29] Today, Tom Kelly asserts that if you're going to plant a chufa patch, "you might as well just go down to the A&P and buy a turkey."[30]

And don't get him started on deer hunting. "You sit there without moving all day and wait for a deer to come into view and then you shoot it like shooting a cow in a field. It's for candy asses. I've been up in deer stands with rocking chairs and magazines in them. It's not a sport. It's not even. Turkey hunting is closer to an even fight, though it would be perfectly even if I could fly and the turkey could shoot back."

Tom Kelly used to hunt turkeys every single day of the spring season, which runs from March 15 to April 30 in Alabama. But at eighty-two years of age, he is forced to take a day off every fourth day or so, which he spends "lying in bed thinking about how I should be out turkey hunting." (Unless it's raining. Then he feels justified.) His favorite days to hunt are the last ten of the season because the hens are constantly on the nest by then and gobblers are more willing to go out in search of them. Kelly claims he is twice as successful calling in gobblers during those last ten days than at any other time.

We drive into the hunting club on April 29. The roads are so rugged that we actually have to ford a small stream. Several rabbits zigzag in front of us until they gain the courage (or the frenzy) to jump the dirt barrier into the woods. "Good shot!" Kelly exclaims when one of them makes the leap. He and his friend Eric have been discussing squirrel problems. Eric shoots them with a BB gun, but Kelly traps and releases them in the woods. He is keeping track of them: fifty-nine squirrels so far. He claims that his wife, whom he sometimes refers to as his roommate, insists on the trapping method, but for some reason, I suspect he wouldn't shoot them anyway.

Outside, the noise from nearby logging trucks would make it difficult to track turkeys, but we don't hear any anyway, so we walk toward an area turkeys might like to be, through terrain so sandy that in low spots it's like walking on a beach through a forest. There are plenty of tracks and strut marks. Kelly tells me that by the end of the season, a gobbler's wingtips look as if they've been clipped with a scissor. He points out a wrinkled place in the sand where a turkey thrashed around, probably trying to rid himself of dust mites. "Now look at this," Kelly says, and we stop beside a large boot print belonging to the young physician who invited Kelly to join this club. "I could tell that footprint anywhere," he says. "Like a damn Sasquatch!" We take turns lining up our own feet next to the print.

We call and wait and walk and call and wait, but we hear nothing. "At this point it's like running out pop flies," Kelly says. So we keep walking. After seventy years turkey hunting and forty-five working in the timber in-dustry, Kelly's knowledge of trees is astounding. We talk at length about the merits of the bygone American chestnut, which scientists are on the brink of reviving with a disease-resistant strain. Kelly tries to teach me the difference between the call of a whippoorwill and a chuck-will's-widow, but they sound identical to me. He points out a purple plant and talks of the impossibility of taking anything from the forest to grow at home. "You just can't replicate the conditions," he says.

Eventually we find a place to set up, and Kelly insists on giving me the camouflage stool while he sits on a small camouflage cloth. He reflects on the plethora of modern turkey hunting equipment. "When I started, I had my army fatigues, a call, and a *Cosmopolitan* magazine to sit on. Now you prac-tically need a wheelbarrow for all the equipment. Of course, I don't get any more turkeys than I used to." He pauses. "And if I tried to buy a *Cosmopolitan* nowadays they'd think I was a dirty old man." I suggest he'd have to switch to *Home and Garden* and he chuckles.

After a while, we decide to drive to a different area as a last-ditch effort to hear a turkey gobble. We run into the young doctor with the big feet, on his way to work. He tells us that the turkey his friend Jim has been after all season has been gobbling this morning. Kelly whispers to me, "If we get poor Jim's turkey, we'll have to bury him. I swear, I'm not telling anyone. We'll

Turkey hunting with
Tom Kelly (photo
by Emily Blejwas)

say we didn't hear a damn thing." As it turns out, we don't hear a damn thing anyway. As we drive out, Kelly tells me to look in the open field we're passing for a turkey laughing and slapping his knee.

Kelly is not one to stick around after the first few critical hours. As planned, we pick up Eric at eight thirty. He hasn't heard anything either. "Not even Henrietta drew 'em in," Eric says of his turkey hen decoy. Kelly suggests getting Henrietta some lipstick and a red dress. As we drive back through the woods, now sunlit, our conversation drifts to the differences between longleaf and loblolly pine. Kelly scans passing trees for a good example then stops the truck, and we get out to study the needle groupings: the longleaf's shaped like a puffball and the loblolly's like a feather.

When we part ways, my turkey season has ended without seeing, much less bagging, a wild turkey. To be honest, I'm slightly relieved. It's hard to imagine killing one considering everything I now know about wild turkeys. I assume this is because I'm not a veteran turkey hunter, but then I stumble across Tom Kelly's words in *The Season*: "You get an opportunity to look in a wild turkey's eye and you see the same thing you see in the eyes of a first-class bird dog. They are not simply the eyes of a dumb brute. There is somebody home in there. . . . Because of a particular set of circumstances, partly on his part and partly on mine, I have managed to personalize him down through the years. He has passed beyond being a bird, he has become a presence. He doesn't just stand around out there, he thinks. But if you let yourself believe in that too much, you run a very real danger. . . . You might get to the point where you could never shoot at one again."[31]

TEN

‖‖‖

Sweet Tea

Birmingham in the Great Depression and the Second World War

Alabamians born during the first third of the twentieth
century would live through the most severe depression and
the bloodiest war in the history of the world. They were a
tough generation and lived in trying times. The world would
never quite be the same again. Neither would Alabama.

—Wayne Flynt, "Hard Times"

"NEVER MARRY A MAN 'til you know how to make his mama's tea," goes the
southern expression. Sweet tea, the trademark beverage of the South, is iced
tea sweetened with sugar while the tea is still hot, allowing it to hold more
sugar than it would under colder temperatures and creating a smoother blend.
It debuted in southern cookbooks in the late nineteenth century. Though
iced tea had been served for decades, it usually appeared as "punches":

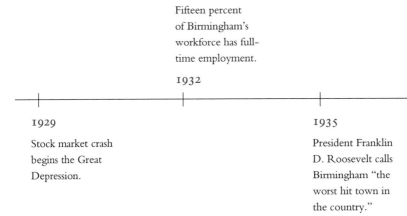

Fifteen percent
of Birmingham's
workforce has full-
time employment.

1932

1929

Stock market crash
begins the Great
Depression.

1935

President Franklin
D. Roosevelt calls
Birmingham "the
worst hit town in
the country."

mixtures of cold green tea and liquor. By the 1860s, southerners drank iced tea without the alcohol, and after 1900, widespread refrigeration boosted the convenience of iced tea (now primarily made from black tea), and its popularity skyrocketed. Prohibition (1920–33) gave iced tea another boost, as southerners sought alternatives to cold alcoholic drinks.[1]

Known as "the house wine of the South," sweet tea has become the most popular and prevalent southern beverage. In fact, some southerners posit that "the sweet tea line" more accurately divides the North from the South than the Mason-Dixon Line. Southerners consume sweet tea year-round, and it is served at every type of gathering, in every type of restaurant. "No self-respecting barbecue house or fish camp would ever stop serving sweet tea," claims food writer Fred Thompson. "Most, for many years, gave no option but sweet tea, and the righteously committed still serve only the sugary brew."[2] At Alabama native and chef Scott Peacock's house, sweet tea "was as elemental as water."[3]

In Alabama, Milo's Tea is a household name. In 1946, Milo Carlton created his famous sweet tea just as he and his native city of Birmingham emerged from the devastating lows and soaring highs of the Great Depression

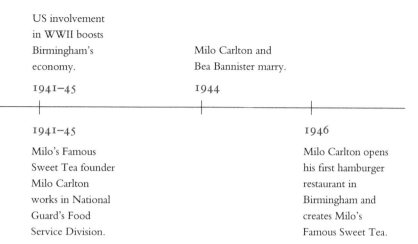

US involvement in WWII boosts Birmingham's economy.

1941–45

Milo Carlton and Bea Bannister marry.

1944

1941–45

Milo's Famous Sweet Tea founder Milo Carlton works in National Guard's Food Service Division.

1946

Milo Carlton opens his first hamburger restaurant in Birmingham and creates Milo's Famous Sweet Tea.

followed by World War II. One of the most dismal places in Alabama during the Depression, Birmingham had rebounded to become "the arsenal of the South" during the war years. The story of Milo's Tea intertwines with the story of the city, and it begins in the depths of the Great Depression.

"Even under the best of circumstances," Alabama historian Wayne Flynt reminds us, "the Great Depression ravaged people's lives."[4] In Alabama, Birmingham absorbed much of the despair. Of the fifty-six thousand Alabama families on relief in 1934, half of them lived in Birmingham. Few emerged unscathed. As resident Hattie Adolphus recalls, the Depression "hit every home in Birmingham."[5] In 1935, President Franklin D. Roosevelt singled out Birmingham as "the worst hit town in the country."[6]

Heavy dependence on industry contributed in large part to Birmingham's suffering. The city was less than sixty years old when the Great Depression hit. Founded at the junction of two railroads in 1871, Birmingham exploded with growth to become the first major industrial center in the South following the Civil War. Several steel companies drove the city's economy and fueled its progress, earning Birmingham its reputation as "the Pittsburgh of the South."

This prosperity collapsed in the wake of the Great Depression, when

Sunday School Punch

Demopolis, Alabama, circa 1880*

Block of ice

1 quart boiling water

2 teaspoons black tea

orange and lemon peel

2 cups sugar

1½ cups orange juice

½ cup lemon juice

tart apples

1 pint ice-cold water

1 pint Muscatel

1 pint best white rum

Place block of ice in punch bowl; decorate rim with flowers. Pour boiling water over tea and citrus peels; steep a few minutes and put in sugar and juice. Place stars and crescent moons cut from tart apples in bowl cavity hollowed on top of block of ice. Strain steeping mixture, add 1 pint ice-cold water, and then add wine and rum. Pour mixture slowly over block of ice. Chill glasses. Provide chairs.

* Eugene Walter's recipe from Goodman and Head 2011:39

Birmingham's industrial output plummeted by nearly 70 percent. Jobs in the steel mills, coke ovens, and mines were cut dramatically. Steel giant TCI reduced the workforce at one of its mines from one thousand employees to seventy-eight. Those lucky enough to keep their jobs were reduced to a "maximum wage." Miners often worked one day out of every fourteen. By June 1932, Birmingham held one hundred thousand workers, with twenty-five thousand of them jobless and sixty thousand working part-time. Further, because black workers held 90 percent of steel industry jobs, effects in black communities were particularly devastating. "Now mills and men are down," aptly states the last line of John Beecher's 1932 poem on the subject.[7]

To complicate matters, farm laborers driven off the land in rural areas streamed into the city in search of work, which was so scarce that when a rare job opened, "people would gather and wait and wait and wait hoping they would get a job," recalls native Orena McBrayer. Obtaining work was nearly impossible. As Alex Bryant recalls, "way up in the thirties it got real bad. Couldn't get a job, couldn't hear a whistle blow, nothing. You couldn't go out there and work a day for a man for nothing." And not only was it difficult to earn money in Birmingham, it was also hard to access it. Banks would shut down without warning, closing one afternoon and never reopening, leaving patrons unable to withdraw money or cash checks. As Elsie Harkins sums up, "We had no money and no way to get it either."

Birmingham residents labored at any job they could find to feed their families. Educated citizens took menial work. The less fortunate dug in trash heaps and garbage cans for junk and scrap: aluminum, iron, copper, rags. They pushed carts around town, picking up anything they could sell. Some collected and sold coal remnants. Others collected and bound small strips of pine to sell as kindling. Though schools remained open, teachers often used their own money to feed hungry children or buy school supplies. Still, many children were forced to quit school, unable to afford the books, fees, lunch money, and transportation. Many also needed to work to help support their families. Children delivered groceries in wagons, sold newspapers on the street, ran errands, and worked in dime stores.

Some in Birmingham became hoboes. On July 1, 1933, two detectives riding a train from Birmingham to Montgomery removed 730 hoboes and 350 trespassers from the train. Some 25 to 30 percent of the riders were teenage boys without work, 10 to 15 percent were teenage girls without work, and some were entire families. Washington Marrisett was a hobo for a time, traveling between Detroit and Birmingham, and recalls seeing all kinds of people, "blacks and whites, men and women in the life." Some rode into the countryside to hunt rabbits to sell back in the city. When rabbits became scarce, they substituted cats. (When rabbits and cats are skinned, it is hard to tell the difference between them.) When cat owners began protesting over missing pets, the city enacted a law that rabbit sellers had to leave the hide on one foot to show that it was really a rabbit.

Getting enough food became a daily concern for a growing number of people. In June 1932, the Red Cross estimated that six thousand to eight thousand Birmingham residents lacked adequate food, fuel, and housing. The Jefferson County poorhouse, designed to hold 220 individuals, held 500. By the following summer, state relief funds were exhausted, forcing the administration to terminate all families with "the slightest opportunity . . . to obtain food from relatives or other sources, even an inadequate amount of food." Out of sixty-eight American cities, Birmingham ranked next to last in per capita expenditures on vital city services. People began leaving babies on doorsteps.

Birmingham residents frequented the back doors of large homes, restaurants, and hotels to ask for food and clothing. Children often came after the evening meal asking for "cold bread." "It was nothing for people to walk up to you and ask you for a nickel for a cup of coffee," recalls Orena McBrayer. "And they were honestly hungry. . . . When people asked you for a nickel or dime they actually needed it for food, and just a cup of coffee, something to warm them 'cause they were out in the cold." Often, they offered to work in exchange for a meal, and it became common to be paid for services in food. "It was lucky if you were paid at all," says Alex Bryant, who considered himself fortunate when he was paid in flour, sugar, or coffee. Even doctors were paid in canned goods and cakes. Though wealthier residents could no longer afford to pay their servants, the servants stayed on, working for food and a place to live.

Rural families gardened and canned during the warmer months to stockpile for the winter, but residents of the city, industrial neighborhoods, and mining camps struggled without space to grow food. When the federal government began distributing seeds, collards, sweet potatoes, radishes, and greens filled the yards and sidewalks in Birmingham, often spilling into the street. The government also issued canned beef, cheese, and eggs and provided lunches for schoolchildren. Soup lines provided one hot meal each day, preventing thousands in Birmingham from starving.

Miners' homes near Birmingham, Alabama, 1935 (photo by Walker Evans, Library of Congress, LC-USF342-001154-A)

In 1934, the Federal Emergency Relief Administration began issuing payments to the neediest Americans. Though Jefferson County soon listed one hundred thousand residents on its relief rolls, payments in Birmingham were far less than in other southern cities. The average monthly relief payment in Birmingham was roughly eight dollars per month, compared with twenty-one dollars in Louisville. Industrial workers complained that bosses and foremen took most of the salaries, with little trickling down to the workers, and African Americans reported difficulty in accessing relief from agency workers. John Beecher illuminates the perverse situation for black residents of Birmingham in the first stanza of his poem "Good Samaritan," when a family of six is given the option to stretch their ration over a week or to "eat well two days and go hungry five."[8]

To make matters worse, many in Birmingham lost their homes after faltering on mortgage payments. During the Depression, fifty to sixty percent of mortgaged houses in Birmingham were in default, the third-highest rate in the nation. Many families moved in together. Adult children returned to their parents' homes, and it was not uncommon for three families to share a house, with all pooling their salaries. The less fortunate stayed in flophouses or slept in parks, under viaducts, or in empty boxcars. Hobo camps, comprised of shacks made from logs, wooden slabs, or cardboard with tarpaper covering the seams, sprang up around railroad stations. Some shacks had corrugated roofing. Whole families lived in the abandoned coke ovens north of the city and cooked over fires built in large oil drums. Others squatted in vacant houses that often lacked doors, which had been looted for firewood.

Birmingham residents lived without basic necessities. As Virginia Bennett artfully noted, "some of them didn't have nothing but breath and britches." Doctors attending home deliveries found pregnant women in beds without sheets. Cars stood on blocks, with no money for gasoline. Children walked with cardboard in their shoes to fill the holes. All of this took its toll. In the summer of 1933, Lorraine Tunstall-Bush, the state director of social services, reported that "pellagra, tuberculosis prevail to undreamed of extents; nervous breakdowns attributed to mental strains resulting from inadequate relief are discernible on every hand."[9] Birmingham residents suffered illness, stress, and early death. There were numerous suicides, mostly by formerly prominent and wealthy businessmen. As Elsie Hope Dillon recalls, "it tested us and a lot of people broke under it. A lot of business people who had a lot of money and were millionaires one day and broke the next just couldn't face it and jumped out of windows and killed themselves. Mostly the little people just rolled up their sleeves and went to work and made it and. . . . We came out of it."

Dillon raises a point that surfaces repeatedly in interviews of those who lived through the Great Depression in Birmingham: the idea that the Depression built character, taught people to work hard, be grateful, and take nothing for granted, and that it fostered unity. As Dillon explains, "I would say that the Depression was a great leveler. Nobody had much and everybody would share and was real conscious of other people's needs. Nobody was high and nobody was low and we were all in the same pan."

In 1935, Bea Bannister was twelve years old when a stranger came to her door carrying her newborn son and said she would have to kill him if Bea's mother didn't take him because she couldn't afford to feed him. Bea's mother took the baby and raised him as her own. Bea and her older sister, who had always wanted a baby brother, "just loved him to death." But life was by no means easy for the Bannister family, who lived in the downtown Birmingham machinery office where Bea's father worked after his hours were cut to one day per month. Bea recalls receiving food donated by the church and going with her siblings to the back door of the Thomas Jefferson Hotel, located five blocks from the office, to ask for food.

When Bea was fourteen, her family moved to east Birmingham, where Bea took to standing outside tent revivals held on vacant lot corners to listen to the music and the preaching. It was there she met Milo Carlton, who was three years older than she. Milo would ride by on his bicycle, sometimes stopping to talk, and Bea thought "he was the cutest thing I ever saw." She was too young to date, but they sat on her front porch and talked and sometimes he would give her a ride on his bicycle. They roller skated on the streets blocked off by the city at Christmastime. Milo was a good skater. "I loved him dearly from the very beginning," Bea says. "He was my first and only real love."[10]

Milo was one of six children. His father worked for a grocer and several of his brothers were in the restaurant business. In 1939, Milo was nineteen years old and working at the Dipsey Doodle, a restaurant run by his older brother in north Birmingham. Around him, the city was slowly getting back on its feet. "It took a long time to pull out of the Depression," recalls Dillon. "It took a long time to get back where you were and for people to get jobs." In the post-Depression era, the federal Works Progress Administration (WPA) was the nation's largest employer, putting more than nine thousand people to work in Birmingham and Jefferson County.

The WPA workers in Birmingham labored at a variety of projects. They

Milo and Bea Carlton (photo courtesy of Patricia Wallwork)

improved streets, roads, bridges, and schools and built highways, airport run-
ways, sewers, health clinics, and public buildings. They expanded recreational
facilities at schools, state and local parks, playgrounds, and athletic fields. They
sealed abandoned coal mines and operated sewing rooms to make hospital
uniforms and clothing for needy families. They created public gardens and
public art. When the WPA program ended in Jefferson County on March 31,
1943, its workers had constructed 566 housing units, paved 81 miles of roads,
and constructed 525 bridges and culverts.

Though the WPA began the work of rebuilding Birmingham, it was the
onset of World War II that jolted the city's economy. Many WPA employees transitioned to war-related work as Birmingham became "the great arsenal of the South." Factories operated eight-hour shifts around the clock.
TCI, already at full capacity in 1939, expanded operations at every plant and
opened a new coal mine. They added seven thousand workers between 1938
and 1941. Bechtel-McCone Aircraft Modification Company opened a factory
that equipped and modified half of the B-29 bombers used during the war. In
fact, the wartime industry in Birmingham was so significant that the city became the second German target after Pittsburgh.

Labor shortages turned serious in 1941, prompting the US government to begin recruiting women for the war effort. One advertisement encouraged every housewife to ask herself: "Can I be of greater service in my home or in a war plant?" Another proclaimed, "The more women at work, the sooner we'll win!" The government's campaign combined with the city's poverty drew quick results in Birmingham. Women joined the war effort in droves, doing everything from fixing radios and engines to building airplanes. At Bechtel-McCone, women made up 40 percent of the workforce.[11]

"Everyone was trying to do their part," Bea recalls. "Everybody was patriotic." Milo's mother made bandages for the Red Cross, both of Bea's brothers enlisted in the navy, and Bea went to work for the Priorities Division of the War Department.[12] In February 1941, Milo's National Guard unit was mobilized. He was engaged to Bea by then, and though he expected to be away for only a year, it was 1944 before Bea saw him again. (She still has all of his wartime letters in a cedar chest.)

Milo's restaurant experience landed him in the Food Service Division. From 1941 to 1945, he attended three cooking schools and cooked on Jeeps, on planes, on ships, in the back of trucks, in mess tents, on beaches, and in four different countries. One day, while sitting under a coconut tree, Milo decided that when he got home, he was going to marry Bea and start his own hamburger restaurant in Birmingham.

Milo had been overseas for nearly three years when a high-ranking officer came into the kitchen one day, saw the jungle rot on Milo's arms, and sent him immediately back to Alabama. He married Bea at the courthouse the day after he returned home in 1944. On April 16, 1946, Milo kept the second half of the promise he made under the coconut tree and opened his first restaurant, Milo's Hamburger Shop, at Thirty-First Street and Twelfth Avenue North in Birmingham. Milo and Bea were partners from the beginning. The shyer of the pair, Milo stayed on the grill while Bea ran the window.

In the mid-1940s, the concept of a hamburger restaurant was revolutionary. Hamburgers were not a popular American food, but Milo thought they made a perfect lunch. He opened the restaurant near Birmingham factories, and it became instantly popular with blue-collar workers, who often called to order for the whole factory. Milo's was also located near a railroad, and sometimes railroad workers would call in an order from a station ahead, then stop the train when they reached Milo's to pick it up.

Milo and Bea could barely keep up. Some days, they posted closed signs in the window when they were actually open. Milo would write out goofy signs like "Closed due to pollution from the Smith Company" (located across the street), and Bea would stand embarrassed at the window while he chuckled back at the grill.

Milo attributed his success to his belief in offering a simple, quality product at an affordable price. He made only a few things but made them well. Milo's offered hamburgers (with onion, sauce, and a pickle), French fries, drinks, and cream pies made from scratch. But Milo also believed in giving customers something extra. When small pieces of meat fell off the cooking hamburgers, he added them to the sandwiches and became known for those extra little pieces. Milo was also careful to raise his prices only a few cents at a time and only when necessary. He paid close attention to the customers' wishes and actually credited them with creating his special sauce: "The customers would tell me it was too hot or too sweet and the next time I made it I would change it by what they had been telling me. When they started telling me to put a lot of that sauce on their burgers I knew I had it just right. All you have to do is listen to your customers because they'll sure tell you what's what. Once you get something they want, you can't run them off with a stick."

Milo followed the same process when crafting his sweet tea and achieved the same success. When the restaurant opened in 1946, sweet tea had been a staple in the South for decades, but the United States had been rationing sugar for the past three years. With the ration in place, Milo didn't have enough sugar for his pies and his tea. So, to conserve sugar, he took the canisters off the tables and began pre-sweetening his tea by mixing it in five-gallon buckets with a wooden spoon. Customers grumbled at first because they were used to sweetening their own tea, but Milo tinkered with the sweetness until it was just right, and soon he was just as famous for his sweet tea as he was for his burgers.[13]

Milo loved his work. He provided for his family, kept his business simple, and never sought to expand. Yet after forty years, Milo's sweet tea had become so popular that customers drove to the restaurant just to buy it. So in April 1989, Milo's son, Ronnie, and his wife, Sheila, founded Milo's Tea Company. They began just as Milo had, mixing tea in five-gallon buckets with wooden spoons and hand filling gallon jugs. They worked in a rented, unheated warehouse where Milo's sauce was made, keeping warm by working alongside steaming gallons of sauce.

Considering the popularity of both Milo's tea and convenience food items, Ronnie and Sheila were sure the tea would sell, though skeptics wondered who would pay for something so easily made at home. Stan Versiglio, the owner of the local Piggly Wiggly, was the first to welcome Milo's Famous Sweet Tea to his shelves. He believed the tea would sell, and he was right. It took off immediately, and Milo's Famous Sweet Tea was soon available in grocery stores throughout the Birmingham area. Over the next two decades, the business grew steadily. A single-serving sixteen-ounce tea was introduced in 1997. The company purchased their own facility and modern equipment in 2002, and tea sales doubled over the next two years. The facility has seen four major expansions since, and distribution has expanded as well. Milo's tea can now be found in thirteen states.

Milo's family still follows his philosophy that if you offer a quality product at a fair price, customers will come back. They brew Milo's tea exactly the way he created it, with three ingredients: tea, water, and sugar. The tea is fresh brewed from leaf. They use pure cane sugar. Milo's tea contains nothing artificial and no preservatives, no added color or flavor. Every batch is tested for its BRIX (sweetness level) to make sure it tastes exactly the way it did over sixty years ago, and Milo's tea is still sold at an affordable price.

Because it's made without preservatives, Milo's tea has a shelf life. It has to be refrigerated and is often sold alongside milk in the dairy section. Few other tea companies brew and sell tea this way because it's an expensive

Tricia Wallwork (photo by Bernard Troncale, *Birmingham News*)

method and limits the market. The Milo's Tea Company's geographic reach is confined to the Southeast. Yet, Milo's family remains devoted to his product and to their customers. As his granddaughter Tricia Wallwork explains, "Every day we make the decision to remain true to the family recipe and to the business by not adding preservatives that would allow the tea to be shipped everywhere. Preservatives change the pH and that changes the flavor, so we'll never use them. It would compromise everything we're founded on. We're not willing to compromise our product to grow the business. We would rather have a smaller reach and a quality product."

Milo's Tea Company is still a family business. Ronnie and Sheila Carlton own the company along with their daughters, Leslie Aven and Tricia Wallwork. Milo's son, Mike Carlton, is the head brewer. When any of the forty-five employees has a birthday, the production line shuts down so everyone can sing and enjoy some cake. Though Milo passed away in 1995, Bea attended all of the company events for another twenty years.[14]

ELEVEN

Sweet Potato Pie

Civil Rights and Soul Food in Montgomery

Sweet potato pies, a good friend of mine asked recently,
"Do they taste anything like pumpkin?" Negative. They
taste more like memory, if you're not uptown.
—Amiri Baraka, *Home: Social Essays*

MARTHA HAWKINS WIELDS an easy grace, rooted in the certainty she is
following the path God laid out for her. Her tranquility fills her countenance,
her voice, even her movements. As the clock edges closer to eleven, when
her restaurant opens, the pace intensifies, with half a dozen kitchen staff
chopping, frying, mixing, or beating bags of vanilla wafers with a rolling
pin. Yet Hawkins moves leisurely between counter and stew pot and oven,
accomplishing all of her tasks, free of haste. She answers her cell phone each
time it rings, telling every caller "I love you" before hanging up.

When she prepares the sweet potato pies, I ask if she follows a recipe and

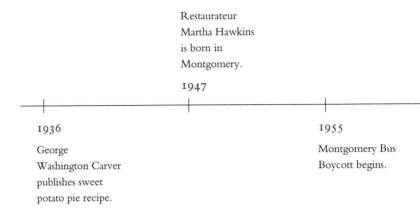

Restaurateur
Martha Hawkins
is born in
Montgomery.

1947

|——————————————|——————————————————————————————|——————————————

1936

George
Washington Carver
publishes sweet
potato pie recipe.

1955

Montgomery Bus
Boycott begins.

she looks at me like I should know better. She makes the filling the way her mother did, eyeing amounts, pouring the ingredients straight into a massive bowl with no measuring cups in sight. Hawkins has been open at her new location for almost a year, but she went eighteen months without a restaurant after closing the first Martha's Place in 2010.

"Did you miss it?" I ask, but she immediately shakes her head. "That season was over," she says, practically. "God told me it had ended and it was time to move on. He always tells you what to do, if you're quiet and listen."[1] She spent the next year and a half traveling the country to promote her book, *Finding Martha's Place: My Journey through Sin, Salvation, and Lots of Soul Food.* Then that ended too, and Hawkins waited for direction for the next phase, which turned out to be a new restaurant on the Atlanta Highway in Montgomery, where a steak place had just folded.

Friends told her to open downtown instead, warning there wouldn't be enough traffic so far from the city center, but it didn't matter. She knew she

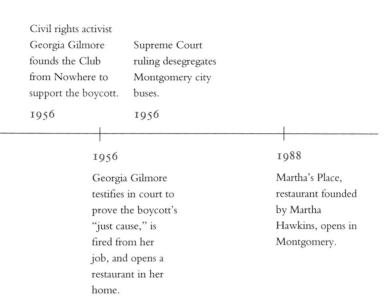

Civil rights activist
Georgia Gilmore
founds the Club
from Nowhere to
support the boycott.

1956

Supreme Court
ruling desegregates
Montgomery city
buses.

1956

1956

Georgia Gilmore
testifies in court to
prove the boycott's
"just cause," is
fired from her
job, and opens a
restaurant in her
home.

1988

Martha's Place,
restaurant founded
by Martha
Hawkins, opens in
Montgomery.

was where she was supposed to be, and she was right. Her old customers showed up in droves, grateful she had reopened and ready to feast on the home cooking that made Martha's Place popular from the beginning. She now serves four hundred to five hundred people daily, closer to six hundred on Sundays. She paid off a $100,000 loan in eight months.

The sweet potato pies emerge from the oven tufted in gold, and Hawkins insists I eat one of the tarts, even though it's still morning. "We serve sweet potatoes in some form four or five days a week," she tells me. "People love them. It's comfort food." The pie is velvety and sweet and heartwarming somehow, making it easy to see why sweet potato pie was a soul food staple from the start.

Sweet potatoes, brought to the New World by Europeans and also likely cultivated by Native Americans prior to European settlement, bear a close resemblance to the African yam. A staple of the West African diet from early

Martha Hawkins (photo
by Valerie Downes)

history, yams were easy to grow and naturally pest resistant, provided high
yields and essential nutrients, and were consumed in a multitude of ways, including fresh, boiled, baked, cooked in ashes, dried, and powdered.[2] Critical
to survival for many, the yam is still revered at harvest festivals, called yam
feast days, throughout West Africa. A symbol of rebirth and renewal, yams
exist at the center of extensive mythology and often accompany ceremonies
relating to birth, marriage, recovery from sickness or injury, and death.[3]

When enslaved West Africans arrived in America, they applied their
knowledge and experience cooking with yams to the American sweet potato,
which quickly became a cornerstone of the southern diet for all classes. Resembling the yam's role in West Africa, sweet potatoes shielded southerners
from hunger during lean times and were especially vital for poor populations,
as they grow easily, produce abundantly (often with little human help), can
be preserved through the winter in a mound of dirt, and, when paired with
greens, provide several essential nutrients. In fact, sweet potatoes give a better

Sweet potato curing house, Franklin County, Alabama, 1927 (Auburn University Libraries, 71.27.5.14)

yield and higher-quality fruit on sandy soil. Consumed from late summer long into winter, sweet potatoes still occupy a primary place on the southern table.

The centrality of sweet potatoes in the southern diet made sweet potato pie a core southern tradition beginning in colonial days, when pies both stretched ingredients and turned humble meals elegant.[4] Europeans, who had consumed pies since the Roman era, made pies in America using apples, lemons, plums, and sweet potatoes by the late 1600s. African slaves, who did the cooking in many colonial households, shaped sweet potato pie by experimenting with spices, techniques, and various ingredients, adding cinnamon, nutmeg, vanilla, cloves, ginger, molasses, orange zest, and coconut to the basic pie filling. Because pigs were abundant in the South, cooks used lard instead of butter in their pie crusts, giving them "a distinct, flaky quality."[5]

In the early decades of the twentieth century, George Washington Carver helped secure the longevity of sweet potato pie in Alabama. As the head of the Agricultural Department at Tuskegee Institute, Carver encouraged farmers to plant crops that would replenish the parched Alabama soil, including sweet potatoes. To spread his message, he produced scores of farming bulletins that were practical, free, and comprehensible. Between 1898 and 1943, Carver issued nearly fifty bulletins on sweet potatoes alone, featuring the 118 products he invented from the sweet potato (including molasses, vinegar, and shoe blacking) as well as various sweet potato recipes. His recipe for sweet potato pie, published in 1936, is a prototype of modern versions.

Twenty years after Carver published his 1936 recipe, and forty miles down the road, Georgia Gilmore used sweet potato pies to support the bus boycott in the racially polarized city of Montgomery, where segregation was mandated in schools, churches, hospitals, restaurants, doctor's offices, restrooms, and even cemeteries. Downtown, African Americans sat in the balcony at the movie theater and in a separate section at the courthouse. They drank from separate water fountains and were prohibited from trying on clothing in department stores. Segregation was required in any public place, making it illegal for black and white people to share a taxi or play checkers together in public.

The Montgomery bus system perpetuated some of the cruelest, most racist treatment black citizens faced on a daily basis. Inside the bus, there were ten seats in front for white riders and ten seats in back for black riders. Black riders could occupy the sixteen seats in the middle only if no white riders were standing. So when the bus filled, black riders gave up their seats. In some cases, two or three black riders were forced to give up their seats for one white person, so the white person did not have to sit next to a black person. Black riders were also required to stand even when there were no white riders on the bus and the ten white seats were empty.

Black riders suffered further abuse at the hands of bus drivers, who often drove off after black passengers had paid at the front and exited the bus to enter through the rear. Drivers routinely refused to make change, purposely dropped change on the floor, and ignored black riders' transfers and made them pay again. They were known to curse, slap, and kick black passengers. In one instance, a black woman with two young children stopped to pay her fare at the front of the bus and her children climbed into the first seat to wait. In retaliation for the black children sitting in a white seat, the driver pushed

Sweet Potato Pie

ABBY FISHER, 1881[*]

Two pounds of potatoes will make two pies. Boil the potatoes soft; peel and mash fine through a cullender while hot; one tablespoonful of butter to be mashed in with the potato. Take five eggs and beat the [yolks] and whites separate and add one gill [¼ pint] of milk; sweeten to taste; squeeze the juice of one orange, and grate one-half of the peel into the liquid. One half teaspoonful of salt in the potatoes. Have only one crust and that at the bottom of the plate. Bake quickly.

[*] Fisher 1995.

Sweet Potato Pie

GEORGE WASHINGTON CARVER, 1936[*]

Boil in skins. When tender, remove skins; mash and beat until light. To each pint of potatoes, add ½ pint of milk, ½ pint of cream and four well beaten eggs; add 1½ teacups of sugar (less if the potatoes are very sweet). Add spice, cinnamon and ginger to taste; one ground clove will improve it. Bake with bottom crust only. The above is enough for five or six pies.[*]

[*] Carver 1936. This recipe appears in the original as "No. 6 PIE (EXTRA FINE)."

the accelerator then slammed on the brake, sending the children tumbling to the floor. In another instance, police shot and killed a black man following an altercation on the bus. His death was ruled a "justifiable homicide."[6]

Despite this treatment, African Americans continued to ride buses because it was the most affordable form of transportation, and most did not own cars. Further, most African Americans could not afford to protest the abuse

Audience at the First Baptist Church in Montgomery, Alabama, during a standing ovation for leaders of the bus boycott, 1956 (Library of Congress, LC-USZ62-135428)

because they could easily be arrested, fined, sent to jail, beaten by police, or fired by white employers. However, a cadre of tenacious black leaders, many of whom taught at Alabama State College (now Alabama State University) in Montgomery, did advocate for integrity on the buses. In 1949, Prof. Jo Ann Robinson founded the Women's Political Council to spearhead the campaign for better treatment of black passengers on Montgomery buses.

On December 1, 1955, Rosa Parks was arrested for refusing to give up her seat to a white passenger on a Montgomery bus. Black leaders in Montgomery, several of whom had actively protested the treatment of black riders for years, rallied around Parks, a respected community member and secretary for the NAACP. The leaders founded the Montgomery Improvement Association (MIA) and galvanized black community support for a bus boycott set for Monday, December 5, the day of Parks's arraignment.

Monday morning dawned cold and dreary, and boycott leaders worried the threat of rain would convince African Americans to ride the buses. But the first buses of the day rolled by empty. Nearly every black person in Montgomery stayed off the buses that day. Black cab drivers charged passengers the bus fare (ten cents) as opposed to the cab fare (forty-five cents), but many African Americans simply walked.

Rev. Robert Graetz, the white pastor of the black Trinity Lutheran Church and the only white minister in Montgomery to openly support the boycott, recalls: "As I cruised the streets that Monday morning, I saw Negro people striding along as if they didn't have a care in the world, their heads held high, their faces covered with smiles. They seemed unconcerned about whether they walked or rode. What they were doing was more important than how or when they reached their destination. I had never seen such proud, confident, happy people. Their message was clear: 'We are colored, Negro, black. We are whatever we decide we are. We are people of value and worth.' . . . A new day had dawned in Montgomery."[7]

The MIA's demands were few. Leaders did not seek the desegregation of buses but requested only three things: courteous treatment of black bus riders, first-come, first-served seating with black riders in the back and white riders in the front, and the hiring of black bus drivers on black routes. White city leaders rejected all three demands. In explanation, bus company attorney Jack Crenshaw stated, "If we granted the Negroes those demands, they would go about boasting of a victory that they had won over the white people, and this we will not allow."[8]

Thus, the boycott continued for nearly thirteen months. To maintain momentum, support, and solidarity for the boycott in the face of white intimidation and violence, black churches held mass meetings on Monday and Thursday nights. Meetings began at seven in the evening to allow working people to attend and often lasted two or three hours, resembling lively church services that included hymns and preaching. At each meeting, a collection was passed to raise money for boycott needs, including gasoline and car repairs to maintain an elaborate carpool system.

Georgia Gilmore, a local cook, raised large sums to support the movement by organizing a group of women into the Club from Nowhere, so named to prevent white people from discovering its purpose and shutting it down. Club members sold Gilmore's pies and cakes to black and white customers alike at beauty shops, laundries, cabstands, doctor's offices, stores, churches, and outside downtown cafeterias. All of the proceeds went to MIA, often $100 to $150 per week. At the mass meeting each Monday night, a club member presented the large cash donation and the crowd gave the Club from Nowhere a standing ovation.[9]

When the boycott began, Georgia Theresa Gilmore was a thirty-five-year-old single mother raising four children. Her friend Nelson Malden remembers her as a kind, generous, well-liked woman who "was hard on her daughters and spoiled her sons." She was friendly and jovial, known to talk at everybody's level and joke around. "And she could dance," Malden adds. "She had rhythm that you'd never seen before."[10] Gilmore was also a member of the NAACP and fearless. Food writer John T. Edge describes her as "a mountain of a woman [made] of girth, grit, and sass."[11] Rev. Thomas E. Jordan of the Lilly Baptist Church recalls: "She was a lady of great physical stature. She didn't take any junk from anybody. It didn't matter who you were. Even the white police officers let her be. She wasn't a mean person, but like it was with many African Americans, there was this perception that she might be dangerous. The word was, 'Don't mess with Georgia Gilmore, she might cut you.' But Lord, that woman could cook. I loved to sit down at her table for some good greasing."[12]

Gilmore worked as head cook at the National Café, a downtown cafeteria that catered to white blue-collar workers. She had been forced off a bus once herself and was active in the boycott from its inception, bringing sandwiches and pies to the first mass meetings. In an interview decades later, Gilmore describes the time,

> You know, you can take things, and take things, and take things. We were
> dealing with a new generation, and this new generation had decided that
> they just had taken as much as they could. They decided that they wouldn't

Georgia Gilmore
(photo courtesy of Rev.
Clarence E. Stewart Jr.)

ride the bus until there be Negro bus drivers and something could be done
about the way that the people would be treated. They decided that they
was tired of it and they wouldn't do it again no more. Sometime I walked
by myself and sometime I walked with different people, and I began to
enjoy walking, because for so long I guess that I had had this convenient
ride until I had forgot about how well it would be to walk. I walked a mile,
maybe two miles, some days. Going to and from. A lot of times some of the
young whites would come along and they would say, "Nigger, don't you
know it's better to ride the bus than it is to walk?" And we would say, "No,
cracker, no. We rather walk."[13]

Nearly three months into the boycott, on February 24, 1956, Georgia
Gilmore testified in the defense of eighty-nine arrested boycott leaders. She
joined other housewives, maids, and laborers in an attempt to prove the boycott's "just cause" by relating the abuses they had suffered. As *Time* magazine
reported, "after a lifetime of taking it quietly, their emotions welled up and
overflowed in their testimony. Some began talking before defense lawyers

asked for their names; others could hardly be stopped. Martha Kate Walker told how her blind husband's leg was hurt when a bus driver shut a door on him and drove on. Sadie Brooks told of seeing a Negro man forced from a bus at pistol-point because he did not have the correct change. Delia Perkins testified that a driver had called her an 'ugly black ape.' Richard Jordan said his pregnant wife had been forced to give her seat to a white woman. Georgia Teresa Gilmore said when she boarded a bus, the driver shouted, 'Come out, nigger, and go in the back door,' and when she stepped off, drove away."[14]

In her testimony, Gilmore identified the bus driver who once kicked her off a city bus. She also uttered Martin Luther King Jr.'s favorite line of the trial: "When they count the money, they do not know Negro money from white money." For her testimony, Gilmore was fired from her job. When she went to King for help, he advised her to start her own business and gave her the seed money. She opened her home as a lunch spot, and business took off immediately. Working at the café had given Gilmore both cooking experience and business sense. Further, African Americans had limited dining options and Gilmore's home was located in the heart of Centennial Hill, a thriving black neighborhood. It was never advertised as a restaurant, and Gilmore never called it one. As Martha Hawkins recalls, "Everybody just said they was going down by Georgia's to eat."[15]

Patrons ate at a large, old-fashioned dining room table surrounded by a dozen card table chairs. When those filled, there were a few stools here and there. Gilmore cooked in cast-iron skillets on a regular four-burner stove and served traditional southern fare, including fried chicken, baked chicken, fried fish, stew meat, liver, collard greens, turnip greens, cream potatoes, beans, potato salad, candied yams, and corn muffins. For a fixed price, customers were given one meat, two sides, cornbread, and sweet tea. Pie was extra, and it was usually sweet potato pie, made extraordinarily smooth with a heavy mixer. Gilmore always added coconut to the filling.

King was one of her regular customers, known for always drinking a second glass of her famous sweet tea. In fact, Gilmore became King's cook in Montgomery and often catered MIA meetings. She would walk from her home to King's parsonage, carrying a large basket full of fried chicken and potato salad. And as white reaction to the boycott turned violent, Gilmore's home became a haven where boycott leaders could converse in peace and knew the food was safe.[16]

After a Supreme Court ruling ended the boycott and desegregated Montgomery buses in December 1956, Gilmore continued to cook in her home. Throughout the 1960s and 1970s, she hosted many civil rights leaders and supporters, including President Lyndon Johnson and Robert Kennedy. Gilmore's had become more than a meeting place. It was a place of rejuvenation, commitment, and strength. As Hawkins explains, "that flavor of what happened inside her walls was what inspired me most. 'Twas something special happening there. The folks writing about Missus Gilmore described meals around her table as more like being at a rally than a restaurant. The feeling in her home became downright sacramental, a camp meeting of sorts with a continual loud and loving conversation about the things that mattered. Folks would feel free to stand or sit or walk about from room to room with plates of food in their hands. It was the fact that a person's cooking could become so much more than cooking—that's what I was aiming to do someday."[17]

Though the ambience at Gilmore's may have been unique in Montgomery, her home occupied a larger place in history, as part of a group of black-owned restaurants that functioned as gathering places for civil rights leaders in the 1950s and 1960s. In southern cities including Atlanta, Memphis, Birmingham, and Montgomery, black-owned restaurants located at the nexus of thriving black communities "became the hub where people from the movement met and planned their strategy," notes culinary historian Jessica Harris. They were "pivot points of history: places where black entrepreneurship met up with the growing national movement for Civil Rights for African Americans."[18]

At these restaurants, activists strategized over plates of traditional southern fare, like fried chicken, collards, macaroni and cheese, pork chops, okra, and cornbread. It was familiar food, grounded in the rural, black experience, food that had sustained the black community for hundreds of years.[19] Sweet potato pie especially represented this southern "comfort" food. As one journalist recalls, "the menu was scratched fresh everyday onto a blackboard and your choice was typically either chicken or ox-tail served up with greens and rice. For an extra dime you could have a piece of fresh homemade sweet potato pie."[20]

The blend of nourishing food, comforting surroundings, and revolutionary plans that defined these restaurants inspired the term "soul food" because, as Harris notes, the food "fed the spirit as much as the body on the long march to institutionalized equality."[21] Soul food, however, was not simply a label for homey African American fare. It was part of a broader national movement anchored in a budding black pride, a sense of black solidarity, and a desire to learn about, honor, and celebrate black heritage.[22] As Harris writes, "for the first time in many lives there was a palpable pride in the uniqueness of the African American experience in the United States. . . . The term 'soul food' harks back to this era, when everything that was black and of the moment had soul."[23]

Spawned by northern, working-class African Americans, "soul" will always be a shifting, enigmatic concept to define, but its roots lie in an authentic, down-home quality rooted in the rural southern experience. Soul was an attempt to recover and pay homage to the hardscrabble lives that many African Americans had left behind during the Great Migration north. Because soul was grounded in this life, it denoted both struggle and endurance. Soul encompassed the ability to survive in a racist society and the triumph represented by the civil rights movement. It was "We Shall Overcome" in a single word.[24]

In addition to uplifting black culture and validating black experience, soul connected urban black populations to their rural roots. It enabled educated African Americans living in northern cities and suburbs to resist assimilation into surrounding white communities, proudly proclaim their unique culture and heritage, and undermine white authority. As civil rights activist Bayard Rustin notes, soul was "membership in a mystical body to which Negroes belonged by birthright and from which whites for a change were excluded."[25]

Soul food lived at the heart of the movement, providing a means for upwardly mobile, urban African Americans to link to their rural ancestors. "Soul food was as much an affirmation as a diet," writes Harris. "Eating neckbones

Staff of Sylvia's, legendary soul food restaurant in Harlem, New York (photo by Carol M. Highsmith, Library of Congress, LC-HS503-4114)

and chitterlings, turnip greens and fried chicken, became a political statement . . . embraced by many middle-class blacks who had previously publicly eschewed it as a relic of a slave past."[26] As culinary historian Frederick Douglass Opie writes, "the survival food of black southerners became the revolutionary high cuisine of bourgeoisie African Americans."[27]

In reality, the dishes that make up soul food are southern dishes, consumed by black and white people alike for centuries. To northerners, soul food certainly appeared to be a black tradition. It was brought to the North by black southerners and consumed largely by African Americans in the North. Yet to white southerners, soul food was the food they had eaten all their lives. It was southern food. In truth, soul food was more class based than race based. As Opie writes, whether black or white, "every poor person struggling to survive [in the South] ate soul food on a regular basis."[28]

Although the actual dishes may be identical, soul food separates itself from southern food by underscoring its African American qualities. Black cooks were largely the ones to fuse African, European, and Native American traditions to create southern food. Soul includes the ability of these black cooks to transform ordinary ingredients, use whatever was at hand, follow the seasons, and spice to perfection. Soul emphasizes the African cooking techniques, food pairings, and seasonings that define southern food. "It was simple food," writes Opie, but "complex in its preparation."[29] Thus, soul food functions as both an emblem of black culture and a means to honor the cooks who created it.

The power of soul food existed at the heart of Martha Hawkins's girlhood dream of opening a special kind of restaurant. When she was still a young girl in Montgomery, this dream emerged amid the relief of returning home to a dinner of pork chop casserole after becoming lost in her new neighborhood. Hawkins recalls,

> Daddy spooned my plate high with the good casserole and I took the first
> bite and it felt like all the comfort of being where I was supposed to be.
> The casserole was salty and smooth from the butter and just about too hot
> to eat but I blew on my spoon and it went down my throat and made me

feel happy inside. All of a sudden, in that very same moment, I knew what I wanted to do with my life. . . . I would make a place where people could eat and I'd serve people comfort food like the pork chop casserole we was having tonight. It wouldn't be no ordinary restaurant neither. When people was out getting lost wandering around Union Circle or doing whatever people do to feel tight inside and worried that they might never find their way home, I would tell 'em to come into my restaurant, and they would feel like they had come home at last. Their mama would be cooking in that restaurant, or someone who seemed just like their mama to them, anyway. And they would sit next to friendly people they knowed, and grace would be prayed over their supper if they was praying folks, and they would settle in and give a big sigh and they would know that when they was eating supper in my restaurant that they had come home for sure. That's what I would do. I knowed it right there like I knows it for sure. I would open a restaurant someday and give people little slices of all that was good.[30]

Martha Hawkins would have her restaurant, but she walked a gritty path to get there. Hawkins was born in 1947, the tenth of twelve children. Her father worked at a fertilizer factory, then as a janitor. His children grew up in a segregated Montgomery. But it was not just the separation that stung. It was the fact that African Americans were constantly given second-class things to remind them of their status: raggedy school books, grubby water fountains, stand-only lunch counters, movie theaters full of rats, hard chairs in the waiting room. It wasn't only that black and white patients were separated in doctor's offices; it was that African Americans were forced to wait until the last white person was seen, regardless of whose appointment was first, or if the white person had an appointment at all.

Hawkins's father followed the civil rights movement in Montgomery, and she can recall every black person killed by white violence during her youth. She heard Martin Luther King Jr. speak several times and was part of a march broken up by Klansmen on horseback who "had whips and started busting the marchers with those whips. It didn't matter who it was or if you were a boy or girl, the whips busted down over and over. I heard them sizzle and zap, sizzle and zap. Folks were screaming now everywhere, all of us frenzied to get away."[31]

Hawkins became pregnant for the first time at age fifteen. She was married on her sixteenth birthday and divorced by eighteen. She gave birth to four boys in six years and quit high school after tenth grade. But despite the odds, Hawkins was determined to make a life for her sons. She worked the night shift at a local factory while her mother kept the boys. She worked despite numerous medical issues and intense pain. But when she fell victim to an unspeakably violent crime, Hawkins became suicidal and entered a mental hospital.

Still, she rose up. She started helping out at the hospital, visiting with residents or fixing their hair. "A job with a purpose," she says, "goes a long way toward healing a body." She also began reading the Bible, which offered "the best flood of healing I was drinking in. . . . That's how I was getting through one day to the next—by reminding myself of God's promises every morning, every afternoon, every evening, just reading, reading, reading. That's how I knew that things was gonna be all right someday."[32]

When Hawkins returned home, cooking became her solace. The kitchen had always been an inspiring, comforting place, where "like magic" her mother, Sally B., took plain garden ingredients and turned them into something incredible, and there was always enough to go around. Sally B. also sold cakes and pies and ran neighborhood fish fries and "heaven and hell suppers," comprised of spicy camp stew followed by pound cake and ice cream. Over decades, she stowed away the profits, until one day she shocked her husband by announcing she had saved the $1,000 necessary for a down payment on a suburban house.

So when Martha returned home, she recalls, "The cooking was flowing out of me as free and easy as breathing." She gives a description of Thanksgiving gravy and butter that parallels her rising hope and happiness as she healed and rediscovered her life's purpose:

> Let me tell you about that gravy I was making. It was simmering hot on
> the stove with the finest turkey pieces bobbing all about—'twas the giblets
> where all the flavor stays—and that gravy, I swear it was so full of joy at the

thought of being poured over that meal it was grinning right along with all my family members seated around my table; that gravy just splashed and laughed its way over peas and dressing and white meat and mashed potatoes. And the butter—it came to the dinner with a smiley personality, too. That good country butter was cooked into that feast with all joy I could beckon. It was melting into rolls and caressing those sauces and hugging the carrots and making everybody feel downright giddy. Have you ever felt giddy about butter? Not many folks realize that butter is an intoxicant. When it's made with love it's transformed along the same lines as that miracle wine Jesus dished up at the wedding in Cana. Butter refreshes the heart and soothes the soul and bursts forth from old wineskins because you can't contain the blessed spirit of good country butter.[33]

As Hawkins grounded herself in her kitchen, she felt increasing dread about her factory job, which she describes as "that thick, dull feeling that there's something more truthful to who you are that you should be doing."[34] So, listening to the "voice of love" moving in her life, Hawkins quit her factory job, gave up her suburban home, went on public assistance, and moved back to the projects. Her friends and family, predictably, thought she was crazy. No longer working the long shifts, however, allowed Hawkins to get involved in community work, and it was through this work that she made the connections that led to the fulfillment of her dream: opening her own restaurant.

Still, it was not a sudden realization. Hawkins waited over a year for the house that became her restaurant to come available. For another year she worked on the house piece by piece with whatever money she could save. Like Georgia Gilmore and Sally B., she sold cakes and pies. She bought one bucket of paint at a time, scraped off wallpaper by hand, and scrounged garage sales for pots and pans. She moved out of her own home and into the upstairs of the house to save money. As she says, "every dime I had went into opening that restaurant."[35]

At the same time, Hawkins remained committed to opening the restaurant her way. She rejected a $50,000 investment offer from a local bank in order to retain control. She vowed to hire those who were down on their

Martha's Place, 2010 (photo by Emily Blejwas)

luck, to make the restaurant "a place of second chances." She still envisioned something beyond the ordinary, "a special restaurant where folks can eat good food and talk about the things that matter and sort through life and feel good afterward."[36] During this time, she read about Georgia Gilmore and became inspired by the way her home had functioned as a place of renewal, unity, and strength during the bus boycott.

Martha's Place opened on October 17, 1988. Rosa Parks was one of the first customers and visited whenever she returned to Montgomery, always taking corn muffins to go. In 1989, Hawkins spoke with her role model, Georgia Gilmore, for the first time. Gilmore told Hawkins to enjoy the restaurant and not to run it for the money but because she loved it. She also told Hawkins how to make her famous sweet tea, with instructions that ended, "'just drink 'til you're tired. You can't have just one glass, you know, Martha. You will never want to stop drinking tea.' That's what she said to me," Hawkins recalls, "her voice all sassy and free."[37]

Sweet potato pie was on the menu the day Martha's Place opened, and she continues to bake five or six sweet potato pies every Wednesday, using her mother's recipe. She ticks off the ingredients: sweet potatoes, Carnation milk, eggs, sugar, butter, nutmeg, and flavor (vanilla extract). But the most important ingredient, she reminds me, is love. Some customers say they can feel it, "an actual tingle when they walk through the front door." It seems Hawkins has created the place she dreamed of as a child, where she would "give people little slices of all that was good" and they would know "they had come home for sure."[38]

TWELVE

||||||||||||||||||||||||||||||||||||||||||||||||||||||||||||||||||||||||||

Barbecue

Black History in the Black Belt

> In Alabama, barbecue is ecumenical. It is both urban and rural,
> black and white, tomato-sweet and vinegar-sour, pulled and
> chopped. It is cinder-block simple and strip-mall slick. A product
> of the working-class culture of the mills and factories, integrating
> all, it is one of the state's most unifying and enduring symbols.
>
> —Fred Sauceman, "Barbecue, Alabama Style"

LANNIE'S BAR-B-Q SPOT is located in a low-lying neighborhood of worn houses that runs along the railroad tracks on Selma's east side. Just before I pull up to owner Lula Hatcher's home, next door to the restaurant, four stray dogs ramble across the road in front of me. Against the cold February drizzle, Hatcher's living room is cozy and warm, full of plush furniture and a gas fireplace at full blast. Lavish Valentine's Day gift baskets made by one of her daughters crowd the dining room table. An image of President Barack Obama,

Lula Hatcher at Lannie's Bar-B-Q Spot (photo by Valerie Downes)

in office just a few weeks, is included among a dozen family photographs atop the TV cabinet, framed so he appears as another nephew or cousin.

Lula Hatcher was born in 1932, when Selma streets were made of dirt, and mules and wagons moved on them. But many Selma residents simply walked where they needed to go. Hatcher thought nothing of walking two hours to her grandmother's house in the country to pick peas and beans for her family. As the eldest of five, she often minded her younger siblings, cooked, cleaned, washed clothes on a rub board, ironed, and carried dinner to her parents at their workplace. By the age of ten, Hatcher also cooked in the homes of two white women. "My mother didn't have to tell me nothing," Hatcher says. "I knew what needed to be done and I did it."[1]

Loosely defined as "meat slow roasted over a smoldering fire," barbecue has existed in Alabama from its earliest days. First as a Native American tradition

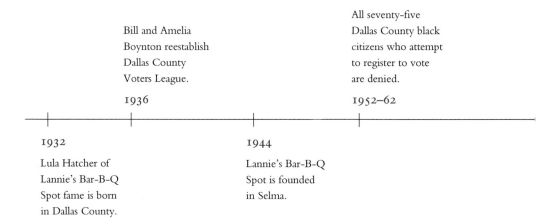

Bill and Amelia
Boynton reestablish
Dallas County
Voters League.

1936

All seventy-five
Dallas County black
citizens who attempt
to register to vote
are denied.

1952–62

1932

Lula Hatcher of
Lannie's Bar-B-Q
Spot fame is born
in Dallas County.

1944

Lannie's Bar-B-Q
Spot is founded
in Selma.

and later as a pioneer, plantation, and working-class staple, barbecue is fundamental to Alabama cuisine. On the frontier, barbecues brought scattered communities together to socialize, dance to the music of fiddles and banjos, and display a growing reputation for southern hospitality.[2] They were festive, entertaining, and boisterous events, sometimes resulting in whiskey-inspired violence and often used by politicians to reach large numbers of voters.

By the 1840s, barbecues had become a southern institution, with the largest gatherings hosting ten thousand guests or more. Marking every stage of the Civil War, barbecues were held to honor new companies, raise war funds, welcome troops home, and raise money for veteran causes and monuments. In the late 1800s, barbecue served as the centerpiece of an expanding range of events, including school celebrations, social club gatherings, estate sales, land sales, community improvement efforts, railroad benefits, veterans reunions, and church and organizational fundraisers.

The year 1920 marked a new phase of barbecue in the South. Sandwich

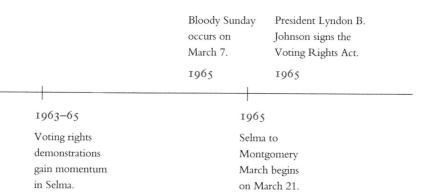

Bloody Sunday
occurs on
March 7.

1965

President Lyndon B.
Johnson signs the
Voting Rights Act.

1965

1963–65

Voting rights
demonstrations
gain momentum
in Selma.

1965

Selma to
Montgomery
March begins
on March 21.

bread and hamburger buns became widely available, giving birth to the barbecue sandwich and giving sauces a new importance. Formerly, barbecue sauce was a simple combination of vinegar, butter, salt, and pepper, used only to baste the meat. Now cooks began experimenting with sauces served directly on the sandwich or alongside it, for dipping. Throughout the 1920s and 1930s, cookbooks and magazines offered a steady supply of barbecue sauce recipes.

Made in infinite variety, particular sauces began to define both individual cooks and regions of the South. Over the next fifty years, distinctive regional styles of barbecue took hold.[3] "Southern barbecue is the closest thing we have in the U.S. to Europe's wines or cheeses," notes New Orleans food expert Lolis Eric Elie. "Drive a hundred miles and the barbecue changes."[4] Alabama alone boasts at least six regional barbecue sauces: tomato-based Tennessee, Birmingham Greek, north Alabama vinegar, spicy orange mustard in the east, pecan seasoned along the coast, and Decatur's specialty white sauce made from mayonnaise, apple cider vinegar, and lemon juice.[5]

These geographic differences have sparked fervent debate among south-erners over what constitutes "real" barbecue, including disputes over the defi-nition of the South, the definition of barbecue, the correct spelling of the word, the type of meat, the type of cut, sauce ingredients, the type of pit, the type of wood, wet versus dry cooking, the best barbecue places, and the method of preparation.[6] And southerners don't take these differences lightly. As food writer Stephen Smith puts it, "barbecue is serious business in the South."[7] Arkansas reporter Max Brantley elaborates: "[Southerners] don't just eat barbecue. They spend hours perfecting home recipes; they burn tanks of gasoline searching for it; they argue about it. Emotions run high. Nothing I've written stirred more comment, or brought down more abuse, than a series of articles about barbecue. . . . For my opinion, I was branded a socialist by a Malvern woman—no kidding—and drew letters of criticism from two states."[8]

Despite the disagreements, southerners are quick to praise the unifying aspect of barbecue, beloved by all walks of life from the nation's earliest days. Some southerners maintain that you can judge a barbecue place by its park-ing lot. If the barbecue is good, the lot will contain a mix of rusty pick-ups, expensive imports, minivans, college kid hatchbacks, and boatlike Buicks. As Tennessee columnist Vince Staten writes, true barbecue lies "in the hands of the rugged individualists who hand-letter their signs and spot-solder their homemade pits. It's still the people's food."[9]

This unifying quality gave barbecue a singular role during the civil rights movement, when some barbecue restaurants became the first interracial insti-tutions in deeply segregated southern communities. The reason was simple. African Americans operated most southern barbecue joints, so white diners wanting barbecue patronized black-owned restaurants, making them the only spaces that black and white people occupied together as equals. No example of this strange pocket of equality is more poignant than Lannie's Bar-B-Q Spot in Selma, Alabama.

The city of Selma sits at the heart of Alabama's Black Belt, which stretches 175 miles across the state's midsection. Though the Black Belt originally took its name from its dark, highly fertile soil, the name now also reflects a high concentration of African Americans. In antebellum years, the Black Belt was a vast region of cotton plantations that held 75 percent of Alabama's slaves, fueled the state economy, and wielded Alabama's political power. It was one of the wealthiest regions in the nation, and Selma was its "Queen City."[10] Located on the Alabama River with critical rail and water access, Selma was the business, banking, and transportation hub of the Black Belt. In the decades leading up to the Civil War, surrounding Dallas County produced more cotton than any other county in Alabama, and Selma held the area's largest slave market.[11]

Cotton prices collapsed during the Civil War, severely wounding Alabama's economy and dampening the prominence, power, and production of the Black Belt. During Reconstruction, a significant number of black citizens served in Selma and Dallas County government, including five county commissioners, four city councilmen, a tax collector, coroner, and criminal court judge. Two black men from Selma, Jeremiah Haralson and Benjamin Sterling Turner, served in the Alabama state legislature. Selma also boasted the first black police officer in Alabama and one of the few black-owned cotton gins in the state.

Reconstruction ended swiftly, however, with the withdrawal of federal troops in 1877. Selma's white residents reasserted their power, pushing African Americans into menial labor. The Alabama Constitution of 1901 disenfranchised nearly all persons of color, Klan violence peaked, and the Jim Crow era of strict segregation took hold. In Selma, segregation was so rigid that only white prisoners were allowed to work in white cemeteries. In 1936, county officials canceled an annual black community sing because white people didn't want so many African Americans congregating in one place.

Selma native and pioneering civil rights attorney J. L. Chestnut reflects on the city in the 1930s, when Lula Hatcher was a young girl: "Your place was obvious: black people sat up in the 'buzzard roost' at the white movie theaters and the white people sat downstairs. My mother and Aunt Lennie couldn't try on clothes in the department stores or use the restrooms. Only one downtown store, S. H. Kress, had a 'colored' restroom. A few of the white cafés had separate little eating rooms for blacks; most just had a window where you placed an order from the sidewalk. Everywhere, black folk had to wait until all the white people were served."[12]

Segregation in Selma was backed not only by law but also by intimidation, violence, and economic reprisal. Longtime resident and voting rights advocate Amelia Boynton Robinson explains: "Having one's office across from a Southern jail for thirty years has quite an effect upon one who is in sympathy with the downtrodden. I could hear cries and pleas of prisoners, and often the sound of straps which lashed their bare backs. Many times I closed the door to keep from hearing the weeping of grown men and women. Brutality and injustice we lived with, every day. The very law and order represented by the enforcement officers was such a travesty that it was no wonder the black man was filled with fear when he saw a white man. Day after day, there were black people who feared meeting an officer on the street, because he might suddenly begin beating, kicking, or clubbing him unmercifully, seemingly without cause."[13]

In 1930s Selma, white people lived on the west side of town and African Americans on the east, where almost all of the roads were unpaved because the city required black residents to pay for their own paving and few black neighborhoods could afford it. Most African Americans worked as domestic aides or as field laborers, toiling from early morning until nightfall. An unspoken agreement existed among white people never to sell land to African Americans, so black residents of Selma rarely had the chance to own land. Instead, they were confined to sharecropping, consigned to a life of debt and dependence.[14]

In the early decades of the twentieth century, black southerners began running barbecue stands as a means of income and as "a route toward self-sufficiency and independence in a society that offered few other opportunities."[15] Early stand owners built on a deep historical link between African Americans and barbecue, as detailed by Robert Moss in *Barbecue: The History of an American Institution*. From the 1600s, West African slaves brought barbecue methods gleaned from Taino-Arawak Indians in the Caribbean to the United States and

Sidewalk scene in Selma, Alabama, 1935 (photo by Walker Evans, Library of Congress, LC-USF342-001142-A)

are largely responsible for developing the techniques and recipes of southern barbecue. On plantations, pitmasters were predominantly black male slaves who cooked for white crowds. Slaves also held their own barbecues during Sundays and holidays when they were typically free from labor.

Following the Civil War, barbecue remained a core food tradition for African Americans. It was the centerpiece of a wide range of community celebrations and the most important black social events, including Emancipation Day (typically held on January 1 in Alabama) and the Fourth of July (a holiday then ignored by most white southerners). As African Americans began migrating to northern cities and to the West Coast, they carried barbecue to new parts of the country.

By the late 1800s, barbecues had become the primary form of summer entertainment and quintessential form of public gathering in Alabama. A soaring demand for pitmasters prompted the emergence of "barbecue men":

experienced pitmasters who earned a living traveling regionally to cook for large private gatherings and public events. Barbecue men were in high demand, and event organizers routinely advertised the pitmaster to draw more participants, as having a famous "barbecue man" was a huge draw. Many barbecue men were black, and though they presided over massive events for the white community, they were prohibited from dining at the main tables.

Before 1900, barbecue was almost always given away at events hosted by organizations or prominent citizens. This began to change, however, in the late 1880s, when barbecue stands cropped up at fairs, expositions, and festivals. Some southerners began selling barbecue out of their backyards, while others sold from stands on vacant city lots or alongside the nation's new highways. By World War I, barbecue stands were commonplace throughout the South. Stand owners soon expanded operations, adding dining areas and brick and cinderblock pits elevated to waist level. Early barbecue restaurants were often weekend businesses: owners barbecued a whole hog on Thursday and sold it through the weekend until the meat ran out.[16]

Lannie's Bar-B-Q Spot was typical of the times, founded in 1944 when Lula Hatcher's mother and stepfather, Lannie and Will Travis, pulled a storage shed from the back of their property to the front and started selling barbecue from it on the weekends. Lula, a young teenager, was often charged with riding her bicycle to the stockyard and carrying the hog home in her basket. She laughs as she recalls how a stockyard man would tie the hog's legs together so he couldn't jump out. She also used her bicycle to carry the block of ice from the icehouse to the barbecue shed for the drinks. "Back then," Hatcher says, "everything you did, you did it the hard way."

When Lula returned home with the hog, her stepfather boiled it in a wash pot, then scraped it clean to remove all the hair and hung it from a tree to cut it open. The hog was killed on Thursday and cooked overnight, over coals in a hole in the ground covered by wire, to be ready for Friday morning. Lula and her siblings helped to clean the chitterlings (intestines), and their mother used the hog's organs to make a gumbo for the family.

While Will Travis cooked the hog, Lannie did everything else. "She

Barbecue men in Montgomery, Alabama, 1928 (Auburn University Libraries, 71.25.5.18)

worked all the time," recalls Hatcher, who is hard pressed to recall any memory of her mother when she was not working. Hatcher has been told she looks like her mother and is similar in manner, quiet and calm. But the resemblances don't end there. Hatcher has also worked all her life. She began selling barbecue at the age of twelve and never stopped.

Some things got easier over the years. An above-ground block pit was constructed for cooking the meat. The shed was replaced by a wooden building, then a block building, then the restaurant in 1987. Hatcher laughs about how much easier it is with the ice machines they have now. But some things didn't change, like the constant work and long hours. Hatcher spent decades minding her eight children during the day, then working at the restaurant from four in the afternoon to eleven at night. Though it was hard work, she maintains that "it was better to be my own boss than to have to work somewhere else."

Sumter County Barbecue Clubs

Sumter County, situated at the Black Belt's far western edge, is home
to the only existing barbecue clubs in Alabama. They date to the
1800s, although the oldest continuous clubs formed between the late
1920s and the early 1950s. No one seems to know why the clubs are
confined to Sumter County. They may be unique to Sumter, or other
Alabama counties may have once had barbecue clubs that died out. As
southern food writer John T. Edge notes, "finding these barbecue clubs
is the foodways equivalent of finding a country juke in the Mississippi
Delta where Muddy Waters is still playing an acoustic guitar."*

Indeed, the barbecue clubs are a decidedly rural phenomenon. Although
home to fewer than fourteen thousand people, Sumter County boasts
seven barbecue clubs, all belonging to towns with up to a few hundred
residents. The newest club, formed in Sumterville in 2001, is comprised
of members of other clubs who did not want to travel so far (six miles) to
attend monthly club dinners. Sumter County's two largest towns have
never had barbecue clubs, making it likely the clubs emerged as a means
for rural communities to reunite after the winter rains, which turned Black
Belt roads into sticky, impassable muck. Further, barbecue was a natural
event choice in farming communities where hogs were once abundant.†

Today, the clubs still revolve around meeting the social needs of rural
people, with all seven clubs citing fellowship as their reason for being.
As Gump Ozment of the Sumterville club remarks, "in the country,
the only time you see folks is when you go to church, go to a funeral,
or go to a barbecue club." The clubs hold monthly dinners from May
through October (although some skip July because of the heat). They
purposely convene on different nights to allow Sumter County residents
to attend more than one dinner each month. According to a Cuba club
member, the dinners are "just country people having a good time."‡

Only club members and their guests are allowed to attend, and only hog meat cooked over an open fire is served. All of the clubs used to roast their own hogs, but as hogs became less widely available and members less willing to spend all night roasting one, many clubs switched to buying meat from local vendors. In all of the clubs, however, the men still gather to pull the meat. The "fellowship of the pulling process," notes Alabama historian Valerie Pope Burnes, "is as important to the club as eating the meal."[§] At the barbecue's end, any leftover meat is divided between the hosts. The meat is never sold, out of a sense that it is "priceless." As a member of the Epes club says, "it's more about the feeling of community than the product."

Many of the clubs meet in community houses transformed from old schoolhouses or churches. Each member brings a side dish or two, which commonly include coleslaw, white bread, baked beans, potato salad, deviled eggs, and sweet tea. Over the years, club members have become well-known for certain dishes and are expected to bring them, like Miss Sarah's lemon cake at the Emelle club. Members also expect dishes to be homemade. An Epes club member once dumped a store-bought cake in the trash before it could be served. All of the clubs also maintain gendered activities. As Burnes notes, the men often prepare the sauce and cook and pull the meat "while women prepare the rest of the food and coordinate the serving line. In the Epes Club, the men serve the meat and the sauce, while the women serve the tea. In the Boyd Club, the men go down one side of the table, while the women and children go down the other side."[**]

All of the Sumter County clubs serve a tomato- and ketchup-based sauce, reflecting the era in which they were formed, when barbecue sauce recipes began including sugar and commercially prepared products like ketchup and Worcestershire sauce. The sauces also reflect the culture of Sumter County, largely settled by emigrants from

North Carolina who brought a tomato-based sauce tradition to the area. However, each club serves its own distinct sauce of which members are feverishly proud. A Cuba club member claims her club's sauce "is so good you can drink it."†† Club sauce recipes are handed down through the generations and are sometimes kept secret.

Bud Williams began coming to Epes, Alabama, to visit his grandparents when he was a newborn, in 1933. His father was an Epes native, and Bud spent most of his childhood summers and holidays here. He recalls 1940s Epes as a bustling place, home to downtown shops and a bank, hotel, barrel staves mill, and stockyard to which cattle were driven on horseback through the fenceless countryside. In 1982, Williams returned permanently to Epes, where two of his cousins still lived and still made the Epes barbecue club's original sauce, created by Stanton Motes.

Williams fell into making the Epes sauce and soon became well-known for it. By 2010, he was making three gallons a week and keeping mason jars of it ready at the house to sell or give away, in addition to the sauce for the barbecue club's monthly dinners. He starts by melting a pound of margarine in a large steel pot, over low heat. The margarine, he tells me, holds all of the ingredients together. He then mixes the ketchup into the margarine before adding the rest of the ingredients: white vinegar, Worcestershire sauce, mustard, salt, black pepper, and red pepper. He mixes all of it using a drill with a paint stirrer attached. (He cut down the paint stirrer handle so the whole contraption would fit neatly in the pot.) The sauce is heated but not boiled, to prevent it from sticking to the bottom and burning.

When the sauce is ready, Williams tucks the pot into the corner of the bed of his pickup truck and we drive to the Epes community center. He tells me about making plum jelly and sauerkraut, and about his life before he returned to Epes: twenty years in the military, driving a city

Uncle Thump's Original Barbecue Sauce

BUD WILLIAMS; ORIGINALLY MADE BY STANTON MOTES*

1 lb. butter or margarine

2 gal. ketchup

1 gal. white vinegar

10 oz. Worcestershire sauce

6 oz. mustard

2 oz. black pepper

1 oz. red pepper (not Cayenne)—to make spicy, add another ounce

Yields 3 gallons.

   * This recipe was given to me by Bud Williams.

bus, working on a horse farm in Virginia. We pass a small white house that holds his first memory of Epes: he used to sit on its front porch swing with his grandparents, listening for trains to blow for the river bridge, then watching them pummel across. "Trains don't sound the same anymore," he tells me, since they switched from steam to diesel.

The community house is a one-room schoolhouse built in the early 1900s. After Williams' parents married in 1929, his mother taught school here. An old firehouse sits behind it, off to one side. Beyond that, teenagers gather for pick-up basketball and base-ball games held on a single court and adjacent field. Directly behind the schoolhouse sits the new community center, unfinished.

The men (and one woman) have already gathered to pull the meat. Thunder rumbles far off and the humidity is intense. The men's shirts and brows are soaked with sweat. They stand quietly around a wooden table that Williams recently fashioned with new legs. They are grateful for the added height, and they discuss Williams' next idea: to install a drain in the center to stop the meat juices from running off the table edges and onto their shoes.

"Alabama barbecue is synonymous with pulled pork," one of the men tells me. "In North Carolina, they chop it. It's worthless."

The social aspect of the barbecue club is immediately apparent. The men talk about people they know: who is in the hospital, who braved the storm last Sunday to attend church. They talk of family names and county history and when structures were built. They recall how Epes used to be and tell stories about the past, including one about former county commissioner Stump Steamwinder. Inside the schoolhouse, where the women set out the food as it arrives, the talk is much the same, minus the recollections of military service and guns.

Even though the barbecue starts at seven, families begin arriving much earlier, all of them carrying a few side dishes tucked into large picnic baskets. The side dishes are set on a long row of tables set end to end and covered with pink tablecloths. The last table holds two large galvanized washtubs, one for sweet tea and one for unsweet. Anyone who has brought a gallon of tea simply pours it into the right tub. The women cut desserts and arrange dishes, ensuring each has the proper serving utensil.

At seven, the members and their families gather around the steps of the community house. Members introduce any guests they have brought and a blessing is given. Then, they file through the line that starts with barbecue and continues with baked beans, vegetables, salads, fruit, and numerous desserts. Most members carry wide plastic lunch trays brought from home to hold all the food. Outside, families have marked their places at three rows of picnic tables using tablecloths. Vases of flowers and cans of bug spray serve as centerpieces. There is a casual feeling among the participants who wear everyday clothes and talk of everyday things.

Many of the members are older. Participation has dwindled over the decades, as rural people became increasingly mobile and able to access new forms of entertainment and as younger generations continue relocating to cities. But the Sumter County barbecue clubs are

Pulling meat at Epes Barbecue Club, Bud Williams pointing to center of table (photo by Emily Blejwas)

determined to survive. Becky Robertson, president of the Epes club since 2003, has diligently worked to increase membership, especially among the younger generation and the black community. Like many of the barbecue clubs in Sumter County, Epes has dropped the requirement that members must live within town limits. Most of the Epes club members are from the nearby college town of Livingston. The clubs have also benefited from a surge of recent attention, as word spreads about this singular barbecue phenomenon way out in west Alabama.[‡‡]

* Spencer 2008:6A.

† History of barbecue clubs in Sumter County based on Burnes 2011 and McAlpine and Burnes 2009.

‡ McAlpine and Burnes 2009; Spencer 2008:6A (Gump Ozment); McAlpine and Burnes 2009:11 (Cuba club member).

§ Burnes 2011:36.

** Burnes 2011:39.

†† McAlpine and Burnes 2009:11.

‡‡ Description of Epes Barbecue Club drawn from personal interviews with Becky Robertson and Bud Williams, 2010, Sumter County, AL, and participation in Epes Barbecue Club dinner.

Lannie's was always one of the most popular barbecue spots in Selma, frequented by black and white patrons alike despite the city's strict segregation code. In the 1960s, when Selma was the scene of violent clashes between black demonstrators and white deputies, Lannie's was one of the only places in town where black and white people shared space as equals. Black diners in the voting rights movement ate alongside local white people and out-of-town freedom workers. When I ask whether Selma police ever gave Hatcher any trouble for violating the city's segregation law, she chuckles. "I guess not. They was eating here too."[17]

Despite serious economic retaliation and threats of violence, the Dallas County Voters League had been encouraging black residents to register to vote in Selma for decades by the time the voting rights movement gained momentum in the early 1960s. Between 1952 and 1962, seventy-five African Americans in Dallas County attempted to register to vote and all were rejected. In 1963, black residents began lining up almost daily at the courthouse to register and were routinely harassed, beaten, arrested, and pushed away by police officers using sticks, fists, and cattle prods.[18]

Jim Clark, the Dallas County sheriff at the time, was known to be racist, high strung, and belligerent. He donned a military helmet and usually carried a billy club. In addition to the courthouse violence, Clark and his officers routinely harassed black citizens attending voter registration meetings, recording their names and threatening to inform their employers. During one meeting, Clark and his men smashed the taillights on every car parked outside the church, then arrested black drivers on their way home for driving without them.

In February 1965, voting rights demonstrations in the nearby town of Marion, Alabama, turned deadly when a young demonstrator named Jimmie Lee Jackson was shot by police and died a few days later. The cry to carry Jackson's body to the steps of the state capitol evolved into a memorial march for voting rights. On March 7, hundreds of marchers started out from Selma, intending to make a four-day pilgrimage to Montgomery.

As the marchers reached the apex of the Edmund Pettus Bridge in Selma,

John Lewis (*lower left*), Bloody Sunday, Selma, Alabama, 1965 (Library of Congress, LC-USZ62 -127732)

they saw what marcher John Lewis called "a sea of blue."[19] Alabama state troopers had formed a blockade, gas masks on their belts and billy clubs in hand. They stood three deep across all four lanes of the highway wearing dark-blue shirts and sky-blue hard hats. On the sidelines stood Sheriff Clark and his deputies, some on horseback and some on foot. All of the officers were under order from Alabama governor George Wallace to stop the march.

When the marchers came within twenty-five yards, after a brief exchange, the troopers moved forward in a rush, knocking the first dozen demonstrators off their feet. Marchers panicked, screamed, and ran. Tear gas clouded the scene. Police beat marchers with billy clubs while deputies charged their horses into the fleeing crowd. On the sidelines, some white people cheered and let out rebel yells. The police continued beating people all the way down the street, chasing them on horseback up the steps of Brown Chapel American Methodist Episcopal Church and in the door. With no city ambulances for African Americans, three black funeral homes used hearses to transport the injured to the church, which was turned into a makeshift hospital for seventy-eight injured marchers.

Eventually, all of the marchers had taken refuge in the church or in their homes while deputies continued to parade back and forth outside Brown Chapel and in the surrounding neighborhood. State troopers stalked the downtown streets, beating on the hoods of African Americans' cars and ordering them to "get the hell out of town. We want all niggers off the streets." According to the *Selma Times-Journal*, "thirty minutes after the marchers' encounter with the troopers, a Negro could not be seen" on the streets of Selma.[20]

News coverage of the assault broke into regularly scheduled television programming that evening and stunned the nation. The day was dubbed "Bloody Sunday," and for the first time, Americans across the country stood behind the civil rights movement. Some rushed to Selma to show their support. As Selma minister Rev. Frederick Reese recalled,

> About 10:30, 11:00 that night, we were still at the church. If you can,
> imagine a congregation being somewhat subdued and the spirits low.
> And all these question marks whether or not we should continue in this
> same vein. Then you hear the door of the church opening and there is a
> group of people, black and white, who came from New Jersey. They had
> chartered a plane. And they walked into the church, down the aisle to the
> front, and said to us, "We are here to share with the people of Selma in this
> struggle for the right to vote. We have seen on the television screen the
> violence that took place today, and we're here to share it with you." There
> was a round of applause in the church and you could feel a change in the
> atmosphere—a spirit of inspiration, motivation, hope, coming back into the
> eyes and into the minds of these people—and then renewed commitment to
> the nonviolent method.[21]

Eight days later, President Lyndon Johnson appeared in a national televised address viewed by seventy million Americans and asked Congress to pass new voting rights legislation. The following day, Montgomery federal court judge Frank Johnson approved the march from Selma to Montgomery

Marchers on Edmund Pettus Bridge during the Selma to Montgomery March, 1965 (Alabama Department of Archives and History, Montgomery, Alabama, Q3013)

and sent 1,800 Alabama National Guardsmen, 1,000 army troops, 100 FBI agents, and 100 federal marshals to protect the marchers.

On March 21, 1965, marchers gathered in Selma to begin the historic Selma to Montgomery March for voting rights. Black and white marchers and religious leaders of all faiths participated. As one reporter related, "In the procession, whites and Negroes, clergymen and beatniks, old and young, walked side by side. There was a blind man from Atlanta on the arm of his 64-year-old mother. There was a one-legged man from Michigan swinging along on crutches."[22] Martin Luther King Jr. gave the send-off, saying "walk together, children, don't you get weary, and it will lead us to the Promised Land. And Alabama will be a new Alabama, and America will be a new America."[23]

Lula Hatcher participated in the voting rights demonstrations, or as she calls it, "standing in line all day trying to get to the courthouse. We did that for weeks," she says. She was not marching on Bloody Sunday but recalls the horror of those who were, including children, afraid the men and horses would run them right off the bridge and into the water. Hatcher did join the Selma to Montgomery March two weeks later. She walked until she reached the air force base at the edge of town, then turned for home. She had, after all, children to mind and a business to run.

Today, Lannie's is still one of the most popular barbecue restaurants in Selma. When natives who have moved away return home, they often stop at Lannie's to pick up barbecue before even reaching their destination. Hatcher's son, Floyd, now runs the restaurant and makes the sauce Lannie created in the 1940s. "I guess the Lord give her that recipe," Hatcher says. A family secret, the recipe is being passed through the generations, and patrons can only find it at Lannie's. Hatcher tried having it bottled once, but it just didn't taste the same.

Though the sauce hasn't changed, the neighborhood has. Hatcher hardly knows any of her neighbors anymore. Most of the older residents have died, and the young people "move in and out, in and out," she says. Last year, Hatcher discovered she had cervical cancer. Though she is impeccably and stylishly dressed, she is self-conscious about her short hair, still growing back after chemotherapy. "Miraculously, it didn't spread," she says. "It was truly a blessing from God." In fact, this whole interview has taken on a sense of blessing. As if this particular moment has been stopped, preserved, and held up to the light for one last look. This sense solidifies when Hatcher happens to mention that Annie Cooper, age ninety-nine, is sitting at the kitchen table in the next room.[24]

Annie Cooper, a Selma native and well-respected member of the black community, was fired from her job the day after she attempted to register to vote. A few weeks later, on January 25, 1965, she marched with four hundred demonstrators to the Selma courthouse. When Sheriff Clark grabbed her roughly, she told him: "Don't jerk me like that!" He responded by hitting her in the back of the head. Cooper began punching the sheriff repeatedly until a few of his men grabbed her and threw her to the ground, then smacked her

Annie Cooper outside Lannie's Bar-B-Q Spot (photo courtesy of Lula Hatcher)

in the eye with a billy club and handcuffed her. Cooper told Clark, "I wish you would hit me, you scum!" and Clark clubbed her head so hard that the sound echoed down the street.

Clark's men dragged Cooper away as she sang "Jesus, Keep Me Near the Cross." She stayed in jail eleven hours, singing through much of it, until the jailer (who was afraid Clark would kill Cooper) released her late at night. After Cooper's violent exchange with Clark, civil rights leaders in Selma reminded followers of the movement's call for nonviolence. But the photograph of Cooper bloodied by Clark brought national publicity to the movement, and Cooper became a folk hero in Selma, known affectionately as "the lady who beat the hell out of Clark."[25]

I shake Annie Cooper's hand before walking next door to Lannie's with a strange gravity, certain that few will step into Lula Hatcher's house as it is today ever again. J. L. Chestnut once described Lannie's sauce as having "a tangy, tomatoey, molasses tinge type taste."[26] I will add that it is not for the faint of heart. It is as Chestnut described but also has a serious vinegar kick that takes my breath away for a split second each time I taste it, almost like a tiny electric shock. I can feel that sauce in my chest all the way to Montgomery.

THIRTEEN

‖‖

MoonPies

Mardi Gras in Mobile

> The South of every country is different, and the south of every
> South is even more so. I come from that stretch of Gulf Coast South
> which is another kingdom. Mobile is a Separate Kingdom. We are
> not North America; we are North Haiti. Because we are so different
> from the rest of the United States. The spirit is closer to the Caribe
> than it is even to Montgomery. . . . You've got pirates and drama
> and Carnival and fishing fleets and smuggling and so many different
> skies and thunderstorms, like this constantly changing pageant in the
> background. It's another country. And that's where I come from.
>
> —Eugene Walter, *Milking the Moon*

DURING THE MONTH-LONG Mardi Gras season in Mobile, the birthplace of
Mardi Gras in America, more than thirty parades roll through the downtown
streets, each featuring a dozen floats. And at every parade, off of every float,
the prized catch is a MoonPie, a traditional southern snack made from graham

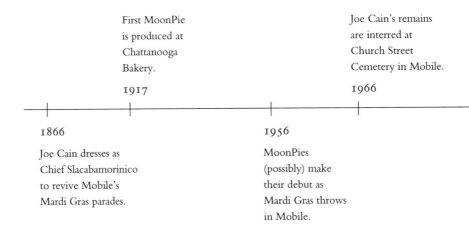

First MoonPie
is produced at
Chattanooga
Bakery.

1917

Joe Cain's remains
are interred at
Church Street
Cemetery in Mobile.

1966

1866

Joe Cain dresses as
Chief Slacabamorinico
to revive Mobile's
Mardi Gras parades.

1956

MoonPies
(possibly) make
their debut as
Mardi Gras throws
in Mobile.

cookies and marshmallow that comes in a variety of flavors. Parade crowds chant and clamor for MoonPies. "You can throw a MoonPie at a two-year-old child and a fifty-year old will knock them out of the way to get it," says city councilman Fred Richardson. "If you run out of MoonPies, you might as well just lay down on the float. You can throw beads for a little while, but the people will start calling for MoonPies."[1]

MoonPies missed in the air are still in play upon hitting the ground. As Mobilian Carrie Dozier explains, her MoonPies "aren't caught in the air, but by scraping my fingernails like a rake on the pavement. It didn't hurt! All that mattered was that I got a MoonPie!" Dozier even claims that MoonPies "from the parades have a different taste. These are the real things!" And when MoonPies land "tauntingly outside the traffic barricade," notes parade goer Kim Kearley, they are retrieved "by savvy children able to perform the fluid 'under the barricade leg scissor.'" Others bring rakes.

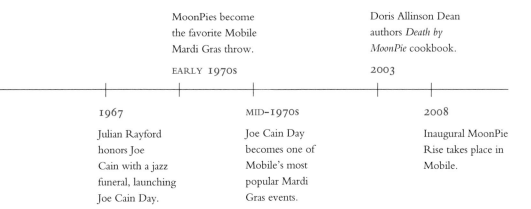

MoonPies become the favorite Mobile Mardi Gras throw.

EARLY 1970S

Doris Allinson Dean authors *Death by MoonPie* cookbook.

2003

1967

Julian Rayford honors Joe Cain with a jazz funeral, launching Joe Cain Day.

MID-1970S

Joe Cain Day becomes one of Mobile's most popular Mardi Gras events.

2008

Inaugural MoonPie Rise takes place in Mobile.

The magnitude of MoonPies in the Mardi Gras experience occurred suddenly to Fred Richardson, who had been searching for a way to brand Mobile since joining the city council in 1997. "I was talking with someone one day about MoonPies and it hit me," Richardson explains. "The MoonPie is us. It's synonymous with Mobile. They don't throw MoonPies in New Orleans. The MoonPie is ours. It was right under our noses, but we hadn't done anything with it yet."

Fred Richardson exudes charisma, punctuating his stories with bursts of laughter, eye rolls, hand gestures, and mimicked voices. Throughout our interview, he gives the impression of not really sitting in his chair, but perching there, as if he could leap up at any second, with too much energy for a simple chair to contain him. As it turns out, Richardson's ideas are as big as his personality. His first MoonPie idea: to throw a giant MoonPie off the tallest building in Mobile.

Mobile Mardi Gras parade (photo by Lyle W. Ratliff, *Mobile Press-Register*)

"I told him, Fred, we are a city of *integrity*, we need to do something to *enrich* our image," recalls Barbara Drummond, executive director of Community Affairs for the City of Mobile. Richardson's MoonPie idea was also rejected on the grounds of safety, cleanup, and liability. But he was nowhere close to giving up. He gathered Drummond and other city leaders around a table in Drummond's office to brainstorm about the MoonPie.

The group wanted to do something sustainable and came up with the idea of an electronic MoonPie. They also wanted to do an event on New Year's Eve, which had become a slow time for downtown businesses and hotels, with few attendees at First Night activities. The group dreamed up a MoonPie Rise (as opposed to a ball drop) over the city of Mobile on New Year's Eve, which would also serve to kickoff the Mardi Gras season. Drummond contacted veteran float builder Steve Mussell about building the giant, electronic MoonPie.

A Mobile native, Mussell began his float-building career at the age of five when he pulled wheels off of toy army Jeeps and attached them to dragons made from toilet paper tubes. After studying art and architecture in Atlanta, Mussell returned immediately to Mobile in 1975 to build Mardi Gras floats, the only job he's had since. He now works year-round, manages a staff of ten full-time employees, and constructs sixty to seventy floats per season. And he's still a bit nostalgic about those dragons, the emblem float of the Mystics of Time: "They always seemed so mysterious. And you know they've changed a lot over the years. People don't recognize it, but it's just like a child growing. You don't notice it on a daily basis, but if you look back at pictures, you see the changes."

"At first I thought it was kind of silly," recalls Mussell, of the MoonPie idea. "I think everyone did." Yet after realizing Richardson and Drummond were in earnest and meeting with excited city electrical and construction workers, "it changed my attitude," Mussell says. "Their enthusiasm was contagious." In fact, many in Mobile changed their outlook on the project upon learning Mussell was on board. His reputation as a float builder helped to secure support for the MoonPie Rise.

And the MoonPie Rise needed all the support it could get. Richardson's decision to spend $9,000 of discretionary funds on an electronic MoonPie made him the subject of intense criticism. One Mobile county commissioner condemned Richardson for spending taxpayer money on a MoonPie in a recession year when people were hungry and jobless. Yet, Richardson insisted he was well aware of the needs of the citizens of his district, and in the MoonPie, he saw opportunity. He hoped the MoonPie Rise would be an economic engine for the city, improving the economy and creating jobs in Mobile in the long term. To Richardson, the MoonPie was an investment in the future.

So despite the condemnation and mockery, Richardson remained locked on his vision of the MoonPie Rise. In fact, he claims the criticism increased community and media attention for the event, and Richardson himself is a master of hype. "I don't care what anybody says," he told reporters in the middle of the ruckus. "We will raise the MoonPie at the stroke of midnight." After that, reporters followed Richardson around the clock, demanding to see the MoonPie, which was under construction in Steve Mussell's float barn.

Mussell built the MoonPie in four weeks, between Thanksgiving and Christmas in 2008. First, the city's building department constructed an aluminum framework twelve feet in diameter that resembled a spool. Mussell added double circles of plywood on each side to represent the outer cookie layers and filled the middle with cardboard to resemble marshmallow. He added a papier-mâché layer to make a smooth surface for painting. Though chocolate is the most popular flavor, Mussell made a banana MoonPie so it would be easier to see at night. Finally, 1,200 golf ball–sized lights were added to illuminate the MoonPie, which weighed 900 pounds upon completion.

On New Year's Eve, 2008, Richardson, Drummond, and other city leaders hoped that five thousand people would turn out for the MoonPie Rise. They had five thousand MoonPies and five thousand RC Colas to give out, which lasted about twenty minutes. The crowd was estimated at nearly thirteen thousand despite the unusually cold weather, with temperatures in the teens. Local companies donated coffee and hot chocolate, and the Chattanooga Bakery had created the largest MoonPie in history for the event. It was nearly four feet in diameter, contained forty-five thousand calories, and weighed fifty-five pounds.

As Richardson had promised, just before midnight, the electronic banana MoonPie rose a hundred feet into the air. When it reached the top, the countdown began, and as the year changed to 2009, so did the lights on the MoonPie. As luck would have it, a CNN reporter was visiting his wife's family in nearby Foley, Alabama, and the electronic MoonPie soon appeared on CNN across the country. Richardson was fielding calls from family and friends nationwide, all shouting, "I see the MoonPie! I see the MoonPie on CNN!"

In its second year, attendance at the MoonPie Rise doubled, reaching twenty-five thousand. The MoonPie was placed on the city side of the river, to make it more visible, and the weather was mercifully warmer. The event

City councilman Fred Richardson at the MoonPie Rise (photo by *Mobile Press-Register*)

had expanded to include music and dance performances, children's activities, open nights at local museums, a ball, and webcams of the event. The Rayz, a Mobile-based band, wrote a song for the event titled "MoonPie over Mobile," which was performed by Marcus Johnson and the Bay City Brass Band. When the MoonPie's lights changed to 2010, fireworks boomed behind it.

At the next city council meeting, downtown hotel owners thanked city council members. On a normally slow night, the MoonPie Rise had made a $45,000 impact on hotel sales, with all of the downtown hotels full. When I ask Drummond if she was surprised by the MoonPie Rise's success, she replies, "We didn't know what to expect. We've been completely blown away. We just happened on it. Everyone was laughing about it and we were laughing too, but it was an extraordinary idea that yielded an extraordinary success."

Richardson and Drummond cite several factors to explain it. The Moon-Pie Rise has the monopoly on the central time zone. The MoonPie is the only thing rising on New Year's Eve instead of dropping. The MoonPie is innovative, different, kooky. Southerners are deeply connected to it in a nostalgic way. Mobile is the metropolitan hub of the region and draws people from a wide area. But Richardson is also quick to credit the universal appeal of the MoonPie: "Cracker Jacks are for kids, but MoonPies are for everyone. The MoonPie cuts across barriers of age, race, economics. The MoonPie brings people together. If I had picked some other object, it could have divided the community. But nobody has anything against the MoonPie. Everybody loves the MoonPie."

MoonPies were first produced in 1917 at the Chattanooga Bakery, founded in Tennessee in the early 1900s to use leftover flour from the Mountain City Flour Mill. The MoonPie traces its origins to a sales call in a Kentucky coal mining region, where workers toiled "all day long in soot-soaked underground shafts, chiseling the coal into chunks and loading them into waiting carts, which were whisked away one after another in an endless, monotonous ritual," writes MoonPie chronicler David Magee. "When the break whistle blew, these mining men wanted a hearty snack, not a small package of lemon cookies or ginger snaps."[2]

When the commissary manager showed no interest in Chattanooga Bakery products, company salesman Earl Mitchell approached a group of miners to ask them what they wanted. One miner replied that they wanted something solid and filling for their lunch pails, then held his hands up to the sky so they framed the moon and said, "about that big." When Mitchell returned to the Chattanooga Bakery, workers were dipping graham cookies into vats of marshmallow and setting them on a windowsill to harden and dry. With the miners in mind, Mitchell put two graham cookies together with marshmallow in the middle and chocolate on top. He took samples of the new snack back to the miners and received a positive response. At the time, MoonPies were one of two hundred confection items made at the bakery, but they quickly became a top-selling product.

MoonPie logo (courtesy of
the Chattanooga Bakery)

The MoonPie was more than four inches in diameter and sold for a nickel. Because it was affordable and filling, it was especially popular among the working class. Similarly, in 1934, the Royal Crown Company in Columbus, Georgia, began selling RC Cola in sixteen-ounce bottles instead of the usual twelve, also for a nickel. With the MoonPie as the biggest snack cake for a nickel and RC Cola as the biggest soda, together they became a popular ten-cent combination, especially as a workingman's lunch. Though neither company made any effort to link the two products, the phrase "an RC Cola and a MoonPie" became well-known across the South, bolstered by the 1951 hit country song "RC Cola and MoonPie" by Big Bill Lister.

Transportation improvements in the 1950s, including new state and federal highways, more road-worthy vehicles, and more gasoline stations, "served as a boundary breaker for the MoonPie."[3] The snack was soon sold and consumed nationally, though it was still most popular in the South and in areas with high numbers of southern emigrants including Detroit and Chicago, where the MoonPie was a staple snack for industrial workers. By the late 1950s, the MoonPie had become so popular that the Chattanooga Bakery produced nothing else.[4]

MoonPie Legends

One legend claims that children on the Queen's float in the Comic Cowboys parade were the first to throw MoonPies in a Mobile Mardi Gras parade in 1956. Another gives the honor to Jerry Curran, who rode in his first parade in 1958 on an Infant Mystics float that carried several employees of Smith's Bakery, who tossed wrapped bakery products like coconut balls and cupcakes to the crowds. Before the next year's parade, Curran visited Malbis Bakery, where his father worked, to ask if they had anything good to throw for Mardi Gras. Malbis made their own version of MoonPies, which Curran threw the following year, in 1959.

Referred to by his nephew Glen as "the granddaddy of MoonPies," Robert "Bob" Harrison is also credited with being the first to throw the MoonPie. In 1967, Harrison was talked into joining the Stripers but had little money to spend on throws. At the time, he worked as a distributor for the Murray Biscuit Company and could obtain MoonPies at a low cost. He brought boxes of MoonPies to the float, a little

Around this time, MoonPies made their debut as throws in Mobile Mardi Gras parades. Early Mardi Gras throws, dating to the 1800s, were French bon bons or trick prizes like small bags of flour that burst when caught. These were eventually banned, and throws reached a lull until post–World War II, when they became an increasingly integral part of Mardi Gras parades. In the 1940s and 1950s, taffy candy and serpentine (rolls of unraveling confetti) were the most common throws, and it was considered a feat to catch a whole roll of serpentine. "Throw me a whole roll, mister!" became a common parade shout.

In the late 1950s, city officials banned serpentine claiming that people choked on it, but some Mobilians insist the serpentine actually choked the gutters and was a chore to clean up. To replace the missing serpentine, float *embarrassed to do so, but the crowd loved them, and the next year, all of the Stripers threw MoonPies.*

Another legend credits the Maids of Mirth with throwing the first MoonPies in the late 1960s. As the story goes, Louise "Sister" Mc-Clure and Elizabeth "Dibber" Lutz went to Tom's Candy Sales in search of something different (and less costly) to replace the whole candy bars they had thrown in the past. As McClure relates, MoonPies "were so cheap—two or three boxes for a dollar, a lot less than some throws. We didn't even try to get a deal from the store—we just bought a dozen or so boxes and started throwing them. They were easy to throw. You could take hold of the cellophane and flip them just like a Fris-bee."* The crowd loved the MoonPies, especially the children who could easily catch them, so the next year, the whole float threw them, and soon other societies were throwing MoonPies as well.†

* Farnell 2009.

† Information on MoonPie legends drawn from personal interviews.

riders began throwing new items like rubber balls, beanbags, candy kisses (chocolate, molasses, and peanut butter), doubloons (coins bearing mystic society insignia), bags of peanuts, bubble gum, hard candies, and Cracker Jacks.

The thrower of the very first MoonPie is up for debate, and several local legends have sprung up around it. Complicating the issue is the fact that many of the legends' "first" MoonPies were actually local bakery versions of the Chattanooga Bakery's MoonPie. Even more perplexing is that all of the legends are probably true. By the 1960s, the Mardi Gras season was two weeks long and featured seventeen separate parades, each with numerous floats, making it highly likely that different people on different floats in different parades began throwing MoonPies (or versions of them) at the same time.

Catching Moon-Pies at Mobile Mardi Gras (photo by Emily Blejwas)

MoonPies' real popularity as throws came in the early 1970s when the city of Mobile banned Cracker Jacks (the then-favorite Mardi Gras throw) because the sharp box corners were injuring spectators. MoonPies perfectly filled the Cracker Jack void. They were soft, easy to throw and catch, affordable, and had been a southern favorite for decades. They were an instant Mardi Gras hit. "Oh, to catch a MoonPie!" writes Marie Arnott, who attended parades in the 1970s. "Something that was actually edible and sweet! They were doled out sparingly and the chant in the crowd was always for MoonPies."[5]

Over the next few decades, MoonPies grew into a Mobile Mardi Gras institution. Today, each float rider throws roughly nine hundred MoonPies during a single parade, estimates Stephen Toomey, owner of the primary Mardi Gras supply store in Mobile.[6] Toomey's alone sells 4.5 million Moon-Pies each Mardi Gras season. And though the streets are littered with beads at the parade's end, there are usually no MoonPies to be found. For months after Mardi Gras, Mobile children find MoonPies in their lunchboxes and trade each other for favorite flavors. Local newspapers print MoonPie recipes. In 2003, Doris Allinson Dean published *Death by MoonPie*, a cookbook full of creative ways to consume post–Mardi Gras MoonPies. Though desserts

Rev. Chief's Mystic Mint Chip Ice Cream

DORIS ALLINSON DEAN*

4 pts. half & half

3½ c. sugar

1 T. vanilla extract

1 T. green food coloring

1 T. mint extract

4–6 oz. pk. chocolate chips pieces

6 chocolate MoonPies

Mix first 5 ingredients together in medium size bowl and place in ice cream machine freezer. In the meantime cut MoonPies into small, bite-size pieces. When ice cream is frozen to your liking, add MoonPie pieces and chocolate chips stirring in gently. Ice cream can now be served or placed in container in freezer.

★ D. A. Dean 2010.

Banana Butterscotch Elexis

DORIS ALLINSON DEAN*

4 MoonPies split in half

1 c. dark brown sugar

2 T. light cream

3 T. butter

⅛ tsp. vanilla extract

4 bananas

½ c. whipping cream

¼ c. chopped nuts

Place ½ of each MoonPie in individual dessert dishes, pricking each MoonPie all over with a fork. Slice bananas over MoonPies. Heat the sugar, light cream, butter and vanilla, stirring constantly until the sugar is melted and bubbling. Pour sugar mixture over MoonPies. Place other ½ of each MoonPie on top. Add whipped cream and nuts. Serve immediately.

Makes 4 servings.

★ D. A. Dean 2010.

make up most of the book (Dean pairs ice cream and MoonPies in several), the book also features recipes for dressings, salads, and sandwiches, including a vanilla MoonPie, ham, and pineapple melt.

Parades have always been the greatest access point to Mardi Gras for the masses, and as the MoonPie quickly became the beloved Mardi Gras throw, another parade tradition, also centered on the public Mardi Gras experience and also unique to Mobile, took root. Joe Cain Day was the brainchild of Mobile native and folklorist Julian Lee Rayford, who stumbled upon the little-known story of Joe Cain in the 1950s while researching Mobile Mardi Gras history.

Born on Dauphin Street in downtown Mobile in 1832, Joseph Stillwell Cain came of age when Mardi Gras parades and the city itself were in their prime. In 1711, members of the Boeuf Gras Society had staged the nation's first Mardi Gras parade in Mobile by fashioning a large bull's head and pulling it by ox-drawn cart down the city's downtown Dauphin and Royal Streets.[7] The parade was beloved by Mobile citizens, who continued to observe it annually. In 1830, the Boeuf Gras Society imported a heavy papier-mâché bull's head from France (it took sixteen men to lift it) that was garlanded and made the parade centerpiece.

Over the next decade, when Mobile's population quadrupled and the city enjoyed an economic boom and unparalleled prosperity linked to the cotton trade, parades continued to grow larger and more elaborate. Horse-drawn floats and themed parades appeared. Mystic societies flourished, and new societies constantly emerged. (Mystic society members ride on Mardi Gras floats but keep their identities secret by masking). At age fourteen, Joe Cain became a founding member of the Tea Drinkers, a mystic society whose founders were all between the ages of thirteen and sixteen.

The onset of the Civil War in 1861, however, ended parades in Mobile for the war's duration and marked a drastic change in the city's fate. When a blockade of Union warships cut off Mobile's cotton trade, the city's economy was thrown into chaos. By the time the war ended, cotton's worth had plummeted by half. The French papier-mâché bull's head had allegedly been used for cannon fodder.

Joe Cain (Caldwell Delaney Collection, Doy Leale McCall Rare Book and Manuscript Library, University of South Alabama)

Into this dismal scene stepped Joe Cain, then thirty-four years old, a clerk in the local market, and a Civil War veteran. On Mardi Gras in 1866, Cain gathered with six other Tea Drinkers and Civil War veterans to rub their faces with red clay and soot, bedeck themselves with Spanish moss and dead leaves, and don Chickasaw costumes. Cain called himself "Chief Slacabamorinico" and dubbed his friends "the Lost Cause Minstrels." They rode into Mobile in a decorated charcoal wagon, banging on abandoned Union military band instruments and stunning occupying troops. Cain announced that he had traveled from Wragg Swamp to the city to put an end to the suffering and gloom of the war years and to declare the return of Mobile's parades.

Cain sought to revive the soul of Mobile, proclaiming to northern troops and Mobile citizens alike that the city would reclaim its spirit and return to its former glory. He personified a Chickasaw chief because the Chickasaw were never defeated in battle. The Lost Cause Minstrels referred to the lost cause of the Confederacy. In 1867, Cain helped to organize the Order of Myths (now the oldest continuous mystic society in Mobile) whose emblem float portrays the figures of Folly chasing Death around the broken column of Time. Cain allegedly portrayed Folly on the first emblem float. At the end of the parade, Folly wins.

Folly won in Mobile as well. On Mardi Gras in 1867, Cain appeared at the head of sixteen Lost Cause Minstrels, each with a musical instrument. Cain played a bass drum so big he could hardly see over it, and laughing children followed him around all day. New mystic societies formed to join the Lost Cause Minstrels, and over the next few decades, Mardi Gras became Mobile's primary event. Parades, floats, costumes, balls, and tableaux (dramas) grew increasingly elaborate. In 1872, the first King of Mardi Gras was crowned in a ceremony modeled after European coronations. Even during the Great Depression, pounds of Dutch gold leaf were applied to Mardi Gras floats.

Mobile historians Melton McLaurin and Michael Thomason surmise that

by adopting Mardi Gras as their major holiday, Mobilians were seeking to escape the psychological trauma of defeat. They returned, emotionally, not to the spirit of Mobile, the antebellum cotton port, but to the spirit of Mobile, the capital of French Louisiana. The Old South had, after all, been defeated, its dreams of glory shattered on the battlefields of a bloody civil war. But French Mobile, now a part of a distant past, evoked far different visions. Mobilians envisioned French lords and ladies, swathed in gold, ermine, and silk, dancing at glittering balls. The reality that colonial Mobile had been inhabited primarily by hard-bitten Canadian adventurers, fur trappers, and a handful of under-supplied French soldiers no longer mattered. To face the future, Mobile required an inspiring past. And so, defeated and dispirited, they created one.[8]

The infusion of a royal element established Mardi Gras as "the premier event of the city's social elite."[9] Mystic societies were largely comprised of the wealthy, membership was by invitation, and society activities were open only to members and their invited guests. In the 1930s and 1940s, attempts to establish public balls were quashed by mystic societies who believed public balls "conflicted with their own traditions" and "diminished the prestige that came with membership in the secretive and highly selective societies." In addition to being closed to the working class, mystic societies were also off limits to black Mobilians, who began establishing their own societies in 1894 and paraded for the first time in 1938.[10]

When Julian Rayford happened on the story of Joe Cain in 1955, he saw an opportunity to counteract the entrenched elitism of Mardi Gras and revive the community ethos he felt while attending Mardi Gras parades in his youth in the 1920s. Though Rayford hailed from a working-class background, he recalled these parades as true community events, with everyone dressing in costume and masking for five days of revelry. Rayford quotes Louis deV. Chaudron, who wrote that "in Mobile, Mardi Gras is everybody's day, and prince, priest, and peasant jostle each other with perfect equality and complete good humor."[11] Rayford himself describes the scene in *Chasin' the Devil Round a Stump*:

> Brass bands blowing out marches and ragtime. People hooting and talking
> excitedly, children running, clowns, clowns, clowns and funny faces,
> mustaches, big noses, derbies, and conical hats. Battleships in port, sailors
> rolling about, clowns directing traffic, people laughing, and red-white-
> and-blue horns, green-and-red horns, confetti, crazy costumes, and gayety,
> hilarity, all the somberness of winter cast aside and spring roped in and
> dragged in zany confusion. . . . In the moment a float comes abreast of
> you and passes with a great burst of flaming torchlight, the bands blaring
> their brass horns, gold and blue and red flashing in the scintillation of gold
> leaf—and maskers on the float jigging in fantastic costumes, while candy is
> thrown over the crowd like rain—in that moment you stand there raised

into ecstasy, trying to comprehend all you can in a blur of joy gone almost as soon as it began. What is Mardi Gras? It is an ecstasy—not an ecstasy for some shy poet to cherish, and not a moment for a couple of lovers to fondle—it is a great hurly-burly filled with all the grace of art and all the compounded vulgarity of mobs.[12]

Though mystic societies were certainly exclusive during Rayford's youth, the parades, as he describes them, were not. And though Joe Cain was part of the elite mystic societies of Mobile, Rayford chose to portray and honor him as the people's hero. Perhaps he viewed Cain's 1866 ride in a charcoal wagon with his ragtag band as symbolic of the true spirit of Mardi Gras. Or perhaps Cain's 1867 parade of musical minstrels resonated with the parades of Rayford's childhood. Either way, Rayford labored for eleven years to gain permission to exhume Cain's remains and reinter them in Mobile's Church Street Cemetery, located on the Mardi Gras parade route. Cain had been buried in 1904 in Bayou La Batre (twenty-five miles south of Mobile), where he had retired in 1885 to grow native oranges and make claret wine.

In 1966, one hundred years after Joe Cain dressed as Chief Slacabamorinico and led his minstrels into downtown Mobile, Rayford succeeded. Joe Cain's remains (along with those of his wife, Elizabeth) were reburied in the downtown Church Street Cemetery. His grave reads, "Here lies Old Joe Cain, the heart and soul of Mardi Gras in Mobile." It is said that Rayford carried Cain's skull in the pocket of his large overcoat on the ride to Mobile and wore the wooden key to Cain's coffin on a string around his neck until his death.

On February 6, 1967, Rayford honored Cain with a traditional jazz funeral. The Excelsior Band, Mobile's oldest Mardi Gras marching band, played "When the Saints Go Marching In" in a procession to Cain's grave, followed by throngs of mourners. The funeral was so popular that Rayford decided to make it an annual event, held the Sunday before Mardi Gras. The following year, Rayford himself portrayed Chief Slacabamorinico and led the parade to the graveyard, where participants listened to the band and danced on Cain's grave.

Joe Cain Day gave all Mobilians a chance to participate in the city's most

Dancing on Joe Cain's grave at his jazz funeral, 1967 (photo courtesy of Clarence Keller, Doy Leale McCall Rare Book and Manuscript Library, University of South Alabama, C4201)

important holiday, regardless of mystic society membership. Rayford modeled the Joe Cain Day parade after the parades of his youth, with all of society masking and clowning. He dubbed it "The People's Parade" and made it a walking parade so all could join in free of charge, without mystic society membership. All they had to do was put on a costume and start walking.

As historian Samuel Kinser notes, "the dishevelled, helter-skelter quality of Joe Cain parades was partly [a response] to the stiffness of the Carnival societies." Though some viewed Joe Cain Day as "the lodestone of the disorderly," many Mobilians welcomed the opportunity to participate.[13] By the mid-1970s, Joe Cain Day had become one of Mobile's most popular Mardi Gras events, with thousands congregating in the cemetery at the end of the parade. In 1991, a Joe Cain Day Classic 5K road race and a street party outside Cain's former home on Augusta Street were added to the public events. Today, one hundred thousand people attend the Joe Cain Day Parade, still led by a Mobile native portraying Chief Slacabamorinico and traveling by wagon.[14]

Joe Cain's Merry Widows (and Floozies)

In the first Joe Cain Day parade, a local librarian joined in by veiling herself in black to portray Cain's widow. Ironically, this solitary and spontaneous act morphed into a traditional mystic society: Joe Cain's Merry Widows. Every year, a few hours before the Joe Cain Day parade, twenty widows, dressed and veiled in heavy black, gather in the Church Street Cemetery to mourn Cain's passing. They arrive by police escort, and as they walk, wailing, into the cemetery, scores of onlookers offer condolences and embraces. No one is allowed inside the cemetery except the widows, two men in tuxedos carrying flower arrangements, and a lone jazz saxophonist, so spectators line the gates and perch on the cemetery wall.

The widows walk slowly into the cemetery, as if in a funeral procession, each carrying a single white lily. When they arrive at Joe Cain's grave, a few widows clear away the Mardi Gras beads that are a constant presence there. The head widow reads a tribute to Joe Cain over the sniffling of the others, which crescendos into weeping whenever Cain is mentioned by name, and especially so when the widow mentions that Joe Cain Day has fallen on Valentine's Day this year. The widows, who go by grand southern names like Mahalia, Magnolia, and Camellia, are then called to place their lilies one by one on the grave.

Then, in the true spirit of Joe Cain, who declared an end to suffering, the head widow announces, "Joe would want us to be happy." The mood instantly reverses and the widows start whooping and dancing on Cain's grave. The saxophonist plays a lively rendition of "When the Saints Go Marching In," and the widows walk alongside the cemetery walls tossing black and silver beads to the crowd. Some hand out black roses and, in honor of Valentine's Day, heart-shaped beads and red lollipops.

Cain's Merry Widows, 2010 (photo by Emily Blejwas)

The widows, however, are not the only women in attendance who loved Joe Cain. A mystic society comprised of Cain's mistresses who call themselves "Joe Cain's Merry Floozies" play against the elegant widows. Dressed in all red, including red hats with red veils and sandbags decorated to resemble breasts hanging around their necks, they work their way through the crowd loudly declaring, "Joe loved us best!"

* Information on Joe Cain Day drawn from personal interview with Wayne Dean and attending the event in 2010.

Slac IV

In a solemn, secret, and symbolic ceremony held in the Church Street Cemetery in 1970, Julian Rayford "passed the feathers" of Chief Slacabamorinico to Red Foster, who in turn passed them to Wayne Dean in 1986. Dean has now spent thirty years personifying the Chickasaw chief, also known as "Old Slac," "Professor Slac," and "Old King Carnival of Mobile." When I ask how he was chosen to be Chief Slacabamorinico, Dean replies simply, "Slac III gave it to me."

Wayne Dean was born in Mobile in 1942. His parents were never members of mystic societies and never attended any balls, but when Dean was a child, his grandfather took him to Mardi Gras parades. His grandparents lived on Virginia Street, and Dean often watched floats ride by from their front porch or rode his bike to the nearby barns to watch floats being constructed. In high school, Dean sketched and built his own miniature floats. He typed out the histories of mystic societies and wrote his first letter to the editor of the Mobile Press-Register *in protest of the city's serpentine ban.*

Today, Dean sports a manicured white mustache and tweed jacket with elbow patches that make him look more like a British professor than a Chickasaw chief. But when he portrays Old Slac, he is mindful to keep the costume as close as possible to a photograph of Joe Cain's representation. He uses the same materials Cain would have used, including a turkey feather headdress, deer tail belt, shell necklace, kilt, long johns, and brown moccasins, all of which are kept in a worn, oversized suitcase.*

Although Dean has been challenged on the political correctness of portraying a Chickasaw chief, he points out that Joe Cain chose the Chickasaw because they were a proud and undefeated people. To Cain and to Dean, Chief Slacabamorinico is the symbol of the irrepressible spirit of the city, which Dean views as a positive portrayal

of Native Americans. Plus, the ruling chief of the MOWA Band of Choctaw Indians, Chief Wilford "Longhair" Taylor, once rode on the coal wagon with Dean at the head of the Joe Cain Day parade.

Throughout the year, Dean portrays Chief Slacabamorinico for various social, educational, and charity events, including Red Cross luncheons, veterans' reunions, and museum programs. He visits many fourth-grade classrooms where students study Alabama history, and he has starred in a television ad against drunk driving. He also regularly marries and buries the Mardi Gras faithful as Old Slac. During Mardi Gras season, Dean keeps a packed schedule. In addition to leading the Joe Cain Day parade, he makes appearances at various Mardi Gras events, careful to attend a wide variety so as not to show favoritism. One year, he attended twenty-four balls.

Wayne Dean as Chief Slacabamorinico, 2010 (photo by John David Mercer, *Mobile Press-Register*)

Even though Dean does not plan on passing the feathers anytime soon, he has given some thought to Slac V and has even been approached by some seeking the title. "But it's not something you can seek out for yourself," Dean says. "All I can say is that it will be someone who has the true spirit of Mardi Gras." And how does Dean define that? "In a word, creativity."[†]

★ Andrews 2010.

† Information on Slac IV drawn from personal interview with Wayne Dean.

FOURTEEN

||||||||||||||||||||||||||||||||||||||||||||||||||||||||||||||||||||||||||

Shrimp

Seafood in Bayou La Batre

You cannot comprehend the superlative quality of this town
until you have seen the Bayou, the Bayou itself, that wrinkled,
crumpled skin of the lacquered water. Early in the morning, there
is a peace, a quiet in the marshes that cannot be disturbed even
by the roaring of the engines of the boats. The trees are so dense
that behind the wall of foliage it is like night. . . . Some mornings,
the Bayou is so intensely green and clean, with a savage, fierce
cleanness . . . like an animal or a bird that is always preening itself.

—Julian Rayford, *Whistlin' Woman and Crowin' Hen: The
True Legend of Dauphin Island and the Alabama Coast*

IN AUGUST 2010, two months after tar balls from the BP oil spill washed
ashore in Bayou La Batre, Alabama, I visit the Boat People SOS office in
town, unsurprisingly abuzz with activity. I soon sit with four Vietnamese
American seafood processors and Vinh Tran, a Bayou La Batre native who

Shrimping boats at harbor in Bayou La Batre, Alabama (photo by Carol M. Highsmith, Library of Congress, LC-DIG-highsm-06495)

translates for us. All four of the processors have worked in the seafood industry since their arrival in Bayou La Batre at least twenty years ago. They have been out of work since the oil spill nearly four months ago and have received checks from BP, but these provide a bare minimum of assistance.

With no other job skills and no English language skills, their opportunities for other work are extremely limited. Yet they have no thought of leaving Bayou La Batre. Their families are here, their communities, their homes, and hopefully someday soon, their jobs. So there is nothing to do but wait until they can work again, though they have received no indication of when this will be. They regard the oil spill as far worse than Katrina because its effects have lasted so much longer than any hurricane. "Everything is a wait," one woman explains. "We sit and wait for the shops to call us back. It is suffocating."[1]

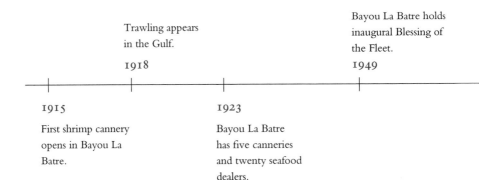

Trawling appears
in the Gulf.

1918

Bayou La Batre holds
inaugural Blessing of
the Fleet.

1949

1915

First shrimp cannery
opens in Bayou La
Batre.

1923

Bayou La Batre
has five canneries
and twenty seafood
dealers.

A large ocean inlet with naturally protected harbors, the Mississippi Sound stretches for ninety miles along the southern coasts of Mississippi and Alabama, from Waveland, Mississippi, to the Dauphin Island Bridge in Alabama. Its southern edge is bordered by the barrier islands: Cat, Ship, Horn, Petit Bois, and Dauphin, separating the sound from the Gulf of Mexico, which harbors one of the richest shrimp fisheries in the world. As Alabama chef Frank Stitt writes, "the warm waters of the Gulf Coast are teeming with an amazing array of sea life. Freshwater marshes and rivers join and mix with the sea, creating pools of differing salinity and unique ecosystems. Mobile Bay and Apalachicola Bay, in particular, are natural hatching grounds for shrimp, crab, speckled trout, red snapper, grouper, and redfish. Old ships and scrap metal—an inland junkyard—are dragged out into the bay to create a barrier reef that, over time, becomes encrusted with barnacles, providing refuge for all sorts of sea creatures. . . . The Gulf is a magical place."[2]

Native Americans prospered along the Mississippi Sound for nearly eight thousand years, drawing the mainstays of their diet from the sea. In the shallow waters of the sound and farther into the Gulf, they shrimped, fished, and

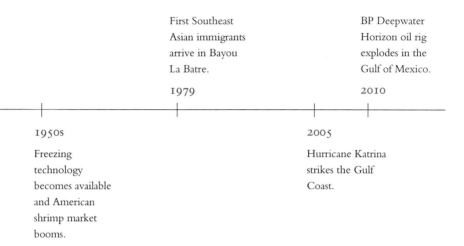

First Southeast Asian immigrants arrive in Bayou La Batre.

1979

BP Deepwater Horizon oil rig explodes in the Gulf of Mexico.

2010

1950s

Freezing technology becomes available and American shrimp market booms.

2005

Hurricane Katrina strikes the Gulf Coast.

gathered oysters and clams. They harvested shrimp using nets woven from the fibers of Spanish moss and palmetto fronds. When European explorers arrived in the seventeenth century, they followed suit, venturing into the sound in wooden skiffs, alone or in pairs, using cast nets braided by hand and dyed with red oak bark.[3]

At the center of the Mississippi Sound's twelve-mile shoreline in Alabama sits the town of Bayou La Batre, likely named for a battery of French cannons that once guarded the coast. Bayou La Batre (pronounced *bye la battree*) was founded in 1786 by Joseph Bosarge, a French native, who settled the Spanish-owned land along with his wife and seven children. Though more families followed, Bayou La Batre remained a frontier throughout the 1800s. Frye Gaillard, Sheila Hagler, and Peggy Denniston describe the history of Bayou La Batre and the neighboring town of Coden in their 2008 book, *In the Path of the Storms*. As they note, "the Bayou was a rough-and-tumble place in those days and remained so through much of the century. Even much later, the old-timers would gather to tell their stories of pirates and ghosts and Saturday-night fights in the Bayou saloons."[4]

Though legends of pirate knife marks in the trees and buried treasure in the bayou persisted, the frontier lifestyle faded as the nineteenth century drew to a close, and Bayou La Batre became a fishing village. At the same time, the new Bay Shore Railroad from Mobile gave tourists easy access to the coast and Bayou La Batre grew as a resort town, famous for its medicinal spring water. As Gaillard et al. note, these were Bayou La Batre's "glory years of posh hotels and tree-shaded streets and tourists pouring in from all over the country."[5]

Then, in 1906, the worst hurricane in living memory hammered Bayou La Batre for more than twenty-four hours. It was a storm so devastating that the memories of it "linger even now in the oral history of the Bayou."[6] Newspaper accounts describe tidal surges tearing homes apart, flooded streets, uprooted trees, drowning people and animals, snakes writhing in the water, and bodies lined up along the shoreline. According to one reporter, those who survived "resembled great chunks of liver-colored beef, so badly were they battered and bruised."[7] Another wrote that "those who escaped with their lives saved nothing, absolutely nothing, even the few clothes they had on being stripped and torn into threads and fragments."[8]

In the decade following the storm, the tourist industry in Bayou La Batre and Coden withered as resorts began to close. As Gaillard et al. write, "the Bayou, in a sense, slowly but surely turned in on itself, returning to the source of its identity and survival: extracting its sustenance from the sea. The work was hard, but the people found satisfaction in the harvest—shrimp and oysters, fish and crabs."[9] Two more horrific storms, in 1916 and 1925, sealed the town's identity as a small fishing village on the tenuous Alabama coastline. And Bayou La Batre held itself apart from the rest of the state. Though only twenty-five miles from Mobile, "Bayou la Batre never felt any relationship between itself and Mobile," writes Alabama native Julian Rayford. Mobile "was simply the city to which fishermen took their catch."[10]

Early large-scale shrimpers in Bayou La Batre cruised Gulf waters in schooners towing smaller boats "piled high with huge beach seines. When they saw white shrimp jumping along the shore and muddying the waters, crews of a dozen men jumped overboard, circled the shrimp with seines,

Skipper on an oyster barge, Bayou La Batre, Alabama, 1911 (photo by Lewis Wickes Hine, Library of Congress, LC-DIG-nclc-04681)

dragged them up on shore by the ton, and sailed back into ports . . . to unload their catch."[11] Beginning in 1915, several shrimp canneries opened in Bayou La Batre, making it the center of Alabama's seafood industry.[12] Yet, as environmentalists Jack and Anne Rudloe note, even with "the canneries going full steam, shrimping remained a local fishery. Bag seines and nets work only in shallow water, and when the season was over and the shrimp left the beaches, the nets came up empty, so the supply was always erratic, inconsistent, and limited. For shrimp to develop into one of the world's most popular foods, it took the simultaneous development of the otter trawl, petroleum, and the internal combustion engine."[13]

Trawling first appeared in the Gulf in 1918. The trawl net allowed for the harvest of large quantities of shrimp but required an engine strong enough to pull it. As boats evolved to become more powerful and engines switched from gasoline to diesel, shrimp boats began pushing beyond the limits of the sound to trawl in deeper Gulf waters. Here, shrimpers could access an abundance of shrimp year-round, and catches off the Alabama coast steadily increased.[14]

Trawling technology also shifted boat ownership from factories to fishermen. Seine nets were up to 1,500 feet long and 18 feet deep and required 6 to 20 men, a schooner, and several skiffs to handle them. Trawls required only two men and a small powerboat, affordable for individual shrimpers. By the end of the 1930s, schooners and seines had fallen out of use, the number of trawlers continued to rise, and fishermen had gained significant autonomy.[15] As a Bayou La Batre shrimper explained in 1939, "working a factory boat is like being a share cropper. . . . Jist suppose that the crew has been out for a week and don't catch no shrimp. What have they made? Well next time they go out they'll probably catch a good haul but they'll owe two weeks grocery bill as well as a oil bill and maybe they've lost a troll or a net wu'th say fifty dollars. They ain't made nothin'. Me I'll take my own boat every time. I furnish everything and sell the shrimp to the factory and what's mine's mine."[16]

Trawl and powerboat technology transformed Gulf Coast shrimping.[17] With an abundant and reliable supply for processors, shrimping became a fixed industry on the Gulf Coast. By 1923, Bayou La Batre boasted five canneries and twenty seafood dealers. "Some three hundred families make a living working in shrimp in the dreamy, drifting town of Bayou la Batre," wrote a WPA worker in 1939. "Drifting in a sense of knowing no other thing to do but catch, pick, pack shrimp and wait for the next season to do it over."[18] Another report from the early 1940s describes Bayou La Batre (population 964) as "a small community of winding streets and cottages set in gardens of roses, poppies, geraniums, larkspur and golden glow. Small musty shops, dim with age, are reminiscent of a Basque village. The road curves down to a water front littered with piles of oyster shells dumped by the canning factories where many of the townsfolk work. Smelly oyster and shrimp boats, their scarred hulls salt-stained and drab with age, crowd the shore line while discharging cargoes, or rock quietly at anchor in the bayou."[19]

Man working in a shrimp-processing plant, Bayou La Batre, Alabama (Alabama Department of Archives and History, Montgomery, Alabama, Q7744)

Wild shrimp in the United States are usually one of three closely related species known as pink, brown, and white. White shrimp dominated Gulf Coast shrimping until the late 1940s, when shrimp boats began dramatically increasing in size. As Gaillard notes, the new steel-bottomed trawlers, many of them sixty-five feet in length, could handle the open, choppy waters of the Gulf. Shrimp catches expanded to include large quantities of pinks and browns discovered in deeper Gulf waters as well as royal reds off the coast of Alabama and Florida.[20]

At the same time, freezing technology appeared. Frozen shrimp coupled with large catches from the new, powerful boats gave birth to the modern shrimp industry. Mass quantities of shrimp traveled inland for the first time, causing a shrimp boom in America. In the 1950s, shrimp became commonplace in cookbooks and restaurants across the nation. Shrimp production increased 60 percent in Alabama in 1950 and reached an all-time high in 1952. Bayou La Batre had replaced all of its canneries with freezing plants by 1965.

However, the same freezing technology that created the modern shrimp industry in America also paved the way for foreign imports. US shrimp processors responding to the high demand began relying on imported shrimp to ensure a steady supply to American consumers. In 1939, 3.7 million pounds of shrimp were imported to the United States, representing 4 percent of shrimp consumed. By 1959, Americans consumed 107 million pounds of imported shrimp: 43 percent of shrimp consumed.

By 1960, foreign imports had become a problem for Gulf Coast shrimpers. Shrimp from forty nations flooded inland markets, and because it entered the United States untaxed and below market value, foreign shrimp slashed the demand and the price for Gulf Coast shrimp. Desperate to keep up, many Gulf Coast shrimpers purchased larger boats to get farther into the Gulf, substantially increasing their personal debt. Furthermore, because processors no longer relied solely on domestic shrimp, Gulf Coast shrimpers lost bargaining power over prices and unions collapsed.

At the same time, the cost of fuel skyrocketed along with operating expenses and loan interest rates. The year 1974 was a solemn one for Bayou La Batre shrimpers. Several processors went out of business, and sixty to seventy boats out of the fleet of three hundred were sold. Ironically, shrimp were abundant that year, but it didn't pay to catch them because diesel was expensive and prices were low.[21] Beginning in 1975, shrimp farming took off, adding more pressure to Gulf Coast shrimpers. As one Bayou La Batre resident stated, "the boats don't go out from here much anymore. Fishermen sit idle or else occupy themselves with odd jobs on stymied vessels. The seafood capital of Alabama is in trouble."[22]

In the late 1970s, an influx of Southeast Asian refugees, including Vietnamese, Cambodians, and Laotians, settled in the Gulf Coast after fleeing war and genocide in their homelands. Gulf Coast geography, weather, and landscape resembled the tropical wetlands of Southeast Asia, and many of the refugees arrived with highly developed fishing skills, "usually the product of several generations of experience at sea." In fact, "some were born on fishing boats, spent most of their lives on them, and [would] not be content with their new life in America until they [could] again make their livelihood on the sea."[23] Further, fishing did not require English language skills and offered both independence and the chance to become a successful entrepreneur.

Bayou La Batre saw its first wave of immigrants in 1979. Within five years, Southeast Asians made up one-third of the town's population. Roughly half of the new arrivals were Vietnamese, one-third were Cambodians, and one-sixth were Laotians. Most took jobs in the seafood industry, first as processors, and later as fishermen and shrimpers. Vietnamese immigrants began buying shrimp boats in 1982, and after five years, had amassed a fleet of sixty boats. In 1984, a Vietnamese processing plant opened. As authors of a 1987 economic study report, "since their initial involvement in local processing plants, the Vietnamese, in particular, have been quick to take advantage of other economic opportunities in the community. . . . It is in the area of shrimp fishing that the Vietnamese have gained the greatest attention along the Gulf Coast."[24]

Local reaction to the newcomers was mixed. Some local shrimpers resented Southeast Asian shrimpers who increased competition over a limited resource in a difficult market. Language barriers caused clashes over the rules of the sea. On the whole, however, the immigrants were regarded as diligent and tireless workers in a town that had always prided itself on hard work. Southeast Asians are credited with solidifying Bayou La Batre's stature as a seafood processing hub by boosting its workforce and breathing "new life into the local economy."[25] As seafood broker Rodney Lyons explains, "it made Bayou la Batre even more of a seafood production town. The Asian workers would pick 100 to 120 pounds of crabmeat a day. They doubled the production of American pickers. It made the crab business grow. If they were shucking oysters, they sometimes worked twelve hours a day, and changed the whole complexion of oyster production. They shrimped also. They bought up old boats and worked hard and upgraded their boats. They were heavy producers, and people had to respect that."[26]

Indeed, in 1985, $43.3 million worth of shrimp was landed in Bayou La Batre and four times that amount was trucked in from other states to be processed. The town was home to major crab, oyster, and fish harvesting and processing industries as well, making seventeen seafood dealers and processors in all, as well as a significant ship building industry. By 1987, the labor force required for shrimp processing alone exceeded the capacity of Bayou La Batre's population, giving the town's seafood processing industry a regional economic significance. As one of the top ten ports in the nation based on the value of its landings, Bayou La Batre was certainly Alabama's most significant fishing community.

Southeast Asian immigrants also infused local communities with a new cultural element. They opened Asian markets, restaurants, and shops that now pepper the Alabama coastline around Bayou La Batre. The area is home to three Buddhist temples, one for each of the Asian cultures living on the coast. This cultural exposure helped to desegregate seafood processing work in Bayou La Batre. New job opportunities opened for African Americans, who were traditionally marginalized in lower paying work.[27]

But although Southeast Asian immigrants carved out homes and livelihoods along the Gulf Coast, shrimping was never an easy profession. From 1980 to 2007, American annual consumption of shrimp jumped from 1.4 pounds/person to 4.1 pounds, largely due to the increasing popularity of seafood restaurant chains.[28] But foreign imports, governmental shrimping regulations, high gas prices, insurance costs, and interest rates continued to shrink profit margins for Gulf Coast shrimpers.[29]

In December 2003, the Eat Alabama Wild Shrimp Committee formed to support Gulf Coast shrimpers who found themselves battling "the worst economic slump in the industry's history" due to an influx of inexpensive foreign imports that had dropped the price of domestic shrimp to lows not seen in thirty years. But before the committee's work could begin in earnest, came Hurricane Katrina.

On August 29, 2005, Bayou La Batre found itself at the eastern edge of Hurricane Katrina's path. The storm surge, the worst on record in American history, swelled to nearly twenty feet and flooded the town. As Mayor Stan Wright put it, "what Bayou La Batre experienced from Hurricane Katrina was pure hell."

Eight hundred homes were flooded beyond repair, only 8 percent of which were covered by flood insurance. More than 2,000 of the town's 2,300 residents were forced from their homes, at least temporarily. A total of 200 of Bayou La Batre's 300 shrimp boats were destroyed, dozens of which lay eerily stranded in trees along the coast. Virtually all of the waterfront businesses were in ruins. As one reporter wrote, "all along the bayou, shrimp boats lay tossed onto dry land, masts and rigging tangled in tree branches. Crumpled piles of lumber marked where homes had stood, and a wash of slime inches deep seeped from the open doors of shops and restaurants."[30]

Yet, despite the wreckage, most Bayou La Batre families stayed to rebuild. This was, after all, their home. And it wasn't the first hurricane to devastate their community. Hurricanes were, and are, a way of life along the Gulf Coast. As Mayor Wright says, "it seems like these people here are special, they can take a lickin' and keep on tickin'. They're tough folks."[31]

It was a difficult road back, with boats, traps, fishing equipment, houses, stores, and offices destroyed. Two months after the storm, the Federal Emergency Management Agency (FEMA) had refused to remove twenty-nine of the thirty-two moored shrimp boats and had delivered fewer than half of the trailers promised to stranded Bayou La Batre residents. Many simply returned to their storm damaged homes. As Amber Hill, a ninth grader at the time, relates, "there was no running water, no gas, no power, and no way of keeping cool. Smothering from the heat, I was forced to sleep sweaty and in nothing but a bathing suit. My parents and I could not bathe and had nothing to eat. We nearly starved, . . . but food wasn't our only concern. We had no place to call home anymore. Instead, we were forced to sleep in our old home where mold had begun to grow on the walls."[32]

But where FEMA failed, relief organizations and average American citizens triumphed, pouring time and resources into struggling Gulf Coast communities. As a resident of Coden wrote, "so many people came to our aid, friends and strangers alike. These individuals sent food, water, cleaning supplies, monetary gifts and helping hands. Our survival was made possible through the unselfish acts of love."[33] Bayou La Batre citizens themselves also organized a shelter, meals, and medical attention for those in need. Dr. Regina Benjamin, a local family physician who would later become US Surgeon General, set up a makeshift clinic on the stage of the local community center after her clinic was destroyed and began seeing patients immediately.

The stranded shrimp boats were ultimately recovered in September 2006 through funds raised by former US presidents Bill Clinton and George H. W. Bush. Yet, those who returned to shrimping found the industry tougher than ever. The cost of fuel was still high, the price for shrimp still low, and the hurricanes kept coming. The year 2008 brought Hurricanes Gustav and Ike and gas prices higher than four dollars per gallon. Shrimp production fell to its lowest level since 1975. In 2009, domestic shrimpers struggled to bring in 250 million pounds of shrimp while foreign imports surpassed 1.2 billion pounds. Some 70 percent of shrimp consumed worldwide was now farmed, largely in Asian countries.[34] Further, a nationwide recession reduced domestic demand for shrimp. But incredibly, there was more to come.

On April 20, 2010, a British Petroleum Deepwater Horizon oil rig exploded in the Gulf of Mexico, one hundred miles from Bayou La Batre. For three months, an oil well 5,000 feet below the ocean surface pumped crude oil into the Gulf Coast, reaching a total of 205.8 million gallons. The spill quickly became one of the worst ecological disasters in American history.

On May 2, 2010, less than two weeks after the oil spill, Bayou La Batre citizens gather for the town's annual Blessing of the Fleet. A centuries-old tradition originating in southern European fishing communities, a local Catholic priest administers the Blessing of the Fleet to ensure a safe and bountiful season. A plaque at the center of Bayou La Batre reads, "This old world custom is a public acknowledgement of God as his blessings are asked for a bountiful harvest and the safety of the men who go to sea." The Prayer for the Blessing of the Fleet, part of which is inscribed on a granite marker at the Bayou

La Batre coastline, reads: "May God in heaven fulfill abundantly the prayers which are pronounced over you and your boats and your equipment on the occasion of the Blessing of your fleet. God bless your going out and your coming in; The Lord be with you at home and on the water. May He accompany you when you start on your many journeys: may He fill your nets abundantly as a reward for your labor, and may He bring you all safely in, when you turn your boats homeward to shore."

St. Margaret's Catholic Church instituted the Blessing of the Fleet in Bayou La Batre in 1949 at the urging of parishioner Clarence Mallet, who believed God's blessings are essential to a good harvest from the sea. Like Bayou La Batre, St. Margaret's has faced its share of turmoil. Built in 1905, it was destroyed by the 1906 hurricane. Rebuilt on its present site in 1908, it was devastated by Hurricane Katrina in 2005. Rebuilt again, the church was completed in time to hold its first mass on Easter Sunday, April 16, 2006. Inside the new church, wood paneling curves from ceiling to walls, mimicking the interior of a boat. At the altar, portraits of Jesus and Pope John Paul II are labeled "Fishermen of the Father."

I slip in for the final minutes of mass. The church is cool, bright, and crisp with the scent of incense, a blunt contrast to the groggy rural summer festival outside: the food aromas, spurts of music from the stage, and the train fashioned from a tractor with plywood cars that children ride for a dollar. On this first muggy day of summer, sun and clouds alternate, and storms are forecast for the afternoon. "Even in this time of anxiety," the archbishop announces, "we give thanks." The recessional emanates from a folksy guitar in the balcony and the lyrics "we are called" are repeated as the Fleet Blessing Court, made up of local eighth-grade girls, processes out of the church along with the Knights of Columbus.[35]

Outside, the festivities stretch from the Vietnamese food booth behind the church to the boats decorated and moored at the docks. Stands offer local products, religious artifacts, crafts, and baked goods. There are children's games and face painting, boat tours, music, a gumbo contest, and a quilt raffle (the quilts always have a nautical theme). The land parade features the Fleet

Annual blessing of the shrimp fleet in Bayou La Batre, Alabama (Alabama Department of Archives and History, Montgomery, Alabama, Q36751)

Blessing queen and her maids, joined by Miss Seafood, Miss Toddler Seafood, Miss Baby Seafood, local politicians, and anyone else who cares to join in. One man throws red plastic crabs to the crowd from a motorized scooter.

When the moment arrives for the Blessing of the Fleet, the archbishop of Mobile, Thomas Rodi, and the Vietnamese American priest of St. Margaret's, Rev. Bieu Nguyen, stand together at the podium of a raised platform in front of the water and festooned boats. The altar boys of St. Margaret's and the girls of the Fleet Blessing Court gather around them. Archbishop Rodi calls to mind the biblical seas teeming with life and asks God to bless these boats, their equipment, and all who use it. He asks for protection from wind, rain, and the perils of the deep. He asks God to fill the nets of his disciples, to give

Boat festooned for the Blessing of the Fleet, Bayou La Batre, Alabama, 2010 (photo by Emily Blejwas)

them an abundant catch. And he addresses the palpable anxiety over the oil, which has not yet reached Alabama's shore. No one knows whether it will, or what to expect if it does. Rodi prays, "We ask God to bless those who are working to contain and to stop the oil leak. We ask God to protect us, to protect the livelihoods of those who make their living in the seafood industry and the tourism industry. And we ask God to protect our way of life, which is imperiled by this danger of the oil slick."

The national anthem is played, followed by a bell toll for each Bayou La Batre fisherman known to be lost at sea. There are twenty-eight in all; many share the same last name. Archbishop Rodi, Reverend Nguyen, and the Catholic laity then process to the lead boat for the blessing. The archbishop sways incense over the water where a wreath of flowers is dropped. The group stands at the bow, unwavering against the jostle of the boat as it moves forward, eyes to the water. A dozen brightly adorned boats follow, and when the last boat is out of sight, the crowd quietly disperses.

About a month after the Blessing of the Fleet, on June 6, the oil reached Bayou La Batre, with tar balls washing ashore. A federal moratorium on shrimping and fishing came just before the start of the 2010 shrimping season. The extent of the ecological damage is still unknown. The economic damage, however, is tangible. At the start of the oil spill, thousands of Gulf Coast shrimpers and fishermen struggled to get reimbursed for lost wages. Because they were usually paid in cash under the table, most did not have the documentation required to make claims against BP for lost wages. BP responded by accepting affidavits from boat captains in lieu of tax returns and W2 forms to evidence a fisherman's income. But because these affidavits would have been signed admissions of tax evasion, most boat captains did not provide them.

The oil spill was particularly devastating for coastal Southeast Asian American communities, 80 percent of whom worked in the seafood industry, including many whole families. The lack of English language skills prevented many fishermen from navigating BP forms, resources, and customer service lines. Claims forms and posters initially appeared in English only. The whole claims system was online, and many fishermen lacked internet access. Fishing area closings were announced on English-speaking radio stations, costing Southeast Asian American fishermen citations from the coast guard.

At the time of the spill, Southeast Asian Americans operated at least one-third of the fishing boats on the Gulf Coast, and Vietnamese Americans owned roughly half of those. The first Vietnamese American translators BP hired for safety and cleanup training spoke with a North Vietnamese dialect and used Communist terminology to address Vietnamese American shrimpers who had fled the North Vietnamese Communist regime thirty years earlier. These translators were replaced, but a general shortage of translators persisted.

Some Southeast Asian American fishermen and shrimpers did receive the standard BP checks providing $5,000 for boat owners and $2,500 for

Outside Vietnamese Buddhist Temple, Bayou La Batre, Alabama (photo by Emily Blejwas)

deckhands. For families falling behind on home and boat mortgages, how-ever, these payments offered little comfort. Others worked for the Vessels of Opportunity program, which chartered local boats and paid fishermen for oil spill cleanup. Yet, this work was only temporary and only a small fraction of those who enrolled were activated.[36]

Even so, the people in the Boat People SOS office do not wear a posture of defeat. They greet and talk with each other, play with the babies, smile at me. Upon leaving, I drive to the Vietnamese Buddhist temple, located down a nondescript red dirt road. In the depth of summer, the figure of Buddha shines a stark white against green pines and blue sky.

Notes

Introduction

1. Cass 2006.
2. Egerton 1993:2.
3. Walter 1971:8–10.
4. Scott Peacock, presentation at the Alabama Historical Association's 64th Annual Meeting, Daphne, AL, April 16, 2011.
5. Neal 1985:3.

ONE *Roasted Corn: The Creek Nation in Alabama*

1. Personal interviews with McGhee family members.
2. Information on corn in the Mississippian Era and Moundville based on Atkins 1994c and Blitz 2008.
3. Dunnavant 1993:7.
4. Hardeman 1981:3.
5. Ibid.: 175.
6. Daniel 1989:33.
7. A "second generation" of cornbreads emerged after the Civil War, when southerners began using butter, milk, eggs, flour, baking powder, and baking soda to make cornbread. These breads included batter cakes, eggbread, corn cakes, griddle cakes, corn muffins, corn sticks, hushpuppies, and spoonbread (Wilson 2007a:152–53).
8. Information on colonial uses of corn based on Hardeman 1981.
9. Taylor 1982.
10. Thomas 1993:102.
11. Davis 2003.
12. History of early Creek society in Alabama based on Atkins 1994c, Braund 2008.
13. Davis 1998:81, 2003:xv.
14. Thrower 2012.
15. Vickery 2009:39.
16. Waselkov 2006.
17. Ibid.:72, 24.
18. Bunn and Williams 2009:11.
19. Braund 2008.
20. Waselkov 2006:203.
21. Ibid.:177, 212.
22. Thrower 2012.
23. Ibid.
24. Bunn and Williams 2009:16.
25. Braund 2008.
26. Description of "Alabama Land Fever" based on Atkins 1994b.
27. Bunn and Williams 2009:10, 17.
28. Atkins 1994a:53.
29. Waselkov 2006:212.
30. Hudson 1976:457, 460.
31. Haveman 2009.
32. Vickery 2009:124.
33. Waselkov 2006:206.
34. Paredes 1979:124.
35. Vickery 2009:141.
36. Vickery 2009:171.
37. Personal interview with Robert Thrower in 2010.
38. Ibid.; Vickery 2009.
39. Paredes 1992.

40. Poarch Creek history from 1970 to present based on phone interview with Alvarez in 2011.
41. Ibid.
42. Ibid.
43. Hoffman 2011.
44. Alvarez 2011.
45. Hudson 1976:374.
46. Historic information on Green Corn Ceremony based on Atkins 1994c, Bowne 2008.
47. Description of modern Green Corn Ceremony based on Alvarez 2011.
48. Ibid. and from observation at the attendance at Poarch Creek Pow Wow.

TWO *Gumbo: Africans and Creoles on the Gulf Coast*

1. Personal interview with Dora Finley, 2010, Mobile, AL.
2. Ibid.
3. Personal interview with Vince Henderson, 2010, Mobile, AL.
4. Hess 1995:78–79.
5. Ibid.
6. Harris 2011:105.
7. S. Thomas 2009.
8. These included *The Virginia Housewife* (1824), *The Kentucky Housewife* (1839), and *The Carolina Housewife* (1847).
9. Gumbo history drawn from Harris 2011.
10. Henderson interview.
11. Gould 1996:31, 34.
12. Ibid.
13. History of Creoles and Creoles of color in Mobile drawn from Gould 1996 and Shelley 1971.
14. Gould 1996:41.
15. Shelley 1971:46.
16. Gould 1996:42–43.
17. Shelley 1971:72.
18. History of Creoles and Creoles of color in Mobile drawn from Gould 1996 and Shelley 1971.
19. Henderson interview.
20. Ibid.

THREE *Chicken Stew: Frontier Life in the Tennessee Valley*

1. Personal interviews with Joey Boyd, Jonathan Hinton, David Scates, 2010, Athens, AL.
2. Chicken stew counties include Lauderdale, Colbert, Franklin, Lawrence, Limestone, Morgan, and Madison in Alabama and Wayne, Lawrence, and Giles in Tennessee.
3. Information on chicken and goat stews drawn from Allen 2009 and 2011, as well as email exchanges with William Allen.
4. Allen 2011:21.
5. Allen 2011:17.
6. Allen, email exchange.
7. Walker 1973:18.
8. Early history of Limestone County drawn from ibid. Quotation from page 20.
9. Ibid.:22.
10. History of Limestone County drawn from ibid. Quotation from page 31.
11. Atkins 1994b:54.
12. Flynt 1989:3.
13. Ibid.:5.
14. Allman 1979.
15. Atkins 1994b:55.
16. Hardeman 1981:53.
17. Ibid.:40.

18. Walker 1973.

19. Ibid.:24.

20. Atkins 1994b:58.

21. Jones 2007.

22. Atkins 1994b:58.

23. Description of pioneer homes and clothing drawn from Walker 1973.

24. Atkins 1994b.

25. Allen 2009:7.

26. Email exchange with William Allen.

27. Personal interviews with East Limestone volunteer firefighters at annual chicken stew.

FOUR Fried Green Tomatoes: Emblem of the Alabama Rural Table

1. Though botanically a fruit, tomatoes are treated as vegetables in cookery and so are considered to be vegetables in this chapter.

2. Description of fried green tomatoes at Slocomb Tomato Festival drawn from event and conversations with participants.

3. Clark 1989:5–6.

4. Southern connection to agriculture based on ibid.

5. Taylor and Edge 2007.

6. Neal 1985:55.

7. Lewis and Peacock 2003:xi.

8. Walter 2001:15.

9. Walter 1971:13.

10. Harris 2007:17.

11. A. Smith 1994:44, 140.

12. Ibid.:57.

13. Ibid.:78.

14. Ibid.:74.

15. Engelhardt 2009:79.

16. Ibid.:79, 82.

17. Girls' tomato clubs history drawn from ibid.

18. Recipes for "fried tomatoes" appear in two popular southern cookbooks from 1844 and 1847, but the earliest known recipe for fried *green* tomatoes dates to an 1835 edition of *New England Farmer* that recommends slicing green tomatoes and frying them in butter as a breakfast dish. This recipe is possibly a version of a Jewish breakfast tradition brought to America in the mid-1600s by Jewish immigrants of Spanish and Portuguese descent.

19. Flagg 1993:74.

20. Ibid.:dedication.

21. McMichael 1995:3.

22. History of the Irondale Café based on ibid. Quotation from page 6.

23. Flagg 1993:7.

24. Ibid.:5.

25. American Profile 2002.

26. Fowler 1995:272.

FIVE Lane Cake: Alabama Women in the Progressive Era

1. http://www.sumtercountyhistory.com/census/1860SumCoCen.htm; http://www.sumtercountyhistory.com/history/CalendarofLocalHistory.htm; https://www.genealogy.com/ftm/p/a/t/Nikki-M-Patrick/GENE2-0005.html.

2. *Heritage of Barbour County, Alabama* 2001.

3. Fowler 1995:310.

4. Mosier 2007a.

5. A 1974 article in the *Montgomery Advertiser* offers some interesting background on the invention of the Lane Cake. The author claims Mrs. W. A. Smart Sr. first made it as a birthday cake for one of her daughters. Allegedly, Emma Rylander

Lane's daughter attended the birthday party and came home talking about the cake. Mrs. Smart shared her recipe with Mrs. Lane, who experimented with the cake in the Parish kitchen before taking it to the county fair in Columbus.

6. Sauceman 2011.

7. Lee 1993:147.

8. http://www.dianasdesserts.com/index.cfm/fuseaction/recipes.recipeListing/filter/gue/recipeID/1503/Recipe.cfm.

9. Lane Cake history drawn from Sauceman 2011.

10. Lane 1898:preface.

11. Blakeslee, Leslie, and Hughes 1890.

12. Gillette and Ziemann 1887:3.

13. History of cookbooks in the Progressive Era drawn from C. Fisher 2006.

14. Fisher's book is the second-oldest known cookbook written by an African American. In 1866, Malinda Russell authored *A Domestic Cookbook: Containing a Careful Selection of Useful Recipes for the Kitchen*. Russell was born free in Tennessee.

15. Biography of Abby Fisher drawn from Hess 1995. Quotations from A. Fisher 1995.

16. Longone 2008.

17. Alabama club women history drawn from M. Thomas 1992, 1995.

18. Jenkins 2000:83.

19. Rorer 1902:3–4.

20. Farmer 1896:preface.

21. Good Housekeeping Institute, n.d.

22. M. Thomas 1992:2.

23. M. Thomas 1995:85.

24. Ibid.:84–85.

25. Robbins 1895:introduction.

26. M. Thomas 1992:219.

27. Flynt 2004:258.

28. M. Thomas 1992:135.

29. Longone 2008.

30. Alabama club women and suffrage history drawn from M. Thomas 1992, 1995. Quotation from M. Thomas 1995:95.

31. Personal interview with Rebecca Beasley, 2010, Clayton, AL.

32. Rogers and Ward 1994:376.

SIX *Banana Pudding: The Banana Docks at the Port of Mobile*

1. Alsobrook 1983; McLaurin and Thomason 1981.

2. Alsobrook 1983:94; Jenkins 2000:16.

3. Alsobrook 1983.

4. McLaurin and Thomason 1981.

5. Jenkins 2000; Soluri 2005.

6. Soluri 2005:33; Jenkins 2000:10.

7. Soluri 2005:36.

8. Ibid.:6.

9. Ibid.:18.

10. Jenkins 2000:18.

11. Ibid.:18–19.

12. Ibid.:19–20.

13. Ibid.:11.

14. Soluri 2005:37.

15. Koeppel 2008.

16. Soluri 2005:37.

17. Jenkins 2000:109.

18. Alsobrook 1983.

19. McLaurin and Thomason 1981.

20. Jenkins 2000.

21. Rayford 1991:188.

22. Description of Mobile's banana docks drawn from ibid.

23. Ibid.:189.

24. Personal interview with Michael

Thomason, 2010, phone interview.

25. Rayford 1991:190.

26. Checkers are the supervisors who weigh and check the bananas before they are loaded onto the boxcar.

27. Terkel 2005:268.

28. "Banana docks" chant drawn from files at the Museum of Mobile. Description of Rayford performing the chant drawn from files at the Mobile Public Library, Local History & Genealogy Branch.

29. Jenkins 2000:101.

30. Poole 1890.

31. Jenkins 2000:84.

32. Ibid.:67.

33. Ibid.:70.

34. Lewis and Peacock 2003:250.

35. Personal interview with Bettye Kimbrell, 2010, phone interview.

36. Personal interview with Cora Berry, 2010, Mobile, AL.

37. McLaurin and Thomason 1981.

38. Ibid.:124.

39. Personal interview with Chris Raley, 2010, Mobile, AL.

SEVEN *Fried Chicken: Decoration Day on Sand Mountain*

1. Egerton 1993:245.

2. Neal 1985:120.

3. Egerton 2007:142.

4. Goodman and Head 2011:2.

5. Neal 1985:120.

6. Egerton 2007:141, 1993:242.

7. Walter 1971:34.

8. Neal 1985:113.

9. Smith and Daniel 2000:262.

10. Edge 1999:232.

11. Carmer 1934.

12. Bragg 1998:83–84.

13. J. Smith 2004.

14. Jabbour and Jabbour 2010:42.

15. Edge 1999:233.

16. J. Smith 2004.

17. Jabbour and Jabbour 2010:41.

18. Ibid.

19. Carmer 1934.

20. Covington 1995:23.

21. Whitehall Decoration Day participant, 2010, Fort Payne, AL.

22. Personal interview with Billie Crumly, 2010, phone interview.

23. Jabbour and Jabbour 2010:25.

24. Ibid.

25. Interview with Crumly.

26. Jabbour and Jabbour 2010:24.

27. Description of crepe paper flowers drawn from Crumly 2009, Jabbour and Jabbour 2010.

28. Jabbour and Jabbour 2010:161.

29. Ibid.:107.

30. Description of Decoration Days in Appalachia drawn from ibid.

31. J. Smith 2004.

32. Smith and Daniel 2000.

33. Description of Whitehall Decoration Day drawn from event and conversations with participants.

EIGHT *Boiled Peanuts: George Washington Carver, the Wiregrass, and Macon County Farmers*

1. J. M. Taylor 2004:244.

2. Peanut history drawn from A. Smith 2002.

3. Dixon 2009.

4. Ibid.

5. History of the peanut in America drawn from ibid.

6. Clark 1989:6.

7. Phillips 2008.

8. Ibid.

9. Pasquill 2008.

10. Exhibit, Museum of Mobile, AL.

11. The Jesup Wagon was named for Morris K. Jesup, the New York philanthropist who funded the project.

12. Information on George Washington Carver based on exhibits at the George Washington Carver Museum in Tuskegee and the Museum of Mobile in Mobile and from email exchanges with Carver expert Mark Hersey.

13. A. Smith 2002.

14. Giesen 2011:105.

15. Ibid.:109.

16. Braund 1989.

17. Giesen 2011:118.

18. Ibid.

19. Ibid.:118, 120.

20. Braund 1989:27.

21. Giesen 2011:119.

22. History of peanuts during World War I based on A. Smith 2002. Quotations from pages 89–90.

23. Ibid.

24. Exhibit, George Washington Carver Museum, Tuskegee, AL.

25. Smith 2002:57.

26. Information on George Washington Carver based on exhibits at the George Washington Carver Museum in Tuskegee and the Museum of Mobile in Mobile and from email exchanges with Carver expert Mark Hersey.

27. Walter 1991.

28. Giesen 2011:127.

29. Braund 1989.

30. Ibid.

31. Giesen 2011:127–28.

32. Ibid.:136.

33. Ibid.

34. Ibid.:172, 141.

35. Ibid.:171.

36. Pasquill 2008:36.

37. History of black farmers in Macon County drawn from ibid.

38. Personal interview with Al Hooks, 2010, Shorter, AL.

NINE *Wild Turkey: Hunting and Wildlife Conservation in Alabama*

1. Personal interview with Steve Barnett, 2010, Spanish Fort, AL.

2. Barnett and Barnett 2009.

3. Bartram 1996:88–9.

4. Leopold 1986: xvii; Williamson 1987:1.

5. Lewis 1987.

6. McIlhenny, Jordan, and Shufeldt 1914:3, 8–9.

7. Lewis 1987.

8. History of the Pittman-Robertson Act in Alabama drawn from Barnett and Barnett 2009.

9. Personal interview with Tom Kelly, 2010, Daphne, AL.

10. Personal interview with Steve Barnett, 2010, Spanish Fort, AL.

11. Ibid.

12. Hutto 1995:1.

13. Ibid.:105.

14. Ibid.; Barnett and Barnett 2009.

15. Hutto 1995:166.

16. Ibid.:128.

17. Ibid.:45, 64, 55, 166.
18. Ibid.:167.
19. Ibid.:174.
20. National Wild Turkey Federation 2009.
21. Kelly 1996:160. From Latin: "As it was in the beginning, is now, and ever shall be."
22. Ibid.:92.
23. Ibid.:94.
24. Ibid.:111.
25. Flack 1999:23.
26. Ibid.:11–12.
27. McIlhenny, Jordan, and Shufeldt 1914:7.
28. Flack 1999:24.
29. McIlhenny, Jordan, and Shufeldt 1914:8.
30. The following information is from my personal interview with Tom Kelly.
31. Kelly 1996:143–44.

TEN *Sweet Tea: Birmingham in the Great Depression and the Second World War*

1. History of sweet tea drawn from Stradley 2004.
2. Thompson 2002:21.
3. Lewis and Peacock 2003:24.
4. Flynt 1994a:466.
5. Quotations from Birmingham residents pulled from oral interviews conducted in 1976. Transcripts housed at the University of Alabama Birmingham Oral History Collection.
6. Flynt 1994a:476.
7. Beecher, n.d.
8. Beecher 1971:25.
9. History of Birmingham during the Great Depression based on Flynt 1994a. Quotation from page 490.
10. Personal interview with Bea Carlton, 2010, Birmingham, AL.
11. History of Birmingham during World War II based on Flynt 1994b.
12. Personal interviews with Bea Carlton, Tricia Wallwork, 2010, Birmingham, AL.
13. Personal interviews with Bea Carlton, Tricia Wallwork.
14. Personal interviews with Bea Carlton, Tricia Wallwork.

ELEVEN *Sweet Potato Pie: Civil Rights and Soul Food in Montgomery*

1. Personal interview with Martha Hawkins, 2013, Montgomery, AL.
2. Cussick 1995:248.
3. Harris 1989; Van Der Post 1978:48.
4. Mosier 2007b:223.
5. Ibid.
6. J. Robinson 1987:21.
7. Graetz 1998:62–63.
8. Gaillard 2004:22.
9. Descriptions of the Montgomery Bus Boycott drawn from Gaillard 2004, J. Robinson 1987, J. Williams 1987, and visits to civil rights sites in Montgomery.
10. Personal interview with Nelson Malden, 2010, Montgomery, AL.
11. Edge 2000:15.
12. Ibid.:15–16.
13. Hampton and Fayer 1990:29.
14. "New Sounds in a Courthouse" 1956.
15. Hawkins and Brotherton 2010:173.
16. Description of Gilmore's cooking drawn from personal interview with Nelson Malden.
17. Hawkins 2010 and Brotherton:173.
18. Harris 2011:200.
19. Ibid.:203, 199, 200.
20. Opie 2008:135.

21. Harris 2011:201.

22. Ibid.:206.

23. Ibid.:206–7.

24. Opie 2008.

25. Ibid.:130.

26. Harris 2011:208–9.

27. Opie 2008:132.

28. Ibid.

29. Ibid.:137.

30. Hawkins and Brotherton 2010:32.

31. Ibid.:42.

32. Ibid.:126–27.

33. Ibid.:137–38.

34. Ibid.:138.

35. Ibid.:178.

36. Ibid.:202, 158.

37. Ibid.:191.

38. Hawkins biographical information drawn from ibid. Quotations from pages ix, 32.

TWELVE *Barbecue: Black History in the Black Belt*

1. Personal interview with Lula Hatcher, 2009, Selma, AL.

2. Auchmutey 2007.

3. Barbecue history drawn from Moss 2010.

4. Elie 2004:4.

5. Sauceman 2012.

6. S. Smith 2004:61.

7. Ibid.

8. Ibid.

9. Staten 2004:139.

10. Tullos 2004.

11. Chestnut and Cass 1990.

12. Ibid.:21.

13. A. Robinson 1991:239.

14. Ibid.

15. Moss 2010:167.

16. History of barbecue drawn from ibid.

17. Personal interview with Lula Hatcher.

18. A. Robinson 1991.

19. J. Williams 1987:269.

20. *Selma Times-Journal*, March 8, 1965.

21. Hampton and Fayer 1990:229–30.

22. "Civil Rights: Protest on Route 80" 1965.

23. History of the voting rights movement in Selma drawn from Gaillard 2004, A. Robinson 1991, J. Williams 1987, and visits to civil rights sites in Selma, Lowndes County, and Montgomery, Alabama.

24. Personal interview with Lula Hatcher.

25. Annie Cooper biographical information drawn from Gaillard 2004. Quotation from page 233.

26. From framed article from *Selma Times-Journal* hanging in Lannie's Bar-B-Q in Selma.

THIRTEEN *MoonPies: Mardi Gras in Mobile*

1. History of the MoonPie Rise drawn from interviews with Barbara Drummond, Steve Mussell, and Fred Richardson, 2009, Mobile, AL.

2. Magee 2006:29–30.

3. Ibid.:45.

4. Historic information on the MoonPie drawn from ibid.

5. Personal email from Marie Arnott, January 25, 2010.

6. Personal interview with Stephen Toomey, 2009, Mobile, AL.

7. The Boeuf Gras Society was Mobile's first mystic society. Membership in mystic societies is by invitation and members keep their identities secret

by masking at society events. In Mobile Mardi Gras parades, each parade is sponsored by a different mystic society, whose members ride on the floats.

8. McLaurin and Thomason 1981:74.
9. Kirkland 2011b.
10. Ibid.
11. Rayford 1962:46.
12. Ibid.:338, 15.
13. Kinser 1990:270.
14. Historic information on Mardi Gras in Mobile and Joe Cain drawn from W. Dean 1967, Delaney 1994, Kirkland 2011a and b, McLaurin and Thomason 1981, Thomason 2001, visits to museums and parades in Mobile, Alabama, a "MoonPie Memories" contest in the *Mobile Press-Register*, and interviews with Doris Allinson Dean, Wayne Dean (2010, Mobile, AL), and Stephen Toomey.

FOURTEEN *Shrimp: Seafood in Bayou La Batre*

1. Drawn from visit to Boat People SOS office and personal interviews with local residents, 2010, Bayou La Batre, AL.
2. Stitt 2004:144.
3. Gaillard, Hagler, and Denniston 2008.
4. Ibid.:15.
5. History of Bayou La Batre drawn from ibid. Quotation from page 16.
6. Ibid.:3.
7. Ibid.:4.
8. Ibid.:16.
9. Ibid.:4.
10. Rayford 1956:32.
11. Rudloe and Rudloe 2010:32.
12. Durrenberger 1992:57.
13. Rudloe and Rudloe 2010:32.
14. Ibid.:33–4.
15. Durrenberger 1992:63.
16. Evans 1997:230.
17. Durrenberger 1992.
18. Evans 1997:235.
19. Gaillard, Hagler, and Denniston 2008:94.
20. Ibid.
21. Durrenberger 1992:109.
22. Shrimping history drawn from ibid. Quotation from page 109.
23. Starr 1981:226.
24. Thomas and Formichella 1987:14.
25. Gaillard, Hagler, and Denniston 2008:34.
26. Ibid.
27. Moberg and Thomas 1998.
28. Rudloe and Rudloe 2010.
29. Gaillard 2007.
30. Gaillard, Hagler, and Denniston 2008:58.
31. Ibid.
32. Ibid.:52.
33. Ibid.:55.
34. Rudloe and Rudloe 2010.
35. Description of the Blessing of the Fleet drawn from attendance at the event, May 2, 2010.
36. Description of the oil spill's impact on Southeast Asian communities drawn from Ravitz 2010.

Suggestions for Further Reading

ONE *Roasted Corn: The Creek Nation in Alabama*

Blitz, John H. 2008. *Moundville*. Tuscaloosa: University of Alabama Press.

Davis, Karl. 1998. "The Founding of Tensaw: Kinship, Community, Trade, and Diplomacy in the Creek Nation." Pp. 81–98 in *Coastal Encounters: The Transformation of the Gulf South in the Eighteenth Century*, edited by Richmond F. Brown. Lincoln: University of Nebraska Press.

Hardeman, Nicholas. 1981. *Shucks, Shocks, and Hominy Blocks: Corn as a Way of Life in Pioneer America*. Baton Rouge: Louisiana State University Press.

Waselkov, Gregory A. 2006. *A Conquering Spirit: Fort Mims and the Redstick War of 1813–1814*. Tuscaloosa: University of Alabama Press.

TWO *Gumbo: Africans and Creoles on the Gulf Coast*

Dormon, James H., ed. 1996. *Creoles of Color of the Gulf South*. Knoxville: University of Tennessee Press.

Harris, Jessica. 2011. *High on the Hog: A Culinary Journey from Africa to America*. New York: Bloomsbury USA.

Opie, Frederick Douglass. 2008. *Hog and Hominy*. New York: Columbia University Press.

THREE *Chicken Stew: Frontier Life in the Tennessee Valley*

Allen, William S. 2011. "Chicken Stew and Goat Stew in Northwestern Alabama." *Tributaries: Journal of the Alabama Folklife Association* 13:16–28.

Atkins, Leah Rawls. 1994. "Land in the Alabama Wilderness Beckons." Pp. 54–66 in *Alabama: The History of a Deep South State* by William Warren Rogers, Robert David Ward, Leah Rawls Atkins, and Wayne Flynt. Tuscaloosa: University of Alabama Press.

Walker, Robert Henry, Jr. 1973. *History of Limestone County, Alabama*. Athens, AL: Limestone County Commission.

FOUR *Fried Green Tomatoes: Emblem of the Alabama Rural Table*

Dean, Don Howard. 2008. *The American Cane Mill*. Jefferson, NC: McFarland and Company.

Engelhardt, Elizabeth. 2009. "Canning Tomatoes, 'Growing Better and More Perfect Women': The Girls' Tomato Club Movement." *Southern Cultures* 15 (4): 78–92.

Flagg, Fannie. 1987. *Fried Green Tomatoes at the Whistle Stop Café*. New York: Random House.

Smith, Andrew F. 1994. *The Tomato in America*. Columbia: University of South Carolina Press.

FIVE *Lane Cake: Alabama Women in the Progressive Era*

Feeding America: The Historic American Cookbook Project. http://digital.lib.msu.edu/projects/
cookbooks/index.html.

Fisher, Carol. 2006. *The American Cookbook.* Jefferson, NC: McFarland and Company.

Flynt, Wayne. 2004. "On and Off the Pedestal: Women." Pp. 251–92 in *Alabama in the Twentieth Century.* Tuscaloosa: University of Alabama Press.

Sharpless, Rebecca. 2010. *Cooking in Other Women's Kitchens: Domestic Workers in the South,
1865–1960.* Chapel Hill: University of North Carolina Press.

Thomas, Mary Martha. 1992. *The New Woman in Alabama: Social Reforms and Suffrage, 1890–
1920.* Tuscaloosa: University of Alabama Press.

———, ed. 1995. *Stepping out of the Shadows: Alabama Women, 1819–1990.* Tuscaloosa: University of Alabama Press.

SIX *Banana Pudding: The Banana Docks at the Port of Mobile*

Jenkins, Virginia Scott. 2000. *Bananas: An American History.* Washington, DC: Smithsonian
Institution Press.

Rayford, Julian Lee. 1991. *Cottonmouth.* Tuscaloosa: University of Alabama Press.

Soluri, John. 2005. *Banana Cultures: Agriculture, Consumption, and Environmental Change in Honduras and the United States.* Austin: University of Texas Press.

SEVEN *Fried Chicken: Decoration Day on Sand Mountain*

Covington, Dennis. 2009. *Salvation on Sand Mountain.* Cambridge, MA: Da Capo Press.

Edge, John T. 2004. *Fried Chicken: An American Story.* New York: G. P. Putnam's Sons.

Jabbour, Alan, and Karen Singer Jabbour. 2010. *Decoration Day in the Mountains.* Chapel Hill:
University of North Carolina Press.

Williams-Forson, Psyche A. 2006. *Building Houses out of Chicken Legs: Black Women, Food, and
Power.* Chapel Hill: University of North Carolina Press.

EIGHT *Boiled Peanuts: George Washington Carver, the Wiregrass, and Macon County
Farmers*

Braund, Kathryn Holland. 1989. "Hog Wild and Nuts: Billy Boll Weevil Comes to the Alabama Wiregrass." *Agricultural History* 63 (3): 15–39.

Giesen, James C. 2011. *Boll Weevil Blues: Cotton, Myth, and Power in the American South.* Chicago: University of Chicago Press.

Hersey, Mark D. 2011. *My Work Is That of Conservation: An Environmental Biography of George
Washington Carver.* Athens: University of Georgia Press.

Pasquill, Robert G., Jr. 2008. *Planting Hope on Worn-Out Land: History of the Tuskegee Land Utilization Project.* Montgomery, AL: New South Books.

Smith, Andrew F. 2002. *Peanuts: The Illustrious History of the Goober Pea*. Chicago: University of Illinois Press.

NINE *Wild Turkey: Hunting and Wildlife Conservation in Alabama*

Hutto, Joe. 1995. *Illumination in the Flatwoods*. Guilford, CT: Lyons Press.

Kelly, Tom. 2005. *Tenth Legion: Tips, Tactics, and Insights on Turkey Hunting*. Guilford, CT: Lyons Press.

McIlhenny, Edward Avery, Charles L. Jordan, and Robert Wilson Shufeldt. 1914. *The Wild Turkey and Its Hunting*. New York: Doubleday, Page.

TEN *Sweet Tea: Birmingham in the Great Depression and the Second World War*

Beecher, John. 1971. *Report to the Stockholders and Other Poems: 1932–1962*. Cocoa Beach, FL: Red Mountain Editions.

Flynt, Wayne. 1994. "Hard Times, 1930–1940." Pp. 465–93 in *Alabama: The History of a Deep South State* by William Warren Rogers, Robert David Ward, Leah Rawls Atkins, and Wayne Flynt. Tuscaloosa: University of Alabama Press.

ELEVEN *Sweet Potato Pie: Civil Rights and Soul Food in Montgomery*

Gaillard, Frye. 2004. *Cradle of Freedom*. Tuscaloosa: University of Alabama Press.

Graetz, Robert S. 1998. *A White Preacher's Memoir: The Montgomery Bus Boycott*. Montgomery, AL: Black Belt Press.

Harris, Jessica. 2011. *High on the Hog: A Culinary Journey from Africa to America*. New York: Bloomsbury USA.

Hawkins, Martha, and Marcus Brotherton. 2010. *Finding Martha's Place*. New York: Simon and Schuster.

Opie, Frederick Douglass. 2008. *Hog and Hominy*. New York: Columbia University Press.

Robinson, Jo Ann Gibson. 1987. *The Montgomery Bus Boycott and the Women Who Started It*. Knoxville: University of Tennessee Press.

TWELVE *Barbecue: Black History in the Black Belt*

Burnes, Valerie Pope. 2011. "Life, Death, and Barbecue: Food and Community in Sumter County." *Tributaries: Journal of the Alabama Folklife Association* 13:29–43.

Chestnut, J. L., Jr., and Julia Cass. 1990. *Black in Selma: The Uncommon Life of J. L. Chestnut, Jr.* Tuscaloosa: University of Alabama Press.

Elie, Lolis Eric, ed. 2004. *Cornbread Nation 2: The United States of Barbecue*. Chapel Hill: University of North Carolina Press.

Moss, Robert F. 2010. *Barbecue: The History of an American Institution*. Tuscaloosa: University of Alabama Press.

Robinson, Amelia Platts Boynton. 1991. *Bridge across Jordan*. Washington, DC: Schiller Institute.

Webb, Sheyann, and Rachel West Nelson. 1980. *Selma, Lord, Selma*. Tuscaloosa: University of Alabama Press.

THIRTEEN *MoonPies: Mardi Gras in Mobile*

Brown, Margaret, dir. 2009. *The Order of Myths*. New York: Cinema Guild.

Dean, Doris Allinson. 2010. *Death by MoonPie*. Mobile, AL: Wayne Dean Productions and Masked Mystic Creations.

Dean, Wayne. 1967. *Mardi Gras: Mobile's Illogical Whoop-de-do*. Chicago: Adams Press.

Rayford, Julian Lee. 1962. *Chasin' the Devil Round a Stump*. Madison, WI: American Printing Company.

FOURTEEN *Shrimp: Seafood in Bayou La Batre*

Durrenberger, E. Paul. 1992. *It's All politics: South Alabama's Seafood Industry*. Champaign: University of Illinois Press.

Evans, Lawrence F. 1997. "Master Abel, of the Grover Cleveland of Bayou la Batre." Pp. 229–35 in *Up before Daylight: Life Histories from the Alabama Writers' Project, 1938–1939*, edited by James Seay Brown Jr. Tuscaloosa: University of Alabama Press.

Gaillard, Frye, Sheila Hagler, and Peggy Denniston. 2008. *In the Path of the Storms: Bayou La Batre, Coden, and the Alabama Coast*. Auburn, AL: Pebble Hill Books.

Rudloe, Jack, and Anne Rudloe. 2010. *Shrimp: The Endless Quest for Pink Gold*. Upper Saddle River, NJ: FT Press.

References

Allen, William S. 2009. "Chicken and Goat Stew in the Tennessee Valley." Pp. 5–7 in *Alabama Foodways Gathering*, edited by Joyce Cauthen. Montgomery, AL: Alabama Folklife Association. November 7.

———. 2011. "Chicken Stew and Goat Stew in Northwestern Alabama." *Tributaries: Journal of the Alabama Folklife Association* 13:16–28.

Allman, John M. 1979. *Yeoman Regions in the Antebellum Deep South: Settlement and Economy in Northern Alabama, 1815–1869.* PhD dissertation, University of Maryland.

Alsobrook, David Ernest. 1983. "Alabama's Port City: Mobile during the Progressive Era, 1896–1917." Auburn University, Auburn, AL. Unpublished manuscript.

American Profile. 2002. "Fried Green Tomatoes at the Irondale Café." http://americanprofile.com/articles/fried-green-tomatoes-irondale-cafe/.

Andrews, Casandra. 2010. "Big Chief." *Mobile Press-Register*, February 14, 1A, 4A.

Atkins, Leah Rawls. 1994a. "Creeks and Americans at War." Pp. 36–53 in Rogers et al., *Alabama*.

———. 1994b. "Land in the Alabama Wilderness Beckons." Pp. 54–66 in Rogers et al., *Alabama*.

———. 1994c. "Native Peoples of Alabama." Pp. 3–17 in Rogers et al., *Alabama*.

Auchmutey, Jim. 2007. "Barbecue." Pp. 22–26 in Edge, *Foodways*.

Baraka, Amiri. 1966. *Home: Social Essays*. New York: William Morrow.

Barnett, Steven W., and Victoria S. Barnett. 2009. *The Wild Turkey in Alabama*. Montgomery: Alabama Department of Conservation and Natural Resources, Division of Wildlife and Freshwater Fisheries.

Bartram, William. 1996. *Travels and Other Writings*. New York: Library of America.

Beecher, John. N.d. "Ensley, Alabama." https://folkways.si.edu/john-beecher/report-to-the-stockholders-poems-by/poetry/album/smithsonian.

———. 1971. *Report to the Stockholders & Other Poems: 1932–1962*. Cocoa Beach, FL: Red Mountain Editions.

———. 2003. *One More River to Cross: Selected Poems*. Montgomery, AL: New South Books.

Berntson, Ben. 2011. "Boll Weevil Monument." *Encyclopedia of Alabama*. http://www.encyclopediaofalabama.org/article/h-2384.

Besson, J. A. B. 1976. *History of Eufaula, Alabama.* Spartanburg, SC: Reprint Company Publishers. Originally published, 1875.

Bivens, Shawn A. 2004. *Mobile, Alabama's People of Color.* Victoria, Canada: Trafford Publishing.

Blakeslee, Mrs. E. C., Emma Leslie, and S. H. Hughes. 1890. *The Compendium of Cookery and Reliable Recipes.* Chicago: Merchants' Specialty.

Blitz, John H. 2008. *Moundville.* Tuscaloosa: University of Alabama Press.

Boucher, Ann. 1978. *Alabama Women: Roles and Rebels.* Troy, AL: Troy State University Press.

Bower, Anne L. 2007. "Cookbooks, Community." Pp. 45–46 in Edge, *Foodways.*

Bowne, Eric E. 2008. "Green Corn Ceremony." *The Encyclopedia of Alabama.* http://www.encyclopediaofalabama.org/article/h-1553.

Brackner, Joey. 2010. "Decoration Day." *The Encyclopedia of Alabama.* http://www.encyclopediaofalabama.org/article/h-2316.

Bragg, Rick. 1998. *All Over but the Shoutin'.* New York: Vintage.

Braund, Kathryn Holland. 1989. "Hog Wild and Nuts: Billy Boll Weevil Comes to the Alabama Wiregrass." *Agricultural History* 63 (3): 15–39.

———. 2008. "Creek War of 1813–14." *The Encyclopedia of Alabama.* http://www.encyclopediaofalabama.org/article/h-1820.

Bunn, Mike, and Clay Williams. 2009. "Clash of Cultures." *Alabama Heritage* 92:8–17.

Burnes, Valerie Pope. 2011. "Life, Death, and Barbecue: Food and Community in Sumter County." *Tributaries: Journal of the Alabama Folklife Association* 13:29–43.

Cannon, Vivian. 1974. "Clayton Christmas Cake Started as Home Recipe." *Montgomery Advertiser*, December 22.

Carmer, Carl. 1934. *Stars Fell on Alabama.* Tuscaloosa: University of Alabama Press.

Carrier, Jim. 2004. *A Traveler's Guide to the Civil Rights Movement.* Orlando, FL: Harcourt.

Carver, George Washington. 1936. *How the Farmer Can Save His Sweet Potatoes and Ways of Preparing Them for the Table.* Bulletin No. 38. Tuskegee, AL: Tuskegee Institute Press.

Cass, Julia. 2006. "After Katrina, Cookbooks Top the Best-Seller List." *Washington Post*, March 22.

Chapman, Jeff. 2000. "The Impact of the Potato." *History Magazine*, December/January. http://www.history-magazine.com/potato.html.

Chestnut, J. L., Jr., and Julia Cass. 1990. *Black in Selma: The Uncommon Life of J. L. Chestnut, Jr.* Tuscaloosa: University of Alabama Press.

"Civil Rights: Protest on Route 80." 1965. *Time*, April 2.

Claiborne, Craig. 2007. *Craig Claiborne's Southern Cooking.* Athens: University of Georgia Press.

Clark, Thomas D. 1989. "Agriculture." Pp. 5–7 in Wilson, Ferris, and Adadie, *Encyclopedia of Southern Culture*.

Coppens, Linda Miles. 2001. *What American Women Did: 1789–1920*. Jefferson, NC: McFarland.

Couric, Gertha. 2009. "Alabama Cane Grindings and Candy Pullings." P. 186 in *The Food of a Younger Land*, edited by Mark Kurlansky. New York: Riverhead Books.

Covington, Dennis. 1995. *Salvation on Sand Mountain*. Cambridge, MA: Da Capo Press.

Crumly, Billie. 2006. "Country Living." *Weekly Post* (Rainsville, AL), May 11.

———. 2009. "Country Living: Decorations and Singings." *Weekly Post* (Rainsville, AL), May 21.

Cusick, Heidi Haughy. 1995. *Soul and Spice: African Cooking in the Americas*. San Francisco: Chronicle Books.

Daniel, Pete. 1989. "Corn." Pp. 33–34 in Wilson, Ferris, and Adadie, *Encyclopedia of Southern Culture*.

David Walker Lupton African American Cookbook Collection. 2004. W. S. Hoole Special Collections Library, Tuscaloosa. https://www.lib.ua.edu/collections/the-david-walker-lupton-african-american-cookbook-collection/.

Davis, Karl. 1998. "The Founding of Tensaw: Kinship, Community, Trade, and Diplomacy in the Creek Nation." Pp. 81–98 in *Coastal Encounters: The Transformation of the Gulf South in the Eighteenth Century*, edited by Richmond F. Brown. Lincoln: University of Nebraska Press.

———. 2003. "Much of the Indian Appears: Adaptation and Persistence in a Creek Community, 1783–1854." PhD dissertation, University of North Carolina, Chapel Hill.

Dean, Don Howard. 2008. *The American Cane Mill*. Jefferson, NC: McFarland.

Dean, Doris Allinson. 2010. *Death by MoonPie*. Mobile, AL: Wayne Dean Productions and Masked Mystic Creations.

Dean, Wayne. 1967. *Mardi Gras: Mobile's Illogical Whoop-de-do*. Chicago: Adams Press.

Delaney, Caldwell. 1994. *The Story of Mobile*. Mobile, AL: HB Publications.

Dethloff, Henry C. 1989. "Crops." Pp. 18–19 in Wilson, Ferris, and Adadie, *Encyclopedia of Southern Culture*.

Dixon, Rob. 2009. "Peanut Production in Alabama." *The Encyclopedia of Alabama*. http://www.encyclopediaofalabama.org/article/h-2016.

Dormon, James H., ed. 1996. *Creoles of Color of the Gulf South*. Knoxville: University of Tennessee Press.

Douglass, Frederick. 2001. *Narrative of the Life of Frederick Douglass*. New Haven, CT: Yale University Press. Originally published, Boston: Anti-Slavery Office, 1845.

Dunnavant, Robert, Jr. 1993. *Historic Limestone County: A Collection of Stories, Incidentally, Some History from Limestone County, Alabama, and Surrounding Counties*. Athens, AL: Pea Ridge Press.

Dupree, Nathalie. 2004. *New Southern Cooking*. Athens: University of Georgia Press.

Durrenberger, E. Paul. 1992. *It's All Politics: South Alabama's Seafood Industry*. Champaign: University of Illinois Press.

Edge, John T. 1999. *A Gracious Plenty*. New York: G. P. Putnam's Sons.

———. 2000. *Southern Belly: The Ultimate Food Lover's Companion to the South*. Athens, GA: Hill Street Press.

———. 2004. *Fried Chicken: An American Story*. New York: G. P. Putnam's Sons.

———, ed. 2007. *Foodways*. Vol. 7. Chapel Hill: University of North Carolina Press.

Egerton, John. 1993. *Southern Food: At Home, on the Road, in History*. Chapel Hill: University of North Carolina Press.

———. 2007. "Chicken, Fried." Pp. 141–43 in Edge, *Foodways*.

Elie, Lolis Eric. 2004. *Cornbread Nation 2*. Chapel Hill: University of North Carolina Press.

———. 2005. *Smokestack Lightning: Adventures in the Heart of Barbecue Country*. Berkeley, CA: Ten Speed Press.

Engelhardt, Elizabeth. 2009. "Canning Tomatoes, 'Growing Better and More Perfect Women': The Girls' Tomato Club Movement." *Southern Cultures* 15 (4): 78–92.

Evans, Lawrence F. 1997. "Master Abel, of the Grover Cleveland of Bayou la Batre." Pp. 229–35 in *Up before Daylight: Life Histories from the Alabama Writers' Project, 1938–1939*, edited by James Seay Brown Jr. Tuscaloosa: University of Alabama Press.

Family Histories and Memories. 2004. Mobile, AL: Mobile Genealogical Society.

Farmer, Fannie. 1896. *The Boston Cooking-School Cook Book*. Boston: Little, Brown.

Farnell, Kathie. 2009. "MoonPie Matriarchs." *Thicket Magazine*, January/February, 26–27.

Feeding America: The Historic American Cookbook Project. http://digital.lib.msu.edu/projects/cookbooks/index.html.

Ferris, Marcie Cohen. 2005. *Matzoh Ball Gumbo: Culinary Tales of the Jewish South*. Chapel Hill: University of North Carolina Press.

———. 2009. "The Edible South." *Southern Cultures* 15 (4): 3–27.

Fisher, Abby. 1995. *What Mrs. Fisher Knows about Old Southern Cooking*. Notes by Karen Hess. Bedford, MA: Applewood Books. Originally published, San Francisco: Women's Cooperative Printing Office, 1881.

Fisher, Carol. 2006. *The American Cookbook*. Jefferson, NC: McFarland.

Flack, Captain. 1999. "Turkey Hunts in Texas." Pp. 11–30 in *Hunting in the Old South*, edited by Clarence Gohdes. Baton Rouge: Louisiana State University Press.

Flagg, Fannie. 1993. *Fannie Flagg's Original Whistle Stop Café Cookbook*. New York: Ballantine Books.

Flynt, Wayne. 1989. *Poor but Proud*. Tuscaloosa: University of Alabama Press.

———. 1994a. "Hard Times, 1930–1940." Pp. 465–93 in Rogers et al., *Alabama*.

———. 1994b. "A State Forged by War, 1940–1954." Pp. 511–23 in Rogers et al., *Alabama*.

———. 2004. *Alabama in the Twentieth Century*. Tuscaloosa: University of Alabama Press.

Ford, Gary D. 1989. "Barbecue." Pp. 676 in Wilson, Ferris, and Adadie, *Encyclopedia of Southern Culture*.

Fowler, Damon Lee. 1995. *Classical Southern Cooking*. New York: Crown Publishers.

Fussell, Betty. 1992. *The Story of Corn*. New York: North Point Press.

Gaillard, Frye. 2004. *Cradle of Freedom*. Tuscaloosa: University of Alabama Press.

———. 2007. "After the Storms: Tradition and Change in Bayou La Batre." *Journal of American History* 94 (3): 856–62.

———. 2010. *Alabama's Civil Rights Trail*. Tuscaloosa: University of Alabama Press.

Gaillard, Frye, Sheila Hagler, and Peggy Denniston. 2008. *In the Path of the Storms: Bayou La Batre, Coden, and the Alabama Coast*. Auburn, AL: Pebble Hill Books.

Giesen, James C. 2011. *Boll Weevil Blues: Cotton, Myth, and Power in the American South*. Chicago: University of Chicago Press.

Gillette, F. L., and Hugo Ziemann. 1887. *The White House Cook Book*. New York: Saalfield Publishing.

Good Housekeeping Institute. N.d. "The History of the Good Housekeeping Institute." https://www.goodhousekeeping.com/institute/about-the-institute/a17940/good-housekeeping-institute-timeline/.

Goodman, Donald, and Thomas Head, eds. 2011. *The Happy Table of Eugene Walter*. Chapel Hill: University of North Carolina Press.

Gould, Virginia Meacham. 1996. "The Free Creoles of Color of the Antebellum Gulf Ports of Mobile and Pensacola: A Struggle for the Middle Ground." Pp. 28–50 in *Creoles of Color of the Gulf South*, edited by James H. Dormon. Knoxville: University of Tennessee Press.

Gray, Juliana. 2004. "Willodene." Pp. 146–50 in Elie, *Cornbread Nation 2*.

Graetz, Robert S. 1998. *A White Preacher's Memoir: The Montgomery Bus Boycott*. Montgomery, AL: Black Belt Press.

Grauberger, Stephen. 1996. "Rolling Stores Once Were Common in Rural Alabama." *Alabama Folklife Association*. http://www.arts.state.al.us/actc/articles/store.htm.

Hampton, Henry, and Steve Fayer. 1990. *Voices of Freedom: An Oral History of the Civil Rights Movement from the 1950s through the 1980s*. New York: Bantam Books.

Hardeman, Nicholas. 1981. *Shucks, Shocks, and Hominy Blocks: Corn as a Way of Life in Pioneer America.* Baton Rouge: Louisiana State University Press.

Harris, Jessica B. 1989. *Iron Pots and Wooden Spoons.* New York: Simon and Schuster.

———. 1995. *The Welcome Table: African-American Heritage Cooking.* New York: Fireside.

———. 1998. *The Africa Cookbook: Tastes of a Continent.* New York: Simon and Schuster.

———. 2007. "African American Foodways." Pp. 15–18 in Edge, *Foodways.*

———. 2011. *High on the Hog: A Culinary Journey from Africa to America.* New York: Bloomsbury USA.

Haveman, Christopher. 2009. "Creek Indian Removal." *The Encyclopedia of Alabama.* http://www.encyclopediaofalabama.org/article/h-2013.

Hawkins, Martha, and Marcus Brotherton. 2010. *Finding Martha's Place.* New York: Simon and Schuster.

Heritage of Barbour County, Alabama. 2001. Clanton, AL: Heritage Publishing Consultants.

Heritage of Limestone County, Alabama. 1998. Clanton, AL: Heritage Publishing Consultants.

Hess, Karen. 1995. "What We Know about Mrs. Abby Fisher and Her Cooking." Pp. 75–90 in *What Mrs. Fisher Knows about Old Southern Cooking.* Bedford, MA: Applewood Books.

Higginbotham, Jay. 1991. Speech given at Admiral Semmes Hotel, Mobile, AL, April 4.

Hobson, Jeremy, and Celia Lewis. 2007. *Keeping Chickens: The Essential Guide.* Devon, UK: David and Charles.

Hoffman, Roy. 2011. "Poarch Creek Indian Pow Wow Offers Symbols of Ancient Religion." *Mobile Press-Register*, November 19.

Hudson, Charles. 1976. *The Southeastern Indians.* Knoxville: University of Tennessee Press.

Hutto, Joe. 1995. *Illumination in the Flatwoods.* Guilford, CT: Lyons Press.

Jabbour, Alan, and Karen Singer Jabbour. 2010. *Decoration Day in the Mountains.* Chapel Hill: University of North Carolina Press.

Jenkins, Virginia Scott. 2000. *Bananas: An American History.* Washington, DC: Smithsonian Institution Press.

Jones, Loyal. 2007. "Corn." Pp. 151–52 in Edge, *Foodways.*

Kelly, Tom. 1996. *The Season.* New York: Lyons and Burford Publishers.

Kimball, Cheryl. 2009. *The Field Guide to Goats.* Osceola, WI: Voyageur Press.

Kinser, Samuel. 1990. *Carnival, American Style.* Chicago: University of Chicago Press.

Kirkland, Scotty E. 2011a. "Joe Cain." *The Encyclopedia of Alabama.* http://www.encyclopediaofalabama.org/article/h-2923.

———. 2011b. "Mobile's Mardi Gras." *The Encyclopedia of Alabama.* http://www.encyclopediaofalabama.org/article/h-1437.

Koeppel, Dan. 2008. *Banana: The Fate of the Fruit That Changed the World.* New York: Plume.

Kytle, Jack. 2009. "Alabama Eggnog." Pp. 187–90 in *The Food of a Younger Land*, edited by Mark Kurlansky. New York: Riverhead Books.

Lacher-Feldman, Jessica. 2011. "A Taste of Community: Community Cookbooks at the W. S. Hoole Special Collections Library." *Tributaries: Journal of the Alabama Folklife Association* 13:79–88.

Lane, Emma Rylander. 1898. *Some Good Things to Eat.* Clayton, AL: self-published.

Lee, Harper. 1993. *To Kill a Mockingbird.* New York: HarperCollins Publishers. Originally published, Philadelphia: J. B. Lippincott, 1960.

Leopold, Aldo. 1986. *Game Management.* Madison: University of Wisconsin Press. Originally published, New York: Charles Scribner's Sons, 1933.

Lewis, Edna, and Scott Peacock. 2003. *The Gift of Southern Cooking.* New York: Alfred A. Knopf.

Lewis, John B. 1987. "Success Story: Wild Turkey." Pp. 31–43 in *Restoring America's Wildlife.* Washington, DC: US Government Printing Office.

Longone, Jan. 2004. "Great Ladies of American Cooking." http://digital.lib.msu.edu/projects/cookbooks/html/browse_int/browse_interest_great.html.

———. 2008. "The Old Girl Network: Charity Cookbooks and the Empowerment of Women." Lecture, University of Michigan, Ann Arbor, September 21.

Lovegren, Sylvia. 2003. "Barbecue." *American Heritage* 3 (3): 36–44.

Lundy, Ronni. 1994. *Shuck Beans, Stack Cakes, and Honest Fried Chicken: The Heart and Soul of Southern Country Kitchens.* New York: Atlantic Monthly Press.

Magee, David. 2006. *MoonPie: Biography of an Out-of-This-World Snack.* Gainesville: University Press of Florida.

Mariani, John F. 1994. *The Dictionary of American Food and Drink.* New York: Hearst Books.

Martin, Judith. 2003. *Star-Spangled Manners.* New York: W. W. Norton.

Matte, Jacqueline Anderson. 2002. *They Say the Wind Is Red.* Montgomery, AL: New South Books.

McAlpine, Pam, and Valerie Pope Burnes. 2009. "The Barbecue Clubs of Sumter County." Pp. 8–11 in *Alabama Foodways Gathering*, edited by Joyce Cauthen. Montgomery: Alabama Folklife Association. November 7.

McGowin, Earl M. 1953. "History of Conservation in Alabama." Speech given at the Alabama Historical Association, Mobile, April 25.

McIlhenny, Edward Avery, Charles L. Jordan, and Robert Wilson Shufeldt. 1914. *The Wild Turkey and Its Hunting.* New York: Doubleday, Page.

McLaurin, Melton, and Michael Thomason. 1981. *Mobile: The Life and Times of a Great Southern City*. Woodland Hills, CA: Windsor Publications.

McMichael, Mary Jo Smith. 1995. *Irondale Café Original Whistle Stop Cookbook*. Birmingham, AL: Crane Hill Publishers.

Mintz, Sidney W. 1986. *Sweetness and Power: The Place of Sugar in Modern History*. New York: Penguin Books.

Moberg, Mark, and J. Stephen Thomas. 1998. "Indochinese Resettlement and the Transformation of Identities along the Alabama Gulf Coast." Pp. 115–28 in *Cultural Diversity in the U.S. South: Anthropological Contributions to a Region in Transition*, edited by Carole E. Hill and Patricia D. Beaver. Athens: University of Georgia Press.

Moritz, C. F., and Adele Kahn. 1898. *The Twentieth Century Cook Book*. New York: G. W. Dillingham.

Mosier, Angie. 2007a. "Cakes." Pp. 134–36 in Edge, *Foodways*.

———. 2007b. "Pies." Pp. 222–26 in Edge, *Foodways*.

Moss, Robert F. 2010. *Barbecue: The History of an American Institution*. Tuscaloosa: University of Alabama Press.

Nathan, Joan. 1998. *Jewish Cooking in America*. New York: Alfred A. Knopf.

National Onion Association. 2011. "History of Onions." http://onions-usa.org/all-about-onions/history-of-onions.

National Wild Turkey Federation. 2009. "NWTF Presents Tom Kelly 2009 Communicator of the Year Award." https://www.prlog.org/10187775-nwtf-presents-tom-kelly-2009-communicator-of-the-year-award.html.

Neal, Bill. 1985. *Southern Cooking*. Chapel Hill: University of North Carolina Press.

———. 1996. *Biscuits, Spoonbread, and Sweet Potato Pie*. New York: Alfred A. Knopf.

Neuman, Robert W. 1989. "Indians and the Landscape." Pp. 547 in Wilson, Ferris, and Adadie, *Encyclopedia of Southern Culture*.

"New Sounds in a Courthouse." 1956. *Time*, April 2.

Nobles, Cynthia Lejeune. 2009. "Gumbo." Pp. 98–115 in *New Orleans Cuisine: Fourteen Signature Dishes and Their Histories*, edited by Susan Tucker. Jackson: University Press of Mississippi.

Opie, Frederick Douglass. 2008. *Hog and Hominy*. New York: Columbia University Press.

Outlaw, Bill. 2008. "Forward." Pp. 1–2 in *The American Cane Mill* by Don Howard Dean. Jefferson, NC: McFarland.

Owsley, Frank L., Jr. 2000. *Struggle for the Gulf Borderlands: The Creek War and the Battle of New Orleans, 1812–1815*. Tuscaloosa: University of Alabama Press.

Paredes, J. Anthony. 1979. "Back from Disappearance: The Alabama Creek Indian Community." Pp. 123–41 in *Southeastern Indians since the Removal Era*, edited by Walter L. Williams. Athens: University of Georgia Press.

———. 1992. "Federal Recognition and the Poarch Creek Indians." Pp. 120–39 in *Indians of the Southeastern United States in the Late 20th Century*, edited by J. Anthony Paredes. Tuscaloosa: University of Alabama Press.

Pasquill, Robert G., Jr. 2008. *Planting Hope on Worn-Out Land: History of the Tuskegee Land Utilization Project*. Montgomery, AL: New South Books.

Peacock, Scott. 2011. Presentation at the Alabama Historical Association's 64th Annual Meeting, Daphne, AL, April 16.

Perry, Percival. 1989. "Peanuts." Pp. 40 in Wilson, Ferris, and Adadie, *Encyclopedia of Southern Culture*.

Phillips, Kenneth E. 2008. "Sharecropping and Tenant Farming in Alabama." *The Encyclopedia of Alabama*. http://www.encyclopediaofalabama.org/article/h-1613.

Pickett, Albert James. 2003. *History of Alabama*. Montgomery, AL: River City Publishing. Originally published, Charleston, SC: Walker and James, 1851.

Poole, Hester. 1890. *Fruits and How to Use Them*. New York: Fowler and Wells.

Prewitt, Terry J. "Our Immigrant and Native Ancestors." http://uwf.edu/tprewitt/sofood/past.htm.

Purvis, Kathleen. 2009. "Peace and a Smile to the Lips." *Southern Cultures* 15 (4): 28–35.

Raley, Jess. 1981. *My Appalachia*. Boaz, AL: Boaz Printing.

Randolph, Mary. 1828. *The Virginia House-wife, or Methodical Cook*. Baltimore: Plaskitt and Cugle.

Rausch, Christina. *Southeast Asia to Southwest Alabama: Connecting Cultures to Weather the Storm*. A project of MDC in Durham, NC. Washington, DC: Billo Communications. https://www.mdcinc.org/home/projects/economic-security/emergency-preparedness-socially-vulnerable-communities/.

Ravitz, Jessica. 2010. "Vietnamese Fishermen in Gulf Fight to Not Get Lost in Translation." CNN. June 24.

Rayford, Julian Lee. 1956. *Whistlin' Woman and Crowin' Hen: The True Legend of Dauphin Island and the Alabama Coast*. Mobile, AL: Rankin Press.

———. 1962. *Chasin' the Devil Round a Stump*. Madison, WI: American Printing Company.

———. 1991. *Cottonmouth*. Tuscaloosa: University of Alabama Press. Originally published, New York: Charles Scribner's Sons, 1941.

Reed, John Shelton. 2004. "Barbecue Sociology." Pp. 78–87 in Elie, *Cornbread Nation 2*.

Ritter, Jess. 1975. "Going Out." *Kansas City Star*, November 20, p. 19.

Robbins, Mary LaFayette. 1895. *Alabama Women in Literature*. Selma, AL: Selma Printing.

Robinson, Amelia Platts Boynton. 1991. *Bridge across Jordan*. Washington, DC: Schiller Institute.

Robinson, Jo Ann Gibson. 1987. *The Montgomery Bus Boycott and the Women Who Started It*. Knoxville: University of Tennessee Press.

Rogers, William Warren, and Robert David Ward. 1994. "Women in Alabama from 1865 to 1920." Pp. 376–91 in Rogers et al., *Alabama*.

Rogers, William Warren, Robert David Ward, Leah Rawls Atkins, and Wayne Flynt. 1994. *Alabama: The History of a Deep South State*. Tuscaloosa: University of Alabama Press.

Root, Waverley. 1980. *Food*. New York: Simon and Schuster.

Rorer, Sarah Tyson. 1902. *Mrs. Rorer's Philadelphia Cookbook*. Philadelphia: Arnold.

Rudloe, Jack, and Anne Rudloe. 2010. *Shrimp: The Endless Quest for Pink Gold*. Upper Saddle River, NJ: FT Press.

Sagon, Candy. 1996. "Ex-Slave's Recipes Survive in Rare Historic Cookbook." *Chicago Sun-Times*, November 13.

Santvoord, George van, ed. 1922. *The Merry Wives of Windsor by William Shakespeare*. New Haven, CT: Yale University Press.

Sauceman, Fred. 2011. "Lane Cake." *The Encyclopedia of Alabama*. http://www.encyclopedia ofalabama.org/article/h-1340.

———. 2012. "Barbecue, Alabama Style." *The Encyclopedia of Alabama*. http://www. encyclopediaofalabama.org/article/h-1405.

Saunders, James Edmonds. 1899. *Early Settlers of Alabama*. New Orleans: L. Graham and Son.

Severson, Kim. 2009. "Festiveness, Stacked Up Southern Style." *New York Times*, December 15.

Shelley, Dian Lee. 1971. "The Effects of Increasing Racism on the Creole Colored in Three Gulf Coast Cities between 1803 and 1860." Unpublished manuscript, University of West Florida, Pensacola.

Smith, Andrew F. 1994. *The Tomato in America*. Columbia: University of South Carolina Press.

———. 2002. *Peanuts: The Illustrious History of the Goober Pea*. Chicago: University of Illinois Press.

———, ed. 2007. *The Oxford Companion to American Food and Drink*. Oxford: Oxford University Press.

Smith, Jerry. 2004. "Dinner on the Grounds." Stclaircountyal.com, December 6.

Smith, Joel P., ed. 1976. *Eufaula's Favorite Recipes*. Eufaula, AL: Eufaula Tribune.

Smith, Page, and Charles Daniel. 2000. *The Chicken Book*. Athens: University of Georgia Press.

Smith, Stephen. 2004. "The Rhetoric of Barbecue." Pp. 61–68 in Elie, *Cornbread Nation 2.*

Soluri, John. 2005. *Banana Cultures: Agriculture, Consumption, and Environmental Change in Honduras and the United States.* Austin: University of Texas Press.

Spencer, Thomas. 2008. "Barbecue Clubs Kindle a Savory Rural Tradition." *Birmingham News,* April 18, 1A, 6A.

Starr, Paul D. 1981. "Troubled Waters: Vietnamese Fisherfolk on America's Gulf Coast." *International Migration Review* 15 (1): 226–38.

Staten, Vince. 2004. "Real Barbecue Revisited." Pp. 138–40 in Elie, *Cornbread Nation 2.*

Sternberg, Mary Ann. 2009. "Thanksgiving Ghosts." *Southern Cultures* 15 (4): 130–32.

Stitt, Frank. 2004. *Frank Stitt's Southern Table.* New York: Artisan Press.

Stradley, Linda. 2004. "History of Iced Tea and Sweet Tea." http://whatscookingamerica.net/History/IcedTeaHistory.htm.

Taylor, Joe Gray. 1982. *Eating, Drinking, and Visiting in the South.* Baton Rouge: Louisiana State University Press.

———. 1989. "Foodways." Pp. 613–16 in Wilson, Ferris, and Adadie, *Encyclopedia of Southern Culture.*

Taylor, Joe Gray, and John T. Edge. 2007. "Southern Foodways." Pp. 1–14 in Edge, *Foodways.*

Taylor, John Martin. 2004. "Boiled Peanuts." Pp. 239–45 in Elie, *Cornbread Nation 2.*

Terkel, Studs. 2005. "Julian Lee Rayford." Pp. 263–74 in *And They All Sang* by Studs Terkel. New York: New Press.

Thomas, David Hurst. 1993. "Indian Confederacies." Pp. 96–109 in *The Native Americans: An Illustrated History*, edited by Betty Ballantine and Ian Ballantine. Atlanta, GA: Turner Publishing.

Thomas, J. Stephen, and Cecelia M. Formichella. 1987. *The Shrimp Processing Industry in Bayou La Batre, Alabama.* Mobile: Center for Business and Economic Research, University of South Alabama.

Thomas, Mary Martha. 1992. *The New Woman in Alabama: Social Reforms and Suffrage, 1890–1920.* Tuscaloosa: University of Alabama Press.

———. 1995. "White and Black Alabama Women during the Progressive Era, 1890–1920." Pp. 75–95 in *Stepping out of the Shadows: Alabama Women, 1819–1990*, edited by Mary Martha Thomas. Tuscaloosa: University of Alabama Press.

Thomas, Susan. 2009. "Gulf Coast Gumbo Traditions." Pp. 15–17 in *Alabama Foodways Gathering*, edited by Joyce Cauthen. Montgomery: Alabama Folklife Association.

Thomason, Michael V. R., ed. 2001. *Mobile: The New History of Alabama's First City.* Tuscaloosa: University of Alabama Press.

Thompson, Fred. 2002. *Iced Tea.* Boston: Harvard Common Press.

Thrower, Robert G. 2012. "Causalities and Consequences of the Creek War: A Modern Creek Perspective." Pp. 10–29 in *Tohopeka: Rethinking the Creek War and the War of 1812*, edited by Kathryn E. Holland Braund. Tuscaloosa: University of Alabama Press.

Tullos, Allen. 2004. "The Black Belt." *Southern Spaces*, April 19.

Van Der Post, Laurens. 1978. *First Catch Your Eland*. New York: William Morrow.

Vickery, Lou, with Steve Travis. 2009. *The Rise of the Poarch Band of Creek Indians*. Albany, NY: Upward Press.

Villas, James. 2010. *American Taste: A Celebration of Gastronomy Coast to Coast*. Guilford, CT: Lyons Press.

Wainwright, Jim. 2008. "Of Kin and Color." *Zalea*, February.

Walker, Robert Henry, Jr. 1973. *History of Limestone County, Alabama*. Athens, AL: Limestone County Commission.

Walter, Eugene. 1971. *American Cooking: Southern Style*. New York: Time Life.

———. 1991. *Hints and Pinches: A Concise Compendium of Aromatics, Chutneys, Herbs, Relishes, Spices, and Other Such Concerns*. Atlanta, GA: Longstreet Press.

———. 2001. *Milking the Moon: A Southerner's Story of Life on This Planet*. New York: Crown Publishers.

Waselkov, Gregory A. 2006. *A Conquering Spirit: Fort Mims and the Redstick War of 1813-1814*. Tuscaloosa, AL: University of Alabama Press.

Weaver, Sue. 2006. *Goats*. Irvine, CA: BowTie Press.

"Wildlife History." 2004. *Discovering Alabama*. Tuscaloosa: Alabama Public Television.

Williams, Benjamin Buford. 2011. "Julian Lee Rayford." *The Encyclopedia of Alabama*. http://www.encyclopediaofalabama.org/article/h-2588.

Williams, Juan. 1987. *Eyes on the Prize*. New York: Penguin Putnam.

Williams-Forson, Psyche A. 2006. *Building Houses out of Chicken Legs: Black Women, Food, and Power*. Chapel Hill: University of North Carolina Press.

Williamson, Lonnie. 1987. "Evolution of a Landmark Law." Pp. 1–17 in *Restoring America's Wildlife*, edited by Harmon Kallman. Washington, DC: US Government Printing Office.

Wilson, Charles Reagan. 1999. "The South: Where, Who, and What's for Dinner." Pp. xiii–xvii in Edge, *A Gracious Plenty*.

———. 2007a. "Cornbread." Pp. 152–54 in Edge, *Foodways*.

———. 2007b. "Pork." Pp. 88–92 in Edge, *Foodways*.

Wilson, Charles Reagan, William Ferris, and Ann J. Adadie, eds. 1989. *The Encyclopedia of Southern Culture*. Chapel Hill: University of North Carolina Press.

Zuckerman, Larry. 1999. *The Potato: How the Humble Spud Rescued the Western World*. New York: North Point Press.

Index

cabbage, 75, 166

cafés, 4, 78

Cain, Joe, 121, 248–49, 260–68

cake, 5, 67, 77, 82, 84–86, 88–89, 98, 104–5,
    122–23, 125, 135, 145, 212, 220–21;
    coconut, 82, 89, 145; fruitcake, 89;
    Japanese Fruitcake, 84; Lady Baltimore, 84;
    Lane, 82, 85–86, 89, 98–99, 104–5; layer,
    5; Moss Rose, 84; pound, 220; red velvet,
    82; Robert E. Lee, 84; stack, 5; white, 67

Calhoun County, AL, 70, 76

Cambodians, 278–79

candy, 70–71

cane. See sugarcane

canning, 67, 75, 102, 132, 167, 194

cantaloupe, 67

Caribbean, 33, 44, 74, 109, 111, 149, 230

Carlton, Bea Bannister, 191, 197–202

Carlton, Milo, 190–91, 197–202

Carmer, Carl, 135, 137

carrots, 221

Carver, George Washington, 5, 147–49,
    154–62, 165, 204, 207–9; "The Peanut
    Man," 161

cast iron, 34, 47, 50, 69, 133. See also skillet,
    cast-iron

catfish, 133, 141

Cathedral of the Immaculate Conception
    (Mobile, AL), 42

Catholic Church, 1, 39–40, 42, 44, 282, 285;
    St. Margaret's Catholic Church (Bayou La
    Batre, AL), 283–84

celery, 32, 34, 36

cemeteries, 136–46

Central America, 102, 108, 109

Charleston, SC, 106, 126

Chattanooga Bakery, 248, 252, 254–55, 257

cheese straws, 73

Cherokee, 14, 18

Chestnut, J. L., 229–30, 246

Chicago, IL, 71, 111

Chickasaw, 14, 48, 51–52, 261–62, 268; land,
    51–52

chicken, 49, 57–58, 67, 122, 132–33, 141,
    214, 216; fried chicken, 125, 128–35, 141,
    145, 214–15, 218; fried chicken recipe,
    128, 131

"Chicken in Every Pot, A," 131, 133

chicken stew, 2, 4, 5, 47–51, 56–61, 132;
    recipe, 59; sales, 47–48, 51, 56–61

Chief Slacabamorinico, 248, 261, 264–65,
    268–69

chitterlings, 218, 232

Choctaw, 14, 33, 53, 269

Christian, 26–27

Christmas, 86, 88–89, 197

church, 21, 25–26, 49, 86, 91–92, 134–36,
    140, 197, 208, 211–12, 226, 234–35, 238,
    240–42, 283; homecomings, 134

Church Street Cemetery (Mobile, AL), 121,
    248, 264, 266, 268

City Federation of Montgomery Women's
    Clubs, 100

civil rights movement, 21–22, 166, 203,
    205, 211–12, 215–16, 219, 228, 240–45;
    Club From Nowhere, 205, 212. See also
    Montgomery Bus Boycott; Selma to
    Montgomery March

Civil War, 2–3, 14, 66, 74, 92, 106, 136, 143,
    148, 150–51, 191, 226, 229, 260–62

clams, 273

Clarke County, AL, 178–79

Clayton, AL, 82, 105

Club From Nowhere, 205, 212

cobbler, 67

Coca-Cola, 77, 168

coconut, 82, 86, 89, 145, 207, 214, 256;
    cake, 82, 89, 145

game laws, 170, 176, 180

gardening, 68, 87

Gee's Bend, AL, 68

Georgia, 14, 18, 52, 64, 71, 143, 150, 158, 161

Gibbs, Henrietta, 96

Giesen, James, 155, 160, 163–64

Gilmore, Georgia, 5, 205, 208, 212–15, 221–23

girls' tomato clubs, 64, 75

goat stew, 49

goober peas, 151. *See also* peanuts

Graetz, Rev. Robert, 211

gravy, 130, 220–21

Great Depression, 5, 76–77, 132, 189–97, 262

Greek, 227

Green Corn Ceremony, 9, 27–28

greens, 33, 67, 75, 171, 166, 194, 214–16, 218; collard, 1, 67, 75, 141, 166, 194, 214–15; kale, 67, 166; mustard, 67, 166; turnip, 141, 166, 214, 218

grits, 11, 13, 73

Gulf Coast, 5, 29, 35–41, 120, 183, 247, 272–82, 286

Gulf of Mexico, 111, 272–73, 282

gumbo, 5, 29–38, 46, 74, 232, 283; recipe, 36

gumbo hens, 35. *See also* baking hens

ham, 35, 46, 77, 145

hamburgers, 199–201

Harris, Jessica, 2, 33, 35, 71, 215–16, 218

Hatcher, Lula, 224–26, 229, 232–33, 240, 243–44, 246

Hawkins, Martha, 203–6, 214–15, 218–23

hay, 160, 166, 175

health, 94, 123, 153, 160, 167, 196, 198, 220, 282. *See also* nutrition

heaven and hell suppers, 220

Henderson, Vince, 32, 35, 46

hoboes, 193, 196

hogs, 16, 67, 163, 175, 232–35

holy trinity, 32, 34

home cooking, 4, 76, 78, 205

Hooks, Al, 147, 166–68

Horseshoe Bend, 18

hospitality, 2, 29, 87, 133

hot sauce, 34, 50, 130

house raisings, 55–57

hunger, 2, 74, 132, 191–97, 206. *See also* poverty

hunting, 4, 11–12. *See also* turkey hunting

Hurricane Katrina, 1, 271, 273, 280–83

hurricanes, 274, 281–83. *See also* Hurricane Katrina

Hutto, Joe, 181–83

ice cream, 38, 135, 161, 220, 260

Indian Removal Act, 19

indigo, 16, 37, 55

Irondale Café, 64, 76–81

Jackson, Andrew, 17–19

Jackson, Jimmie Lee, 240

Jefferson County, AL, 137, 194–98

Jesup Wagon, 155, 158. *See also* movable school

Jim Crow, 45, 134, 166, 229. *See also* racial segregation

Joe Cain Day, 249, 260, 264–69. *See also* Cain, Joe

Joe Cain's Merry Widows, 266. *See also* Cain, Joe

Johnson, Frank, Jr., 242

Johnson, Lyndon B. 215, 227, 242

Kelly, Tom, 170–71, 179–80, 183, 184–88

Kimbrell, Bettye, 125

potato salad, 46, 135, 141, 145, 214–15, 235

poverty, 2, 35, 74, 151–54, 158, 164–66, 191–99, 206, 216, 230. *See also* hunger

preserves, 38, 91, 135

Progressive Era, 82, 92, 94–95, 98, 100

Prohibition, 88, 190

Protestant, 41, 44

pudding, 125. *See also* banana pudding

quilting, 56–57, 283

racial discrimination, 20, 32, 166, 195, 208–16, 219, 226, 229–30, 232, 240, 242, 245, 263, 280

racial segregation, 20, 32, 43, 45, 113, 134, 164, 166, 208–16, 219, 228–30, 232, 240, 242, 263, 280

racial violence, 208–10, 214, 219–20, 229–30, 240–45

racism, 44, 164, 166, 208–16, 219, 226, 229, 230, 232, 240, 242, 245, 263

radishes, 68, 194

railroads, 20, 21, 76–77, 82, 110–11, 120, 126, 134, 141, 274; Alabama Great Southern Railroad, 76; Bay Shore Railroad, 274; Central of Georgia Railway, 82; Georgia Pacific Company, 76–77; Mobile and Ohio, 118

Randolph, Mary, 74, 128–29, 131

Rayford, Julian, 106, 108–9, 113–19, 121, 249, 260, 263–65, 268, 270, 274

RC Cola, 135, 252, 255

Reconstruction, 14, 44–45, 229

Red Sticks, 17–18. *See also* Creek; Creek War of 1813–14

Reese, Rev. Frederick, 242

Revolutionary War, 88

rice, 14, 35, 37, 216

Richardson, Fred, 248–54

Robinson, Amelia Boynton, 226, 230

Robinson, Jo Ann, 210

rolling stores, 122, 125

Roosevelt, Franklin D., 190–91

rosemary, 34

roux, 30, 34. *See also* gumbo

rum, 88, 122, 192

rural life, 3, 56–57, 62, 66–67, 71, 75, 77–78, 122, 125, 130–42, 147, 151–55, 158–61, 164–65, 194, 216, 218, 225, 234–35, 238, 283

rutabaga, 166

rye, 53

salad, 145, 161, 238, 260

Sand Mountain, 5, 128, 130–31, 135, 137, 139–41, 143, 145

sassafras, 33, 53

sausage, 32, 35–37, 46, 58

Scotch-Irish, 51–52, 56, 136

seafood, 33–34, 270–71; processing, 270–72, 275–81, 286

seine nets, 274–76

Selma, AL, 224–31, 240–45

Selma to Montgomery March, 227, 242, 243–44

sesame seeds, 33

sharecropping, 4, 148, 151–55, 164–66, 230

shipbuilding, 126, 280

shrimp, 30, 33–35, 270, 272–78, 280, 282

shrimping, 4, 271–82, 286

singing, 24, 26, 28, 48, 116–17, 120, 134, 140, 144, 229, 245

Sipsey Wilderness (AL), 183

Sisters' Restaurant (Troy, AL), 123

skillet, cast-iron, 128–29, 132–33

slavery, 2, 16, 18, 30, 32–33, 36–44, 66–67, 74, 88–90, 134, 136, 149–50, 206–7, 229, 231

vanilla wafers, 109, 125–26, 203

vegetables, 2–3, 11–12, 32, 53, 62, 66–67, 74, 77, 122, 147, 166, 238

Vietnamese, 4, 270, 278–79, 283–84, 286–87

Virginia, 41, 52, 143

voting rights, 226–27, 240–45

Voting Rights Act, 227

Walker County, AL, 153

Wallace, George, 241

Walter, Eugene, 2, 3, 29, 68, 119, 130–31, 247

Waselkov, Gregory, 16–18

watermelon, 167

Weil, Adele Kahn, 100–103

West Africans, 2, 34, 36, 39–40, 74, 149–50, 205–6, 230

wheat, 12, 14, 71

whiskey, 12–13, 86, 88, 104. *See also* moonshine

Whistle Stop Café, 76, 79

Whitehall Cemetery (Fort Payne, AL), 130, 141–45

Whitfield family, 71, 73

wildlife management, 170, 176–80

wildlife restoration, 170, 171, 177–80

wild turkeys, 169–75, 178–88; wild turkey recipe, 176–77. *See also* turkey hunting

Williams, Bud, 236–39

Winston County, AL, 173

Wiregrass region, 5, 147, 158–60

women, 12, 32, 77, 82, 84–87, 92–98, 100, 105; Alabama Federation of Colored Women's Clubs, 96; Alabama Federation of Women's Clubs, 84, 93, 95; Alabama League of Women Voters, 98; Alabama Women's Christian Temperance Union, 84–85, 92; Anna M. Duncan Club, 95–96; City Federation of Montgomery Women's Clubs, 100; as cookbook writers, 84, 87, 90–92, 100; as homemakers, 87, 92, 94–95, 100, 123; Montgomery County League of Women Voters, 100; Nineteenth Amendment, 86, 98, 105; roles, 92–98, 105, 199; suffrage, 85, 93, 96–98, 105; Ten Times One Is Ten Club, 95; Tuskegee Women's Club, 96; women's clubs, 4, 92–93, 95, 97–98, 100, 102–3

Women's Political Council, 210

Works Progress Administration (WPA), 71, 197–98

World's Largest Peanut Boil, 151

World War I, 57, 160, 232

World War II, 1, 3, 14, 21, 64, 67, 109, 122, 126, 183, 189, 191, 198–200, 256

yams, 206, 214